The Perfect Turn

and other tales of skiing and skiers

The
Perfect Turn

*and other tales
of skiing and skiers*

Dick Dorworth

WESTERN EYE PRESS
2010

THE PERFECT TURN
is published by
WESTERN EYE PRESS,
a small independent publisher
(very small, and very
independent) with a home
base in the Colorado
Rockies and an office in
Sedona Arizona.
The Perfect Turn *is also*
available as an eBook
in various formats.

© *2010 Dick Dorworth*
Western Eye Press
P O Box 1008
Sedona, Arizona 86339
1 800 333 5178
www.WesternEyePress.com

First edition, 2010
ISBN 978-0-941283-27-4

Cover photo and photo-
based illustrations by
Linde Waidhofer.

Contents

INTRODUCTION

Tales of Skiing and Skiers

THE SKIER SKIS. THE WRITER WRITES. Together, like ski tracks in fresh powder snow on a bluebird day, they delineate the path of a life and its many turns of every conceivable shape and radius, none of them, so far, perfect.

I learned to ski as a boy in the post WWII years in the hills above the south shores of Lake Tahoe by riding rope tows, one T-bar and the traditional way of climbing up. When Squaw Valley opened in 1950 its chairlift was the most exciting, wonderful, beautiful tool of freedom to my young eyes since discovering the ski itself. Along with the first chairlift, Squaw brought Emile Allais as ski school director to the Tahoe Basin. Allais, world champion and French resistance fighter *par excellence* during the war, skied several levels above anything any of us had ever seen. He was magic on a pair of skis and, most important to my evolving young mind and spirit, he radically expanded the boundaries of the possible. Without him saying a word, by watching him ski I came to realize there was far more to this skiing thing than I had imagined. Almost 25 years later, when Allais was an old man with white hair (though not as old as I am now) I was fortunate to ski with him for a Warren Miller film in France, he did it again, expanded the boundaries of the possible. After a lifetime on skis there is still far more to this skiing thing than I had imagined. The learning, experiencing, growing, evolving as a person and making turns through skiing continues. As it does through writing.

Some of that pre-TV boyhood time was spent in Zephyr Cove on

Tahoe's east shore when in winter the nearest neighbors were miles away. Reading was a huge part of daily life for an only child. Mark Twain, Jack London, Mickey Spillane, Argosy Magazine, Field and Stream Magazine, Ski Magazine, Life Magazine and the skiing adventure novels of Monty Atwater and the novel *Hans Brinker: or The Silver Skates* were favorites. Like many people who appreciate the written word as a means to explore, understand and navigate the path of life it occurred to me early on that I could write a few words of my own. In 1952 when I began high school my family moved from Tahoe to Reno where it was no longer possible to ski in the backyard or to ski to school, but I managed to spend even more time on skis. I knew I needed it and appreciated it more as the closest skiing was half an hour by car out of town. And my English teacher for three years of high school, Blythe Bulmer, unlike the teachers of most other subjects, went out of her way to help me fill in the blank spots of the several weeks each winter when I was away from school participating in the all encompassing and crucial ski races. Ski racing was far more important to me than school, or, really, anything else, and in retrospect I see that it provided me a better education with more useful life skills than did the public schools.

Reading at home and during the long road trips to ski races was fundamental to that education, and majoring in English with a journalism minor in college was a natural progression. After a long college career frequently interrupted by the demands of skiing I graduated and spent the next few years ski racing in North and South America and Europe. During those years we set the world speed skiing record (see the chapter, "In Pursuit of Pure Speed") which led to my first published writing in a national publication. But it was published under Ron Funk's name and, though I wrote it, written from Ron's perspective of the events. In those Avery Brundage tainted days I was not on very good terms with the U.S. Ski Team and was with good reason concerned that any association with writing professionally about skiing could get me banned from amateur ski racing. Ski Magazine paid $500 to Ron for the story that I wrote and Ron gave me the money. It took several years before I was able to convince Ski Magazine editor John Fry that I, not Funk, had done the writing and that he should consider publishing my writing. Eventually he did.

Before that happened I finished ski racing, attended graduate school and taught remedial English at the University of Nevada in Reno under a short-lived delusion that I wanted to be a professor and spend my life in academia as a means to support my writing. After a year in grad school I scurried back to the mountains where I belong and have managed to carve out a rich and satisfying life on a meager income mostly earned from teaching and coaching skiing, guiding climbing and writing. In 1969 I wrote the book "The Straight Course" which has never found a publisher. In 1971 I was working as a coach for the U.S. Ski Team when I found myself in a dilemma: I could keep a job I enjoyed, was suited for and really needed (my wife was six months pregnant) by acquiescing to and supporting the Ski Team's unwarranted, unnecessary, dishonest, cowardly, really really stupid (to people interested in American ski racing) destruction of the career of America's best downhill ski racer (3rd in a World Cup, 5th in the Lauberhorn a couple of weeks earlier) because his attitude was neither servile nor obsequious and rubbed some insecure but powerful authoritarian cretins on the staff the wrong way; or I could commit mainstream professional ski coaching self-destruction by resigning in protest and making a fuss. I chose the latter. Skiing is about freedom, not authoritarianism, racing is about the fastest times, not hierarchical codes of etiquette, and it is a shallow (hollow?) ski racing coach who won't/can't stand up (or stand down) for the racers and their best interests. I left in the middle of the season and ski racing continued, the U.S. Ski Team barely noticed my absence, the career of the best downhill skier in America was not saved by my move, and, as he had promised, my least favorite cretin on the staff, made sure that I paid dearly in several realms including the smear for my statement in action. But I never once regretted it for one simple, clear reason: it was the right thing to do.

"Where one door shuts, another opens."
Miguel de Cervantes

A couple of weeks later Bill Tanler, the founder/editor of Ski Racing and a very good man and friend to skiing, asked me to write something for his publication about leaving the Ski Team and my reasons for doing so. I did, but he didn't consider it suitable for Ski Racing and wouldn't print it. He was, however, good enough to take it to Mike Moore, editor of the off-beat, alternative publication Skier's Gazette. Mike loved it, printed it under the title "The Greening of a Ski Coach," and invited me to submit anything else I cared to write. For a writer those were sweet words as well as the beginning of my writing career and a relationship that has endured for 40 years as Skier's Gazette became Mountain Gazette which has survived a few different incarnations and editors and still publishes my work and the work of many others you won't find in the mainstream.

Because of my work in Mountain Gazette, Doug Pfeiffer, editor of Skiing Magazine, invited me to do some writing for him. That exposure and experience opened up other writing opportunities and convinced John Fry that my writing aspirations were legitimate, and my writing has since appeared in Ski, Snow Country, Powder, Ski Heritage Magazine, Climbing, Rock & Ice, Ascent and Men's Journal among others. I live in Ketchum, Idaho, write a regular column for the local bi-weekly newspaper the Idaho Mountain Express. My book "Night Driving" was published in 2007. I write most days and in winter I ski nearly every day on Bald Mountain in Sun Valley or in the back country, still learning, experiencing, growing, evolving, working on that turn and the just right word.

I truly hope you enjoy "The Perfect Turn: and other tales of skiing and skiers."

Dick Dorworth

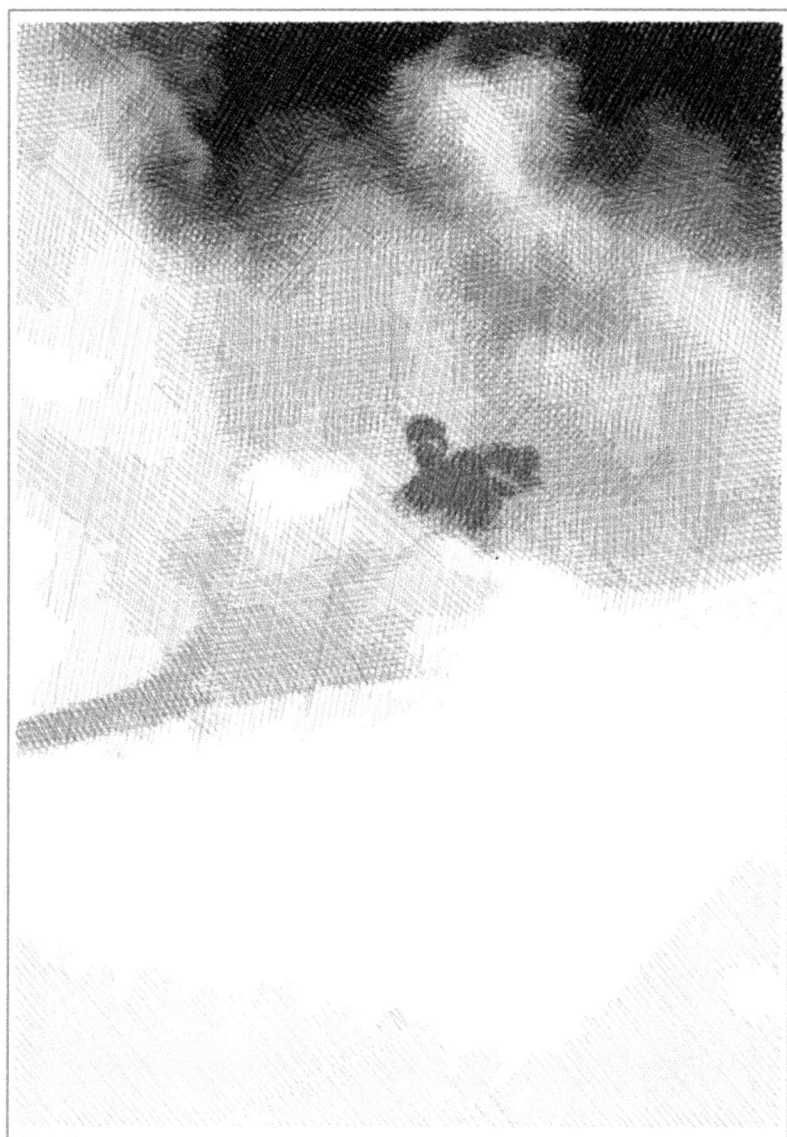

PART ONE

Spirit

CHAPTER ONE

A Life on Bald Mountain

IN LATE OCTOBER 2002 at least fifty people climb the mountain. Those who reach the top rest at the wooden tables outside the ski patrol hut, drink tea from a thermos, eat something, put on a warm layer carried up in a backpack. A social atmosphere prevails, rooted in the recognition between people of like spirit, in this case the arduous attitude, even spiritualism, generated by the efforts of the climb out of the valley, the effects of being outdoors on the human heart. The atmosphere is akin to that of American skiing in the 1930s more than that of a major ski resort of the 21ˢᵗ century, a technological irony to some. Greetings between friends seldom seen are frequent. "Here we are." "Another year." "You're looking strong, like always." Many climb on skis with climbing skins and randonee bindings. Others use telemark skis with skins. Some are on high-tech snowshoes. A few wear crampons. Several carry snowboards. For most, the slide down is reward for climbing up eight inch thick strips of glacier hard snow. The surrounding hills and mountains and the valley below are as brown and green as the landscape of summer. The sky is clear, the sun bright, temperature brisk enough to encourage persistent movement.

This year it is October when the change began from mountain in a mountainous neighborhood to place of magic and dreams and inspired rising from the low land sediments of most human life. In the grand, mysterious scheme which no man comprehends, a "beginning" is just a point in time, a chosen convenience in trying to understand things beyond human perception. In truth, to make of expediency a certainty, to insist on delineating beginnings and endings is a deceit, a conceit or a fearful blindness to life's immensity. Still, as pragmatism and the saying have it, we must begin somewhere. In more innocent times when nature guided action and reverence, it was usually December before enough snow fell to keep a pair of skis above the mountain's dirt and rock and brush, allowing gravity's rider to slide down its contours. Snow's arrival was the onset of winter. The powerful change of seasons happens four times a year, but for skiers winter's is the most enchanting of all. Most years in the mountains of central Idaho snow fit to ski upon will be delivered from the sky by Christmas, though big snows occasionally arrive much earlier. There have been years when snows big and small do not come at all.

The mountain is called Bald Mountain, often referred to as "Baldy." Its flanks are blanketed with trees, the bare top covered with sagebrush, cheat grass, lupine and rock. It is, anthropocentrically speaking, a bald mountain 9150 feet above sea level, rising 3400 feet above the central Idaho town of Ketchum alongside the Big Wood River draining the Boulder Mountains to the north and northeast, the Smokey Mountains to the north and northwest and the Pioneer Mountains to the east. Bald Mountain is part of the Smokey Mountains. Though less than fifteen miles to the south the valley spreads out and becomes part of the great high plains desert of Idaho, Nevada, California, Utah, Arizona, New Mexico and parts of California, Bald Mountain and everything close around is alpine mountain country. Human and all biological life in the vicinity are defined by that geographical/meteorological/cultural fact. Ketchum was once a mining town called Leadville until the U.S. Postal Service determined there were too many Leadvilles in western America and forced this one to find a different name. Ketchum is a mountain town. It could even be called a Bald Mountain town, as it the crown (sic) jewels of the Sun Valley Ski Resort and is festooned with high speed ski lifts. The majority of people who ski Bald Mountain do not climb up. They never have. Most back country skiers who use their own bodies rather than ski lifts to access their skiing high points do not regularly climb Baldy. Back country leg-powered skiing and alpine lift-serviced skiing are different activities favoring different mentalities and skills and offering different rewards. A small number of skiers engage in both. There is tradition, continuity and paradox in 21st century skiers using their own legs to get up Bald Mountain, an historical and perhaps evolutionary irony: In the early days of Sun Valley from 1936 to 1940, back-country skiing in the spectacular mountains around the resort was a significant aspect of its recreation activities. A separate ski school was devoted to taking clients on tours in the different nearby mountain ranges, including overnight trips to the Pioneer Cabin and the Owl Creek Cabin, both built by Sun Valley to accommodate its guests. *(An historical interjection: The first director of the Sun Valley Ski School, Hans Hauser, was an Austrian, as were most but not all of the instructors of that school. Florian Haemmerle, a native Bavarian, was the only German. Since Germany was in the process of annexing Austrian into the Third Reich, there were resentments, anxiety and abundant nationalistic feelings even in America where natives of both European nations were trying to fit in and distance themselves, both literally and perceptually, from Nazi Germany. Like the Japanese of a few years later and the Arabs of today, every German (and Austrian) in America was viewed with suspicion and fear and treated with unjust xenophobia. It was insanity of the kind that marks man's history, but Haemmerle could not be on the normal ski school because he was German. But he was a fine and accomplished skier, a personable and caring man, an asset to America and its fledgling ski industry. Averell Harriman, who built Sun Valley for his Union Pacific Railroad, was not about to lose him. Harriman helped Haemmerle set up the back country ski school and Haemmerle stayed. Some 65 years later, in October 2002, some 50 people are carrying on the tradition on Bald Mountain.)* In addition to Haemmerle, Andy Henning and Victor Gottschalk specialized in taking skiers into the back country in the years before World War II. In modern times Baldy always has the first snows of the season, and skiers, like happy flies to fresh horse manure, go to where the snow is. That is the way of skiers.

The snow on Bald Mountain in autumn is nowhere else because it did not fall naturally and indiscriminately out of the sky on the entire countryside. It was forced out of high pressure nozzles in the form of water spray which turns to snow upon contact with cold air. It falls to the ground more or less (depending, like so much of life, on which way the wind blows) exactly where the directors of the nozzles intend. Sun Valley opened as a ski resort in 1936, and for 40 years Sun Valley skiers were dependant on nature's snowfalls for their skiing, as, of course, were the Sun Valley Company and other local merchants for the skiers' business. That ecological system worked well enough until the gifts of nature became line items in the corporate ledgers of the ski industry. Nature's cornucopia cannot keep pace with the desires of man, a scenario not limited to the world of skiing. In the early 1970s a string of nature's drought years struck western America. Snow fell sparsely or not at all. The economies of ski towns were hit hard, and Sun Valley/Ketchum was not spared. In response to economic disaster (and really poor skiing) Sun Valley began to install what has become one of the world's largest and best man-made snow systems. In 1975 the first artificial snow making system in Idaho was installed on Lower Warm Springs. It has continued to expand in size, technological sophistication and efficiency. Today Bald Mountain has 810 groomable (with fleets of $250,000 to $500,000 snow cats working the snow every night so that morning skiers have skiing as smooth as an Afghan rug) acres of ski terrain. Seventy eight percent or 645 of those acres can be covered with snow that does not come from the sky. This elaborate system is connected by more that 36 miles of underground water pipe and is controlled from one center at the Roundhouse cooling tower. The runs of Bald Mountain are lined with 535 twenty foot tall metal 'snow guns' resembling prehistoric, lanky, wingless birds with yellow bodies composed of thick pads wrapped around the bottom of the tubular guns to protect hapless skiers who collide with them. Sun Valley has enough water rights to use up to 3200 gallons of ground and surface water a minute in their snow making system. Normally, only half that allotment is used. If Sun Valley operates the snow making system eight hours a day, approximately 768,000 gallons of water is turned to snow. If snow is made 60 days a season, approximately 46,080,000 gallons of water is pumped from the ground and from Warm Springs Creek and turned into snow. The potential exists to divert double that amount of water, 92,160,000 gallons, from its natural cycles each year for the enjoyment of Sun Valley skiers. The environmental consequences of this much disruption of the natural water cycles in the immediate area of Bald Mountain are unknown, unstudied and not much discussed. Snow can be made from this water in temperatures ranging from 34 degrees Fahrenheit to 15 degrees below zero Fahrenheit, and temperature is one of several variables determining the quality of the resulting ski conditions. There is some debate as to whether it is more aptly named 'artificial' or 'man-made' snow. I prefer the latter but sometimes think 'technological snow' is closer to the mark. An argument can be made that anything made by man is artificial (except, of course, children); and an argument can be made that since man is part of nature anything he makes is natural. Either way, the mechanics of producing tiny water droplets that turn into snow upon contact with cold air are similar in both nature and man's systems. Each produces six-sided snowflakes of similar but not identical structure, but the configuration of man-made flakes causes them to bond to each other more readily than do natural ones. Thus, the man-made flakes produce a denser snow pack which more easily turns to ice. Man-made snow has saved the community's bacon during some years and enhanced it every year.

Man-made snow systems are expensive. The Sun Valley Company does not disclose in-house financial information to inquisitive writers, but it is clear that it takes many millions of dollars to install and operate a sophisticated snow making system. Even with lift tickets priced at more than $1500 for a season pass and $80 per day, it takes a lot of skiers to pay for technological snow on demand. The economics of Sun Valley and Bald Mountain are beyond the scope of this writing; but among the consequences of the financial realities of Sun Valley skiing is this: Skiers on Bald Mountain either have money to spare or have given up much in life in order to ski. They give physical presence and a cultural face to the old adage, coined, as far as can be determined, by the 1960s Yosemite rock climber Eric Beck, "At either end of the social spectrum lies a leisure class." At the higher end of that spectrum, age and money usually lie together. Capitalism tends to favor robber barons, those who honestly work hard and intelligently to acquire wealth for 30 years or so, the randomly lucky, those who practice capitalism outside the confines of the law, and, of course, members of the lucky sperm club whose parents or previous ancestors fell into one of the afore mentioned categories. Many modern Sun Valley November to April lift riding skiers are retirees who refer to Sun Valley as a ski resort, not a ski area. In the Warm Springs and River Run Lodges on the majority of mornings before the mountain opens more skiers are over 60 than under 40. Many came to skiing late in life, though some are lifetime skiers for whom retiring to ski is part of a natural and logical pattern. For the most part it is retirees who can afford to stay in Sun Valley and ski. It was not always so.

I first saw Sun Valley in 1953 when I was 14 years old after an all-night drive from Reno, Nevada. I have written elsewhere of that first encounter: *"We pulled into Sun Valley on that long-ago March night a couple of hours before dawn, and crashed in the back of the truck. When we woke, chalky-mouthed, fiery-eyed and achey-boned, we crawled out of the camper into a perfect Sun Valley day. The first thing we saw were the 1953 moguls on Exhibition, the most beautiful, exciting sight I'd ever seen. It was love at first vision, me and Bald Mountain, a long-standing love affair that persists to this day, unlike, alas, some others there have been along the road. In a manner that must be felt and sensed rather than explained, riding the narrow, all-night 1953 Nevada and Idaho highways of the mind, in open conversation with my boyhood friend, Bob Lerude, helped prepare me to recognize on sight the finest skiing mountain in America. As a skier, that was an important moment in life. It was an instant akin to that when a guitarist first hears a Martin; a climber sees the Cerro Torre close up; a feared drug addict lays his eyes on eighty acres of his favorite cannabis sativa blowing in the mind; and that magical (mythical?) (myriad?) realization that blinds the heart and mind and sex of every person encountering, for the first time, the love that will never die, the kiss that will never cool. The second time is, all together, re-affirmation, mind-bender, faith-healer and heart-stomper. The third time is pure faith. After that, it is so far out on the edge that only those who have been there know the precarious balance—tightrope walking*

*a thread above the first and last and only abyss—involved in going for it
again, once again, along America's endless highways that go nowhere, end
nowhere, begin nowhere and circle continually inward in a seemingly endless spiral toward the self that should love and must be love and can be
nothing else and is—love—lost along the passageways of the fiery human
heart encased in the crazy human frame blasting down the eternal concrete/
asphalt cables with which we have bound together this beautiful land called
America which must someday burst its bonds the way only love—pure,
unadulterated, simple love—can."*

(During the writing of this my old friend Bob Lerude died, not
unexpectedly. In a telephone conversation with him a few days before
his death, he said to me with a clarity and brightness that cut through
his pain diminishing morphine haze like the pure faith of the love that
will never die: "We've been friends for a long time, Dick, and I'm happy
you're still in Sun Valley. You've made a good life out of the mountains
and they've been good to you. Don't leave them. God bless." After that
conversation, I walked outside and looked at Bald Mountain from Ketchum and thought of more than 50 years of its influence on my life and
wondered at the passage of time and of the sense I often have that time is
a human construct that does not really exist. I thought of the endurance
of mountains and of the abstract but real knowledge that they, too, will
eventually be washed home to the sea in the immensity of a time that
does not really exist.)

We were young ski racers in 1953, boys in love with an activity that
took me out of myself into a world of mountains, snow, and crystal clean
air and focused vision, out of the anger, confusion and encompassing
fury of my particular set of circumstances within a rage-filled generation. Skiing, and, more specifically, ski racing probably saved my life,
allowing me to grow into a social critic instead of the sociopath I might
have become in response to society's violent and small-minded hypoc-
risies, pretensions and shallow smugness. Skiing kept anger, adolescent
hormones and confusion in check enough to focus on a path that was
to take me skiing all over the world. It formed and informed my life at
least as much as the dynamics of family, the structure of schools, the

warmth and generosity of true friends, the betrayals of false friends and the other (and normal) vicissitudes of life. That path always led back to Bald Mountain.

I write these words at my desk in Ketchum, Bald Mountain rising above. There have been changes in more than fifty years, but the basics never change in anything that survives. Changing basics is to flirt with the advance scouts for the armies of extinction. So far, despite wild and rapid refinements in the technology and services of ski areas and even the face of Bald Mountain itself, the basics are the same as when the first Ketchum skiers set skis to snow and hiked up the mountain and skied back down, and, sometimes, did it again. In my mind, Baldy's first tracks are associated with Dick Durrance, an old friend, a fine man, America's first great skier, who did it for the workout, the joy of physical effort, the pleasure of being in the outdoors, and for the exhilaration of the controlled slide back down. In Dick's case, the quality and level of control and, presumably, exhilaration were higher than for most skiers. Mechanical ski lifts replaced human effort with the economic toil of paying for the fuel, machinery and labor to supply and maintain them. A recreation/athletic/fitness endeavor was transformed into more of a recreation/economic matter by technology. This erased the repetitious physical exertion required for climbing up a mountain, allowing more time to enjoy and practice the more 'fun' and exciting skills of downhill skiing. As skiing is a metaphor for life, Bald Mountain is the residence of magic and dreams and inspired rising from the low lands. Often enough, fun and excitement involves a descent of one form or another, but there is nothing like descending a mountain on a pair of skis. There is value, virtue and building of body, mind and spirit in the human powered ascent and something priceless lost with a ski lift ride. I have always been into skiing primarily for the (cheap) thrills of skiing downhill (less so for the physical exercise, the social amenities and the professional options). I will not argue the relative worth of climbing up with riding up and do not apologize for a single ride. A good number of the best things in life are a process repeated, and, like individual snowflakes, each time around is unique, separate, irreplaceable and eternal. It is said that no snowflake ever falls in the wrong place. (Nor does it ever fall in the same place twice.) And no snowflake falls alone. Each transitory snowflake bonds with others to form a snow pack, a cornice, a glacier, in another step of a repeated process that eventually returns to the sea from whence it begins again. Each ride or climb up Baldy and the many other mountains there have been and will be (Ullr willing) and every turn of every descent merges into the whole of a life. Much of the best of it for me has happened on Baldy, always with a spirit and quality of experience unique to that mountain.

We were of a 1953 Sierra Nevada era, place and skiing circle where riding lifts was the norm. From more than 50 years away, it seems a simple age. The Sierra Nevada was and is a lovely, benign range of mountains in which to discover one's place and self and create a path from it. Skiing was not the mainstream activity it is today and its small circles were mostly filled with socially correct nonpartisans. Only eccentrics climbed for the pleasure of the climb. In the early 1950s America was busy putting an automobile in every garage, a toaster in every kitchen, a television in every living room, an atomic bomb in every bomber flying the perimeters of Russia and making a wasteland of the southern part of my home state Nevada by testing those bombs in the winds above its desert sands. And those winds blew everywhere, covering the land and all its inhabitants with invisible poison. Like every American with a modicum of ordinary human instinct, an average amount of natural adolescent skepticism and a God given functioning shit detector, I knew without having the skills to articulate the knowledge that something was deeply amiss with America. It was not even close to being all it could, should and would be, and that pissed me off (it still does), But I now realize it's the human condition and not *just* America. Any positive place to put that sort of angry energy is a gift and a blessing to a young man. One of the central frustrations and challenges of adolescence is having the clarity and insight of innocence without the experience to not be blinded and made crazy by its light. Skiing (downhill, using lifts, often competitively) was, thanks be, the tool at hand by which I dealt with those frustrations and challenges. In my opinion, competitive athletics does more than teach young people interesting and enjoyable skills, instill self-confidence and self-discipline, and develop healthy bodies and discriminating minds. Despite some obvious and unobvious destructive consequence of an over-emphasis on athletics, most of them associated with LLPS (Little League Parent Syndrome), the salient point is that athletics save lives. Skiing was the most beautiful, free, satisfying and sane aspect of my young life, and on a 1953 spring morning I recognized at first sight that Bald Mountain was the ski mountain for me. While skiing long ago ceased to be the all engrossing focus of life, it is still a significant and much loved part of daily winter existence. Most important, it remains beautiful, free, satisfying and sane. There have been many other mountains and uncountable climbs and rides up and turns down those mountains, and I have loved and been enriched by each and every one of them. That I ski Bald Mountain most winter days more than 50 years after first seeing it is not surprising; that I find myself sometimes *climbing* Baldy under my own power is. And it is interesting, rewarding and relevant not only to my life but to the unchanging allure and essence of skiing which transcends technology, technique and the fashionable (and nonessential) illusion of comfort and ease as requisite for the good life. The essential is always available by a return to the basics which never change. The act and the place of skiing contribute both quality and a certain consistency to my life *in the present moment.* That moment is formed by its history which includes for every skier a beloved mountain, the historical and present home of his skiing soul, a place that never leaves his heart, no matter where else his skis, upward or downward bound, may go.

Every mountain has its devotees whose favorite tracks and skiing spirit are carved more cleanly on that mountain than on others. Generations of American (and non-American) skiers have fallen in love with Bald Mountain and that love has formed or at least altered their lives in lasting and profound ways. It is not the evolving technology of ski equipment, lifts, snow making or grooming, nor is it the ever-expanding amenities of lodges, restaurants, art galleries, shops, spas and real estate banditry near its base that makes Bald Mountain a place of magic and dreams and inspired rising. It is the private, immediate, transcendent relationship between skier and mountain that matters. Whether one ascends with personal effort or mechanical ease, whether one descends with the skill and grace of snow geese in flight or with the ineptitude of ignorance and innocence, it is the focus and heart and spirit which one brings to the mountain that determines how high one rises, how hard one falls, how bright, lasting and inspiring the experience. The mountain is always metaphor and mirror to the skier. Accurate reflection requires persistent polishing, and, as indicated, the shape and clarity of Bald Mountain suits me.

CHAPTER TWO

In the Spirit of Dick Durrance

Adventures in the ski film trade with the
Men's Journal Adventure Team

SUN VALLEY, IDAHO, MARCH 1940

In the downhill race of his life, the fourth annual Harriman Cup, Dick Durrance approaches the Warm Springs Steilhang with abandon and speed. The previous year he was beaten after winning the first two years. This year he has trained hard, and with distinctive style—skis apart, body crouched low—he neither slows nor flinches on the steepest face of the hardest downhill in America. Despite his 60 mph speed he wears no goggles. His skis, hand made of laminated hickory with no side cut and short strips of metal screwed into the bottom edges, are about the same length though narrower than a modern ski. As tools of control they are more like a Model T Ford than a BMW. His lace up leather boots provide less ankle support than a modern high-top tennis shoe. He wears baggy gabardine pants and a sweater. A bandanna covers his head. He shusses the entire face with characteristic courage and assurance. "I do remember the fear of God," he said, "and I started talking to myself: Whoa, this is too fast. I was cussing in German and English, This is bad, I'm in trouble. But there was no choice, I had to take it straight." He enters the Warm Springs gully with too much speed. "So I did the best I could to get around the corner, and then I could see this grove of saplings. It was obvious I wasn't going to make it. People say I skied right over one tree. I do know I was knocked backwards, so I was dragging my hands, but I was able to summon enough strength to rise back up. And nobody was as surprised as I was that I came out again." Durrance keeps going, only slightly slowed and bruised by the encounter.

"Himmel, you're a lucky son-of-a-gun," he says to himself, quickly regaining speed and continuing down the course. A potential disaster for the country's finest skier becomes, instead, a defining moment in the spirit (and history) of American skiing, and a cornerstone of the legend of its most respected and influential citizen. America's first great alpine ski racer, skis the rest of the race much faster than his competitors, but just before the finish he goes off the course a second time, falling into a crowd of spectators. He gets back up and walks across the finish line, but manages to win the race, beating World Champion Walter Prager He retires the Harriman Cup. It is the last big ski race of an original champion whose spirit and imagination helped form and inspire American skiing. In fact, it is the last great race of the era before World War II.

America was soon engulfed in World War II. Durrance's generation fought that war and he and his skiing contemporaries returned from it to establish the ski industry in the United States. An art major graduate of Dartmouth University, Durrance was America's original ski filmmaker, as well as its first great ski racer. His films from that time are classics. Post WWII ski filmmaker Warren Miller said it best: "Dick was the one that everyone copied. Dick was, and always will be the influential trend setter wherever he travels."

After the war he became President of the Aspen Skiing Corporation, changing the course of American skiing in the process. He put in new lifts, cut trails to make Ajax Mountain accessible to intermediate skiers, and, most importantly, cut new runs for and brought the 1950 FIS World Championships to Aspen. He also made the best ski racing film of its time about those races, a masterpiece of its genre. He says, "If I've made a contribution to American skiing in general, I think that the 1950 FIS in Aspen would be it.....After that Aspen began to prosper and grow." The rest of American skiing followed and it is not too much to assert that all of American skiing has been molded by Aspen. Shortly after the FIS races, Durrance, remaining true to his own spirit and passion, gave up the security of running America's leading ski resort for the precarious adventure of making films. It was a bold move that defined the rest of his working life.

He later summed up his guiding philosophy, one that takes a certain spirit to follow: "Making a ton of money never was our goal in life, and as a result we never did. We always had enough, and we've lived a good life. We almost always lived in resorts where there was a lot going on.... Our goal in life has been to enjoy doing the things we do, and try to do them well."

MT. SNOW, VERMONT, JANUARY 2001

Zach Crist and his older brother Reggie and four others have reached the X Games skiercross finals. Zach describes skiercross as "the newest cult of ski racing." Six racers leave the starting gate at the same time, negotiating the same course full of manmade terrain bumps and sharp turns, big air and moderately high speeds, each skier running his own race while watching out for the other five.

Reggie says that skier cross "gets back to the purest roots of ski racing—back when we were kids—the first one down wins. I've raced the hardest downhills in the world—the Hahnenkahm, the Lauberhorn, Bormio—, but nothing compares to the adrenaline rush of getting into a starting gate with five other competitors." Skier cross started in the U.S. in the mid-1990s, and, according to Reggie, "In many ways it is similar to the raw spirit of ski racing in Durrance's day."

The luck of the draw found Zach and Reggie in the opening round together. Only three from each round advance to the next round, and Reggie won every one of his heats, while Zach managed to stay in the first three. They have been competing with each other their entire lives, and they agree to select lanes next to each other so that, according to Zach, "we only have to worry about foul play from one side rather than from both." This brotherly cooperation marks their relationship. They are among the pioneers of this event and at least one of them has reached the podium in every skier cross they have entered.

"The intensity jumps up a big notch in the finals," Zach says. "In the X Games finals last year there was body contact right away. Three of us were fighting for the holeshot (the line to the front of the pack.) The big Swede, Tomas Anderson, emerged as the early leader. The top portion of the course consisted of a long gliding section that quickly transformed into a series of rollers ('whoops') that each skier was forced to absorb. That was the turning point. I had regained my composure after the initial contact and made my move through the whoops. I exited the rollers with better speed than the leader and at the first table top jump I knew I would take the lead for good. I left the ground and 60 feet later when my skis touched back down, I was the new leader. At that point I knew it was up to me to finish a clean run with no mistakes to take the gold. As for Reg, I had no way of knowing what had happened to him. It wasn't until the smoke cleared at the finish that he told me of his fall. He had been tangled up in another scuffle that ended in a crash. I was disappointed since I had hoped we would both make the podium, but I couldn't deny the stoke I was feeling. Maybe next year?"

The 2001 Men's Journal Adventure Team

Reggie and Zach and their sister Danielle from Ketchum, Idaho are the core of the MJAT.

Since retiring from the U.S Ski Team in 1996 Reggie has made his living as a filmmaker, writer and professional skier. His articles for Men's Journal about skiing, climbing and kayaking in Nepal, Bhutan, Greenland and British Columbia helped spawn the Men's Journal Adventure Team. "Right now," Reggie says, "I have to return to this year's Winter X Games to battle it out with Zach who beat me last year. It's amazing how much of this is mental. Everybody's in good shape. Everybody knows how to ski. Everybody has good equipment. When it really boils down to it, it's who wants it the most, and who's the most confident on his skis."

Danielle Crist, 30, was a member of the U.S. Ski Team for three years in the late 1980s. She won the third annual ESPN "survival of the Fittest" competition in 1996. In 1997 she won an Emmy Award for "outstanding digital camera work" for her digital video contribution to Outdoor Life's Adventure Quest Series. She is a Class V whitewater kayaker and a wicked skier. She says, "For me, skiing is not about being extreme.

It's about seeing new places, being outside with great people, learning how to enjoy the simple things."

Zach Crist, 28, was a member of the U.S. Ski Team for eight years. He makes his living as a professional ski racer and a film maker. He is currently working on a film about the lifestyles of freestyle skiers in the 1970s in Sun Valley. He says, "I think the most memorable feeling from our adventures is the camaraderie between team members. It's dog eat dog on the race circuit, but in the back country it's all about teamwork. A certain chemistry beyond your own abilities is required. The ingredients for confidence is derived from our teammates' years of experience that you can TRULY trust. Pete's snow safety evaluation, Reggie's tactical advice, and Danielle's expedition experience added a level of comfort (if there is such a thing) that enabled me to focus entirely on the task before me. Confidence in an environment like Alaska usually leads in one of two directions: the most 'real' moment of your life or a complete disaster—seldom in between."

Gerry Moffatt, is a world traveling Scottish filmmaker and world class kayaker. He lives part of each year in Nepal, Sun Valley and Maui. Gerry is the organizer and heart of Equator Productions and the recognized manager of the MJAT. Moffatt is usually the first one up in the morning, the last one down at night, and he uses his seemingly inexhaustible energy to keep the MJAT on track, on the road, and, as he has said, "on the right path," which he defines as, "Have fun. Throw caution to the wind." He first came up with the idea of producing a film about Dick Durrance after reading his biography, "The Man on the Medal."

Pete Patterson, 44, is one of America's most respected alpine skiers. He was third in the combined at the 1978 FIS World Championships and fifth in the 1980 Olympic downhill. He is a climber, a mountain and heli-ski guide and the man his comrades turn to for personal and mountain guidance and judgment calls which tend to be reliable and excellent. Patterson's personal motto is: "If you have a problem, get over it."

Daron Rahlves, 27, is the current World Champion in Super Giant Slalom and America's brightest hope for a medal in men's alpine events in the 2002 Olympic Games in Salt Lake City. He is best of friends with

Zach and Reggie. He "badly" misses their comradeship while traveling and training on the World Cup tour, and he relishes his springtime back country reunions with his "bros," and the Alaska trip was a highlight of the year for them all.

SUN VALLEY, IDAHO, MARCH 2001

Dick Durrance is 86 and walks with a cane and a considerable stoop, a consequence of two car wrecks and three back surgeries. He sits on a bench a mile outside Sun Valley by the Trail Creek Road with Miggs, his wife of more than 60 years, and Reggie and Zach. The Crists have known of and been inspired by Durrance their entire skiing lives, but have just met him in person for the first time. Durrance has traveled from his home in Carbondale, Colorado to meet them and to talk about the Crists' upcoming trip to the back country of Alaska. Dick tells them about the rigors and rewards of his trip to New Zealand and Australia to train in the southern hemisphere winter (northern hemisphere summer) of 1937. It is a sunny, clear day. Bald Mountain and the Warm Springs run are visible a few miles away. Durrance is a small, balding man with tiny, hawkish features and a mind as sharp and clear as his startling blue eyes. He has a keen wit, an innate humility and a no-nonsense, relaxed demeanor that comes from 86 well-lived years and lots of laughter. Dick and Miggs and the Crists talk about skiing and Sun Valley and making films from the 1930s to the present, and of the enormous changes 60 years has brought to the world. They speak of differences and similarities in generations and of human qualities which never change—the spirit of adventure, the courage to follow passion, the commitment of living dreams, the imagination to create higher standards and new adventures.

Reggie asks if Dick has ever skied in Alaska. He has not, but Dick is curious about the skiing Reggie and his contemporaries are doing on its steep, scalloped faces. After hearing about some of the Crists' skiing adventures in the mountains of Nepal, Greenland and Alaska, Durrance concludes that the curious and restless spirit and attitude that pushes limits and explores new grounds is the same in each generation.

Durrance, the original spirit of American skiing, and the Crists are in the same tradition.

In Durrance's day there were few ski lifts. Many ski races consisted of competitors climbing up a mountain and skiing down an unprepared slope by any route they chose. Snow conditions were naturally variable. Boldness and imagination were as valuable as repetitious discipline and ultra-subtle finesse. Reggie, the Olympic downhiller who raced for 10 years on the World Cup tour where courses are precisely proscribed and prepared with $250,000 machines and battalions of workers, is amazed to hear of Durrance's skiing and racing experiences. In Reggie's day, powder mornings on Sun Valley's Bald Mountain see every possible line skied out two hours after the lifts open. Thus, the Crists' attraction to the new untracked frontiers of the back country.

"You must have had a lot of first tracks," Reggie says to Dick.

"That's all there was," Durrance replies without hesitation, his blue eyes flashing with amusement. "Everything we did was all new ground, and we kept coming up with ways to improve our skiing and the equipment and the conditions. Mostly we found ways to go faster and to ski more difficult terrain. That's what we had to do. And look where it has come to. Who knows where it will go from here?"

On the road: April 2001

It's 1500 miles by car and 300 miles by boat on the Inland Passage ferry from Ketchum, Idaho to Haines, Alaska where the MJAT hopes to answer part of Durrance's question. Danielle, Zach, Reggie and Gerry pack all their gear into two Ford SUVs and head first for the Whistler/Blackcomb ski area of British Columbia. There they meet up with Atomic Freeteam rider Rex Thomas whose big air jumps and freestyle moves known as 'jibbing' have, in Reggie's words, "Along with big mountain skiing given a surge of momentum to the sport of skiing."

After a couple of days in Whistler, they head north in a 14 hour push to Prince Rupert on the Alaskan Highway through the coastal mountains of British Columbia.

During the drive, Gerry, ever the organizer looking at the professional big picture, busies himself studying the technical manuals for their new digital and computer software.

Danielle, who has more pure expedition experience than the others, is relaxed and adaptable during long periods of waiting. She reads, experiments with the new digital camera equipment and sleeps in uncomfortable positions when not driving. She describes the journey as, "A day's drive to Whistler for a few days of skiing, following Zach off the back side, into the cliffs and through the trees, warming up for the real thing. Back into the rigs, loaded to the roof with gear, and a night in a cramped two bedroom hotel suite. No one was disappointed to arrive at the ferry dock. Three days of bliss traveling through the Inland Passage with room to spread out, relax, write letters and film the wildlife. Great anticipation as peaks get bigger, weather colder, snow deeper. Everyone buzzing with the excitement of exploring a new set of mountains. Lots of thoughts about Durrance and how much time and travel he put into skiing in a place like New Zealand."

Mostly, they talk. Conversation is the ancient pastime of those bound together for long periods of time. They speak of the steepness of the lines they will ski and of their fears. Danielle says of Reggie's presence, "He is so supportive and encouraging. His knowledge gives me a sense of confidence that I would not have otherwise. He's so experienced that even in light of the horrific fears that race through my mind, he makes me feel I can do it. Sometimes I think he has more confidence in my ability than I do. He is truly my big brother watching out for me. He has got be my favorite person to challenge myself with."

Zach and Reggie talk for hours about their trip and about Durrance and the upcoming skiing. At one point Zach says, "We think we are paying our dues driving up to Alaska and jumping on the ferry, but this is nothing compared to Dick Durance traveling half way around the world by boat to New Zealand in 1937 to make a few turns on a glacier."

To which Reggie, ever the leader and practical man of the moment at hand, replied, "Sometimes it is good to go slow and take the scenic route. I think there is a certain amount of satisfaction when you take the long road from your doorstep in Sun Valley to the top of an unskied peak in Alaska."

They were fortunate to find 10 days of consistently good weather in Haines. A combination of relatively low elevations (2000 to 5000 feet), proximity to the ocean, and incessant storm cycles, puts the coastal ranges of southeast Alaska on the cutting edge of modern adventure skiing. This unique combination causes skiable snow to hold on steeps where it would not stay on the higher, drier slopes of the lower 48. Alaskan steep skiing is the current stage on which the actors/skiers are finding ways to go faster and ski more difficult terrain.

Pete Patterson flew in from Greenland to add his mountain judgment, and Daron Rahlves came from California to complete the team. Pete's hardest skiing days are behind him, but his presence is invaluable. Danielle says of Pete, "He's the guy who never loses his sense of humor. The worse it gets the better his jokes become. He has a way of evening out everyone's hot temperaments. I don't think Pete knows what it means to be uptight or not totally stoked. In the back country there is no one I would rather be with. He is knowledgeable and safety conscious, and he bestows this feeling of pure faith in his followers. Not that you are ever invulnerable, but if there's a chance of surviving it's with Pete that you will."

Danielle, bolstered by Pete's good judgment and Reggie's confidence and devotion, skied all but a couple of the steepest lines. She skied the thousand foot 50 degree slope named "Tomahawk" in recognition of the sight of the several skiers who have fallen down it. Just a few days before, two excellent skiers were seriously injured there.

Zach skied the hardest, steepest lines, even after falling 800 feet down "Tomahawk" on the second day of skiing. The next day a guide fell 600 feet down another slope which was then given the droll name "Rag Doll." Neither was seriously injured, though Zach sprained both ankles. Both knew they were lucky sons of a gun.

When Dick Durrance led the first contingent of American ski racers to New Zealand in 1937 to train on the Ball Glacier below Mt.

Cook, it turned into a combination of high standard technical skiing in a mountaineering environment, a precursor of things to come. Avalanches periodically fell off Mt. Cook onto the Ball Glacier, and they had to pick lines to both climb up and ski down that avoided the not always visible crevasses. Dick said, "It was a very fast-moving glacier. Every day.....our tracks would've moved down a foot and a half during the night....We walked up...skirting all the crevasses—of which there were new ones every day—to hold our downhill race...We followed our own tracks while coming back down, for fear of hitting new crevasses, so the downhill was a little more than just skiing." Durrance concluded, "You just had to be lucky."

While Durrance obviously was lucky, running out of luck was never far from his mind. One member of the 1937 New Zealand trip said, "Almost every night Dick had a nightmare about falling into crevasses."

Luck is a factor in all great adventure, and the spirit of Dick Durrance, like the spirit of the MJAT in Alaska, exemplifies that which tends to create its own good luck by not flinching in the face of high adventure and the unknown.

HAINES, ALASKA, APRIL 19, 2001

Daron is the current World Champion, but in the Alaskan frontiers of modern skiing he follows Reggie's lead. Rahlves says what everyone feels: "I have complete trust and confidence in Reggie, and I respect his judgment. Reggie sets the standard here." Today Reggie has traversed out from a narrow, unnamed ridge in the wilderness 30 miles north of Haines. He was dropped there by helicopter. Below him is a thousand foot face of snow beautifully textured into vertical grooves running the entire length of the slope. They are runnels caused by snow falling, not sliding, down an incline too steep to hold all that lands upon it. The gradient is about 55 degrees, steep enough that Reggie can touch his uphill elbow to the snow without leaning into the hill, the last thing he wants to do. Reggie's Atomic skis are high-tech carbon fiber/steel/plastic instruments of space age efficiency. His Atomic boots are plastic casts that give him a subtlety of control Dick Durrance could never have imagined in lace-up leathers. Reggie's clothes are state-of-the-industry Columbia wear that will keep him warm and dry in the severest conditions. His head is encased in a shock absorbent Boeri helmet and stylish Scott goggles. In some ways he looks more like an astronaut or a race car driver than a slider down improbable slopes of snow. None of it (except, perhaps, the helmet) will be of the slightest use if he should make a mistake, if his will fails or his spirit falters. Like Durrance on Warm Springs 62 years earlier, only spirit, skill and personal commitment to courage will bring him through this moment. A mistake means a thousand foot fall down a snow-covered cliff, with no chance of slowing momentum.

It is Reggie's fourth day on skis since breaking his pelvis in a skier cross race two months earlier. He stands there a long time, analyzing the slope, rehearsing strategy, quelling fears, waiting for word from the photographers that the light is right and they are ready.

When the cameras are ready, Reggie goes.

He makes two turns and then a longer one right to get out of the way of the slough, a small avalanche keeping pace with the skier, created by skis turning on a slope so steep. Two turns and then a longer turn right. And then again. And again. The entire slope is sloughing deep enough that it will take Reggie with it if he can't stay out of its way. Slough management is a requisite skill of the Alaskan skier of the steeps. Watching Reggie is an incredible and thrilling sight. He literally drops a thousand feet at 60 miles an hour in perfect control. He finishes with a loud whoop of accomplishment and relief—"WHAAAAHOOOOOOO"—giving exact voice to a 21st century version of "Himmel, you are one lucky son-of-a-gun."

Then it is Rahlves' turn. He moves from the ridge onto the face where he waits for the cameras. He stands on his uphill leg with enough intensity that the next day his World Champion thigh is sore. That night, he says, "I was definitely more scared than in the starting gate of any World Cup downhill, including the Hahnenkahm, considered the most difficult, dangerous and frightening of World Cup downhills."

Rahlves exudes the confidence of a champion and he has skied all his life, but he is a rookie in the Alaskan steeps. He later wrote of this day and run, "The skies were blue and the snow was ideal. This is what it's all about. I feel like I can handle anything on snow, but for a moment I was concerned if I had what it took."

Standing at the top of the thousand foot face, the runnels appear to Rahlves like speed bumps running the entire length of the descent. Reggie's sage advice comes to mind: "If you don't stick to your tactics and ski the right line you'll be taken out by the slough." He feels the nervous buzz of uncertainty run through him, knowing that if it takes control "then you are in for the ride of your life at the mercy of the mountain."

"Ski it strong," he says to himself.

The radio transmission from the film crew cuts the defining silence—"skier ready, 10 secs—5,4,3,2,1—." He drops onto the run, fighting the first few turns, searching to get a feel for the mountain and to relax. It was his 3rd run on skis in two weeks. After a couple of turns massive amounts of snow are rolling past Rahlves on his left. He skis too far left into the slough. "I felt snow slam into my boots trying to take me down," he said. "It was like a wall of whitewater from a wave. I laid into the turn and got out of there." It was a narrow escape, not without an element of luck, and he said, "From that point on I stuck with my plan to keep working to the right. Near the bottom I pointed my skis straight down the fall line, accelerated and jumped over the bergshrund (a horizontal crack where the glacier pulls away from the base of the mountain) and I had survived my first big line in Alaska."

"Sure, it's a risk"

There are those who would question the wisdom of Daron Rahlves doing this sort of skiing less than a year before his best chance for an Olympic medal. Rahlves says of this issue, "Sure, it's a risk, but it's a great adventure and it's what I want to do, and it all makes you a better athlete. Besides, I can't live my life for those who question my judgment." Indeed, there are those who would question the good sense of *anyone* doing this sort of skiing. But those are the ones for whom security takes precedence over freedom and passion and who would question the intelligence of leaving the safety and prestige of running the Aspen Skiing Company for the adventure and uncertainty of making films, as Dick Durrance did half a century ago and the way the Crists are doing today. Those naysayers are the ones whose WHAAAAHOOOOOOOs lack a couple of 'A's and several 'O's and whose souls will never know just what lucky sons-of-a-gun they are.

CHAPTER THREE

The Joy of Skiing

THE FIRST POINT TO KEEP CLEAR is that skiing and the ski industry are not the same thing. I refer not to the whole of skiing but specifically to the activity and industry of lift-serviced alpine in bounds skiing. The two, activity and industry, do, of course, overlap and intertwine and feed into and off each other, but they are not the same. They need each other. To criticize the ski industry is not to ignore the fact of an imperfect marriage, but it is to emphasize the destructive consequences of the industry's long term excesses and short term greed on its partner, skiing. Every skier and ski businessman (also not, necessarily, the same thing) will have somewhat different definitions and perspectives of skiing and its demographic range of practitioners, but all will agree that there is value in the act of skiing. The value in the act of skiing for the individual skier can be determined only by that skier; it may be exercise, relaxation, escape, family bonding, athletic endeavor or church; but it is private, sacred time, even when surrounded by friends, family and thousands of fellow skiers, each in his and her own private, sacred ski time. The value in the act of skiing for the ski industry can be determined by its accountants. The value in the act of skiing to each individual, the whole of society and the universe at large can be neither quantified nor qualified by any power or entity known to man, though it can be named. In full awareness that one man's name may not fit another man's perception, the name I will put to that value is "joy," and the joy of skiing, like all joy, is invaluable. Life without it is reduced to a drudge or a duty. And he or she who would place duty above joy, like those who would sacrifice freedom for security, deserve and will enjoy the benefits of none of them.

Joy is a noun originating in Middle English, from Old French joie, based on Latin *guadium*, from *guadere* 'rejoice.' Among the definitions of joy listed in the OED are: 1.) A vivid emotion of pleasure arising from a sense of well-being or satisfaction; the feeling or state of being highly pleased or delighted; exultation of spirit; gladness, delight. 2.) A pleasurable state or condition; a state of happiness or felicity; *esp.* the perfect bliss or beatitude of heaven; hence, the place of bliss, paradise, heaven. 3.) A source or object of joy; that which causes joy, or in which delight is taken; a delight. 4.) The quality which causes joy; quality or faculty of delighting.

As the well-known abstract expressionist painter Abby Grosvenor, is fond of saying of her work and other things, "There you have it."

Skiing is a joy, pure and simple.

There you have it.

That, at any rate, is as close to defining *my* experience of skiing as I've seen. Skiing is a joy. If for some reason it is not a delight for some skiers, then it is worth considering that those people might be best served (and best serve) by seeking pleasure and a sense of well-being in other realms. An inner sense of well-being and delight has far more value in life than, say, a joyless, well executed turn, no matter how dutifully performed or loudly applauded. There are skiers for whom skiing is not a joy, but, rather, a sort of self-imposed duty, often a grim duty at that. Many of these skiers have managed to make of joy a duty through confusing skiing with the ski industry, and they are easily recognizable by the gravity of spirit and demeanor with which they mistake form for function while substituting looking good for feeling good.

It is not my intention to write for or about those staid people, for they are a minority in the community of skiing and I do not really understand them. I write for those millions of skiers who ski one or ten or thirty or one hundred fifty days a year with passion and all their soul and, you know, *happiness.*

Skiing makes people happy.

There you have it.

That's why millions of skiers continue to visit the ski resorts of America, despite the over priced impediments the ski industry continues to place in the way of skiers' search for skiing happiness. Skier days are dropping, as are the number of skiers, as any ski industry accountant can verify. This is not because the act of skiing is no longer fun. It is because the industry has turned away from keeping skiing open to the multitudes and made of it a financial gated community. Gated communities are by definition exclusive and limiting, not inclusive and expansive, and they do not thrive on joy and eventually, lacking new blood and oxygen, they die of stagnation.

There are as many ways of skiing joy as there are joyous skiers, those who are in it for the skiing, not the accoutrements, the scene or the cachet. A few sketches of joyous skiers who are specific individuals but not uncommon:

I used to know a man who was the curator for the largest Art Museum in a major metropolitan American city. A busy, high energy man, he was a classic weekend intermediate skier who had come to the endeavor late in life, but his zest for the act of skiing was something to behold. He skied with passion and complete focus and an inspiring enthusiasm that cut through his experiential and technical limitations like they were nothing more substantial than a foot of fresh powder. He expressed what so many skiers know without, perhaps, thinking too much about it: "Nothing else makes me feel as free as skiing." He also said, "It's the only time they can't get me by phone." I haven't seen him in years as he skis in California, but I sometimes wonder how he's faring in the cell phone era, if skiing still sets him free, if 'they' still can't get him.

I have a friend who skis Sun Valley every winter and who takes the joy of his skiing more earnestly than some, and he does not suffer fools or impositions on his free time lightly. One day he was riding up one of Sun Valley's high speed quad chairs with his wife, a friend and a stranger who got on the chair at the last minute. The stranger pulled out a cell phone and asked his chair mates, "Do you mind?" The man who does not suffer fools lightly replied, "Yes, I do." Without hesitation, the stranger then proceeded to dial a number and carry on a business conversation. When he eventually hung up my friend asked, "Is that one of those cell phones?" "Why, yes, it is," said the stranger. "Can I see it?" The stranger handed over his cell phone. My friend looked it over and the phone slipped from his hand, dropping fifty feet to the snow below. "Oh, I'm so very sorry," he said with a smile. "How will I find my phone," said the obviously dismayed stranger. "Call yourself," said my friend, who skied the rest of the day overflowing with even more happiness than usually fills his skiing days. It is not known if the stranger found his cell phone, but when last seen he was neither filled with the joy of skiing nor looking good.

Every large ski area has them, the pack of skiers with the skills and experience to stand out on any mountain, the ones who ski nearly every day all winter and whose lives on every level are organized around the freedom to have those days on skis. They often ski together, but they ski for the love of skiing and the joy of life and the passion of snow and mountains. These are the ones who began as children and when they became adults and had to make choices in life choose to ski, and then they became middle aged and more, and they continued to ski for the love of skiing and the joy of life. They often ski fast. They always ski hard. The social aspects of skiing are not a high priority with any of them, though some of them are sociable, personable, engaged citizens of the world. They are in every ski area in every period of that area. In Sun Valley, where I live, in this era (the beginning of the 21st century) they are Pedro, Cheeso, Harpo, Psycho, Dano, Jimbo, Curly, Matt, Robbie, Jeff, Sallie, Byron, Twyla, Julie, Pat, Reggie, Zach, John, Mary, Mike, Dave, Maggie and Chris, among others. These are the ones for whom the joy of skiing is a serious and lifelong way of life, not a form of casual and enjoyable recreation. In my opinion they are the soul of skiing, visible in every ski area, and one need look no further to answer the question of why people ski.

And then there is technology. Does the evolution of skiing technology enhance the joy of skiing? Enhance the experience? Expand the possibilities? Do fleets of $500,000 grooming machines make a better skiing experience? Do high speed lifts result in a better day of skiing? Do modern ski and boot design expand the possibilities of skiing and enrich the experience for each skier? Do shape skis work and do they make it easier to carve a turn? Do artificial snow making systems create a true skiing environment? Are these technologies evolution, progress and to be applauded, or are they marketing tools driven by the bottom line at the expense of the soul of skiing?

The answer to all of these questions is "yes," the same answer to the questions concerning the inherent and obvious contradictions of modern skiing.

Walt Whitman probably expressed it best:
"Do I contradict myself?
Very well then I contradict myself,
(I am large, I contain multitudes)."
Joy itself contains multitudes of contradictions, thank Ullr.

An old friend, Bob Chamberlain, a brilliant photographer whose work has enhanced the culture of skiing, an avid and long time skier, and husband of poet and writer Karen Chamberlain, once asked me, "Is there any hope for skiing?" Bob was dispirited with the state of skiing, or, at least, the state of the excesses of the ski industry. In this he is not alone, but I maintain that skiing itself is alive and well and as joyous and worthwhile as ever. Bob still had moments of joy using 60s vintage equipment—long skis, soft boots—that don't work as well or as easily as modern gear. There is as much joy in the latest made in China K2 ski as there was in the great for its time Head ski made in Maryland, but, just as you can't go to the same party twice, you can't make the same turn forever.

In 1964 just off the Mt. Rose Highway between Reno and the North Shore of Lake Tahoe Bill Kidd and I raced head to head with members of California's Alturas Snowshoe Club with their 19th century vintage 12 foot hand made wooden skis with one pole. We ran straight down parallel tracks a few hundred yards long and reached probably 60 mph, me and Bill and our 'modern' gear against the boys on their beautifully crafted 19th century models. We found that if we just lifted our poles and got in our tucks and started moving, our modern gear would prevail, but only by a few yards. If we allowed the Alturas boys to pole just once while we refrained they would beat us. In a straight race on skis a century of technology hadn't made that much difference, but, of course, our modern technology of the '60s gave us turning and controlling capabilities and pure skiing freedom the Alturas boys could only dream of, just as the technology of the 21st century gives us turning and controlling capabilities only dreamed of in the '60s of the 20th century.

The answer to Bob's question is "Yes", there really is hope for skiing. There is as much freedom and joy in skiing today in Aspen, Sun Valley, Bear Valley, Squaw Valley, Taos and Keystone as there was in Alturas in 1880, Chamonix in 1924, St. Moritz in 1948, Aspen in 1950, Alta in 1968, Vail in 1975, Jackson Hole in 1985 or in Spar Gulch a couple of years ago before they opened it up to snowboarders. Why, just this morning, January 9, 2003, in the company of a couple of my favorite skiing buddies, I had some skiing on my favorite mountain (Sun Valley's Bald Mountain), that made me happy in a way that nothing else does. We skied on new shape skis and rode high speed lifts and some of the snow we skied upon came from a nozzle and not the sky, and it was groomed by machines that cost more than all the cars I will ever own, and it was really fun. The joy of skiing is in the present, ever changing moment of skiing, and it is that present moment that needs the focus, and gives the freedom, and keeps the faith.

There you have it.

CHAPTER FOUR

Mammoth Par Coeur

It is a deep dive into the mind to remember things of more than 50 years ago, but the heart best retains the past and most strongly connects it to the present and, sometimes, the future. At least so it is for me. Things of the heart do not fade away like old soldiers; they maintain and nourish and are always there to be called upon, learned from, cherished and loved, even when removed by time and distance.

I was a ski racer from Reno, Nevada in the 1950s and '60s, and the mountain and people and experiences of nearby Mammoth Mountain, California were a huge part of my formative years and beyond. Mammoth is part of my heart and life experience, a guide to the mind. Only the inaccuracy of nostalgia allows people to claim that the '50s were a "better" time for American skiers, but both the heart and mind tell me it was a simpler era. Today's Mammoth Mountain skier gets miles more skiing on better and more varied terrain than the skier of 50 years ago, but it does not seem to me that the personal satisfaction, well being and joy of the day's skiing endeavors are any better now than then in Mammoth or anywhere else.

There are reasons besides economic ones that back country skiing around Mammoth and elsewhere is growing in popularity among skiers seeking simplicity, a return to basics and a sense of how it was in the beginning.

In the early years we only came to Mammoth for races, always among the best and best run in the west. The first few years (1952-54) two rope tows got skiers to near where Broadway Express exists today. Holding on to the rope clear to the top was an arduous task that strengthened arms and hands and destroyed gloves and was sometimes as exciting as the ski down. At the age of 13, 14, and 15 ski trips out of town were as much a life quest as a ski racing adventure, and Mammoth was always and easily our favorite place on the western tour. In retrospect it is clear that trips to Mammoth were so satisfying and enjoyable to our young, developing beings not so much because of the excellent skiing and the excitement that marked every ski race but because of the people of Mammoth and Bishop. There was hominess, friendliness and inclusiveness to the Mammoth skiing community that did not exist so readily in other places, and we always felt welcome, worthy and rewarded and thereby inspired to be our better selves. Why this was so is speculative, but it is well remembered.

Among people who stand out in those early years were Bill Kinmont and his family who often invited us to stay at their Rocking K Ranch outside Bishop during ski races. Jill and Bob Kinmont were two of the best young ski racers in America and were friends and contemporaries, and the Kinmonts' hospitality and generosity to young ski racers made many trips to Mammoth a warm pleasure rather than a motel ordeal. One spring I learned to do a back flip off the Kinmont diving board into the swimming pool.

And there was (and is) Dave. Nothing then or now about Mammoth Mountain as a ski resort, a community, a state of mind or a life experience exists without the imprint of Dave McCoy. Dave was never perfect or a saint as some (not Dave) would have you believe, but as a young (and then not so young) Reno based ski racer it was my great good fortune to be associated with Dave, his family, the Mammoth Mountain race team, friends in the community and, of course, the mountain itself and those surrounding it. Others have written sufficiently of Dave's energy, intelligence, enthusiasm and vision that have so formed the Mammoth area. It needs not repeating here. In my opinion, the reason he has affected the lives of so many people in such a beneficial way is that he always thought large, of the greatest good for the greatest number, when he made decisions, and he is a model for many people I know. Even during the late 1960s and through the '70s and, in some cases, beyond, when many of my generation and mind-set (including my closest friend among the McCoy clan, Carl "P-Nut" McCoy) were living a long-haired, unshaven, turn on/tune in/drop out lifestyle and ethic that was a calculated affront to mainstream American and Mammoth culture, Dave never once held back his mainstream square-jawed open smile, curiosity, friendliness and insight, nor was he stingy with his honest, practical opinion about matters that were neither easy or comfortable for him. In heart as well as mind Dave holds the generous position.

The end of innocence in ski racing for me coincided with that of Mammoth Mountain's, or so it seems to me. On January 30, 1955 I was 16 years old and in my first Class A ski race, the Snow Cup in Alta, Utah. I was very excited and almost overwhelmed to be in such a "big" event. It was a stormy day at Alta and the course was fast and tricky, and Jill Kinmont fell and broke her neck and ski racing which was *everything* was never the same again. I fell in the same place as Jill in that race but was unscathed, and I still remember the look of a broken heart and tragedy in Dave McCoy's eyes that evening as we waited in the emergency room of the hospital in Salt Lake City where Jill and several other injured racers had been taken. Paralysis, spinal cord injury and paraplegic became new words in my developing vocabulary, and I never raced again without the awareness that the smallest mistake carried the potential of grave consequences. In all things, including skiing and ski racing, the end of innocence opens up possibilities that allow life to grow and evolve and move on. Innocence can be charming and it may (or not) be virtuous, but there is nothing innocent about organic life or natural evolution. 1955 was the year the first chair lift was built at Mammoth, and the mountain and village and community have grown and evolved from there to a vastly more complicated ski resort megalopolis that certainly serves a greater good for a greater number of people, though whether the simple individual skiing/mountain experience is better today than 50 years ago is not assured. Like many others I knew that first lift as "Chair 1," but the Mammoth website assures me that Chair 1 and others "...all have names now, and exist only in the memories and automatic brain-recall of Mammoth regulars."

Sigh.

What is certain is that in the late '50s and through the '60s the Mammoth Mountain Race Team, first coached by McCoy and then by Philippe Mollard, was in a class of its own and became the standard and the model for subsequent ski race programs throughout America. Mammoth was the first ski area to provide coaching, transportation, room and board and training facilities for its racers, freeing up their minds and hearts and energies for the straight forward task of ski racing. It changed the way ski racing was carried on in the United States, and many of its racers—among them Ken Lloyd, Penny McCoy, Dennis "Pancho" McCoy, Jean Saubert, Joan Hannah, Bev Anderson, Linda Myers, Robin Morning, Katie Morning, Jim Morning, Perry Thompson, Rosie Fortna and others—were among the finest in America. I was never formally associated with the Mammoth Race Team, but as a racer and later as a coach I often wound up traveling with them. I still remember leaving Joanie Hannah in a restaurant in Salt Lake after a stop on the way to Colorado and driving half an hour east before noticing she wasn't with us; we returned to Salt Lake to find her patiently waiting outside. And I recall sitting in the Wort Hotel in Jackson Hole, Wyoming with Mollard in 1968 and whooping with glee while watching on TV Canada's Nancy Greene kill the field in the Olympic giant slalom in Grenoble.

The following summer, August 1969, I climbed the Steck Route on Mt. Morrisson with Mammoth ski racer Steve Wood. More than 20 years later, Steve, a gentle soul and wonderful ski racer, climber, artist, teacher and friend, was brutally murdered by a couple of thrill seeking punks he had never met before they killed him. I've written elsewhere of that climb......"*I left Squaw the afternoon of the second and drove to Mammoth where Steve was working. We got organized and picked up Steve Thompson, who was hiking in to the base with us for exercise, and would carry out sleeping gear which we hoped we wouldn't need on the climb. Steve Thompson, the brother of racers Lance, Perry and Tim, was just re-learning to walk after nearly two years of casts, crutches and operations necessitated after he* straddled the tree-size finish post of a downhill in Steamboat. We drove to Convict Lake in the afternoon and began the four-hours bushwhack to the base of Mt. Morrisson. It was hot and every possible insect abounded. The hike was a drag. We ate dinner quickly and bedded at dark. There was very little sleep that night in the boulders at the base of Mt. Morrisson. The heat was oppressive. The bugs were impossible. Apprehension was perceptible. I figure I slept two hours.

"We were up before dawn and climbing in the first light, after saying so-long to Thompson who wished us luck and hiked out. This day...gave me one of my best mountaineering experiences...We moved fast and didn't get lost once on a very complex route. We ran out of water before noon. By two in the afternoon we were both hurting from the hard-labor summer dries. It began to rain as Steve led up the great red chimney, and I was desperate enough to be grateful for the few raindrops I caught in my open mouth with my head thrown back. At about three o'clock we found water; we stopped and drank our fill, ate, took a ginseng and continued to the summit. We signed and read the summit register, including a terse message from a member of the first party to climb the Steck route in winter: 'never again.' Then we began one of the longest, grungiest, most involved, difficult, **shittiest** descents in the Sierra. We reached Convict Lake about 9:30 that night and went straight to Mammoth. We showered and drank twenty glasses of orange juice from the cafeteria machine. Then I ate some more ginseng, watched Steve ease off to bed and hit the road to Squaw. About 2:30 in the morning I got to my tiny apartment under the tram, woke Jane and stayed up until dawn talking about the climb, Steve Wood, the descent, the orange juice at Mammoth, the drive, the mountains, the ginseng, and what a wonderful life it was to be able to climb and to come home and talk until the summer Sierra dawn, with no thought of what the future might bring or the past may hold, enveloped in the unimaginably perfect present, talking with someone I loved."

A Mammoth good time and memory, and I will always miss Steve Wood's presence in this world and treasure his memory.

In the early 70s I spent a winter in Bishop skiing most days at Mammoth just for fun, a welcome and much enjoyed break from the years of teaching and coaching skiing. It would be 20 years before I got completely out of professional skiing, but that winter of the freedom to ski in Mammoth certainly got me to thinking and helped lead me back to the essential pleasure of simply skiing for the joy of it. For several consecutive springs in the 70s I spent a couple of weeks at Mammoth testing skis for Skiing Magazine. Several of us would ski on 8 to 10 pairs of different skis a day and then write critical evaluations of the performance of each ski. It was great fun and we learned much about skis and which ones worked and which ones didn't. Skiing, of course, couldn't offend any potential advertisers and sometimes bent our reports to suit the mind set that every ski is good for someone. (The brilliant ski maker Mike Brunetto who learned to ski at Mammoth and who made RD and Wolf skis is fond of saying, "If it's turned up at one end it's a good ski.") My favorite bent Skiing ski report read something like, "This is an excellent ski for a 300 pound skier on hard ice." During those test camps we skied every morning until the snow got soft and we climbed in the afternoons and had spirited discussions in the condo at night over dinner with Doug and Ginny Pfeiffer, Wayne Wong, Ralph Harris and others, and one year we watched the Watergate hearings on TV and debated the issues surrounding them.

And then the circuitous paths of life over the next 20 years caused me to visit Mammoth only rarely, though I kept in touch with friends and Mammoth developments. In one recent year (2005) I visited twice, once in spring to climb at Owens River Gorge and a few months later to attend Dave McCoy's 90th birthday party where the past was naturally emphasized and rightfully honored, but the present and the future were represented and looking healthy.

During the spring visit we skied one day on the mountain, mostly on the cornice in abundant and good snow. 50 years ago a skier hiked to the cornice and was lucky to get one run in a day. In 2005 we got several and were grateful and happy for each one. At the end of the day my buddy Sean and I stopped by the terrain park to watch the boarders and twin tip skiers do their thing(s). The Mammoth terrain park (I am told) is world class, with enough half-pipes, kickers, rails, ramps and spectators to keep the sickest snow sliding acrobat in nuclear air heaven. We live in Sun Valley where (at that time; there is now a first class terrain park in Sun Valley) the terrain park is, to put it mildly, lame, and neither of us has paid much attention to this most modern of ski resort activities.

Watching the boarders and twin tippers in the Mammoth terrain park was (for a couple of Idaho rubber-neckers) a revelation, an education, a thrill and a great show. Once again, Mammoth has set the standard and expanded the possibilities of the present and future of ski resort endeavor. The basics never change, and watching some 30 or more baggy clothed 14 to 30 year old Dudes and Bettys perform astonishing (and alarming) inverted 180, 540 and 720s, jibs, McTwists, rodeo airs, wetcats, fakies, Stalemaskies, gay twists and an occasional "boned out a indy," a crippler and a zonk was a fine reminder that innocence never dies and that in the world of mountain people Mammoth is a star and we were and are properly impressed.

A week or so later I was in northern California and talking to Dave McCoy in Bishop by cell phone on an imperfect connection. We were speaking of the vagaries of life and of its rewards and pleasures and endeavors and sorrows and pains, and of what we (Dave at 89, me at 66) have learned and seen and experienced and look forward to in Mammoth and skiing and life. I said, "Well, sometimes in life all we can do is cope."

Faster than lightning came Dave's reply, "No, no, we must never coast."

"No, Dave," I said, "sometimes all we can do is *cope*."

"Dick," he said with seriousness that I pictured as all square jaw and no smile, "I don't want to ever hear of you coasting."

I laughed at the miscommunication, at the swiftness and perfect assurance with which Dave corrected what he thought was a lapse and defect in my thinking. My life has been warmed and informed by the knowledge that coasting is unacceptable behavior. We soon straightened out that I said 'cope,' not 'coast.' And he agreed, "Sometimes in life all we can do is cope."

We must never coast.

CHAPTER FIVE

Ski Instruction in America

A rant to begin a long overdue discussion

"Discussion in America means dissent."
James Thurber

ACCORDING TO THE *HARPER'S INDEX*, fifty-nine percent of American public school teachers hold second jobs. Anyone who has ever taught school knows this statistic does not indicate that being a teacher is less than a full-time occupation, or that time and energy are in abundance at the end of the teacher's day. It does mean that the chosen profession of our school teachers will not support them. What this indicates about America's values, priorities, economics and politics is a matter that probably deserves more reflection than the short, speedy attention span of our culture allows. It shows that learning, or, more to the point of this essay, *teaching* in America is viewed as a commodity rather than a value, a line item expenditure rather than a survival mechanism for civilization if not the individual, of less importance (if compensation is an indication of the significance a society gives the work of its members) than the labor of bartenders, the efforts of realtors or the inherently dishonest drudge of public relations. In America, it seems, the substance of teaching is deemed of less worth than, or, perhaps, viewed in a more kindly light, is confused with, the *appearance* of passing along and expanding the body of knowledge that supports and nourishes what mankind's collective hubris touts as 'civilization'.

Somewhere in the national psyche lurks agreement with George Bernard Shaw's cynical adage: "He who can, does. He who cannot, teaches." Or so it would seem from the shabby and neglectful treatment our society consistently bestows on its teachers.

The brilliant and usually insightful Shaw was wrong on this and other issues. A more accurate summation of the state of things, equally cynical or, at least, skeptical, would be, "He who can, teaches. He who cannot, becomes an administrator."

And it is not only in the public school system that the work of teachers is so ignorantly under valued, unappreciated and relegated to the list of topics, like George Bush's education and astuteness, that right thinking people don't like to think about.

In the stylish, expensive and increasingly privileged world of lift serviced skiing, where the knowledge and efforts of ski instructors generate a substantial cash flow for the ski resorts they work within, few ski instructors are able to live from their profession. Whether it would be more appropriate to use 'even' or 'especially' to begin and make more accurate the previous sentence is, like reflecting on the values, priorities, economics and politics of America, a matter worth more attention that it gets. This is not to equate the significance to American society of ski lessons for the privileged with the schooling of its ordinary children, but only to portray the neglect and disdain our culture bestows upon the teacher's profession, no matter what their subject. (It is also not to ignore snowboard instructors who are in the same boat as ski instructors and are here included for purposes of brevity of prose under the ski school and ski instructor designation.)

So far as I know, there are no reliable statistics on how many American ski instructors hold second jobs in order to make it through winter. Ninety percent would be a conservative estimate. Any skier who has paid for a lesson might find this a bizarre circumstance, given that an all day private lesson at most major American ski resorts at the beginning of the 21st century costs around $400. The most expensive ski instruction in America at this writing can be enjoyed at Deer Valley, Utah where an all day private lesson for one (at the beginning of the century) costs $470 a day, though three to five people can join the lesson for $510. Aspen, traditionally in the forefront of all things skiing in America, has lost face and slipped in status by dropping slightly behind in the most expensive ski lesson division, charging only $449 for an all day private, though it maintains some of its prestige by offering five full days of private lessons for just $2100. Sun Valley charges $415, with $25 for each additional person up to five, though its sister resort, Snow Basin, site of the 2002 Olympic downhill and super giant slalom events, offers all day lessons for $269 for one or two people. Jackson Hole charges its customers $395 for an all day lesson, while Squaw Valley is $399 for one to four skiers and $125 for each additional student. Taos charges $360 a day and $95 an hour for one to four people. Many areas offer class lessons, where up to ten or twelve strangers of similar ability are grouped into the same class. A two and a half hour class lesson in Sun Valley sells for $40. Squaw Valley has an on going group lesson program that works out to $36 an hour, while Jackson Hole has a four and a half hour group lesson for $65. Keystone offers two days of two and a half hour group lessons for $80. Class sizes vary, of course, but it is not unusual to have ten in a class. This means that ten people in a two and a half hour $40 lesson bring $400 to the ski school. These prices are representative of what is available to the skiing public at most major ski areas.

A ski instructor should be able to get by on the $400 a day ski schools charge for his and her knowledge, skill, experience, training, time, labor and wear and tear of body, equipment and psyche. For the majority of ski instructors, this is not the case. While the price of ski lessons have steadily raised at a steeper rate than the price of living, the wages paid ski instructors have not. Without going into a breakdown of all the types and lengths of lesson available in the large and small ski resorts of America, the $400 all day private lesson will serve to illustrate why the American skiing industry is stagnating.

The first question that needs asking is whether a day of ski instruction is rightly valued at $400 (or $470) for the customer/client/student/guest. There is, of course, no definitive answer to such a question that will find universal agreement, but it can be assumed that from the customer's standpoint it is deemed worth it to those who pay and not worth it to those who don't, won't or can't. This is the essence of the free whatever the market will bear capitalist system. The next question is whether a $400 a day ski lesson is properly valued for the long-term health and prosperity of the sport and industry (they are not the same thing) of skiing. Again, no facile answer is available. Lastly, the question arises whether a $400 a day ski lesson is appropriately valued for the labor and time of the ski instructor. The answers to these questions are subjective and meaningful, and they will vary widely from person to person. To confront these questions is as useful as whatever answers emerge from the process. They are interesting questions to pose to people in the world of skiing—instructors, ski school directors, area managers, ski school students, lift operators, ski patrolmen, mechanics, the skier who does not pay for lessons, the school teacher who can only afford to ski a few days a year or not ski at all. I've inserted variations of these questions into many conversations over the past few years, and the replies have never failed to educate, illuminate and entertain. Such questions are not asked, discussed or thought about nearly enough for the health of skiing. They are questions that are not found in the pages of the major ski publications of America. For the well-being of the industry, the sport and the people of skiing, they should be; but, alas, the major ski publications of America, once the wholesome, rosy cheeked lovers of the sport of skiing, have turned into the gaudily rouged whores of industry.

The answers to such questions vary. I know veteran ski patrolmen who view ski instructors as little more than prima ballerinas, overpaid for easier work and far less responsibility than patrolmen bear. One long time corporate ski resort executive, notoriously disdainful of the profession of ski instruction and the persons of ski instructors, refers to his own ski instructing years as his "ski bum" years. There are clients whose answers take the form of long-standing friendship and yearly five figure tips and all expense paid vacations to exotic spas in the off season for their instructors. There are many ski instructors themselves who view ski instruction less as a profession than a means to earn a free season pass, a few extra dollars and, in some cases, status. The latter are necessary to a ski school, as teacher aids and substitute teachers are necessary to public schools; but, in my opinion, they are not the core of a professional ski school and reflect less the ethic of professionalism than a cultural bias that if you can ski you can teach skiing, in somewhat the same manner that believes that if you can read the newspaper you can teach English, history or economics. There are marketing directors who think ski instructors are the best public relations ambassadors a ski area has, and are, thereby, worth their weight in marketing gold. My own answers, for instance, are not likely to be aligned with those of the President of the Aspen Skiing Company, the CEO of Intrawest or the Chief Financial Officer of Vail Associates whose primary responsibility is to the bottom line, short-term, maximum profit for their corporations.

Being obligated to the short-term profits of a company (often the largest single employer of a ski town community) is not the same as being socially responsible to a community or, in the long run, fiscally responsible to the larger industry of (in this case) skiing. The $400 a day ski lesson is symptomatic of the ways in which the modern corporate world of skiing is destroying the social fabric of ski town communities. It is also a clue to why the numbers of skiers is dropping along with the number of ski resorts still in business. The steady decline in number of skiers signing up for ski school has been blamed in the mainstream ski media on several factors—skiing having become too easy due to grooming and artificial snow, better equipment that supposedly makes skiing effortless, a cultural wide stigma attached to going to schools or learning from teachers, a lack of competition within each ski resort and a lack of professionalism among instructors as a result of abysmal wages. There is a sliver truth to each of these points, and a large laminated beam to the last one, but they evade the primary reason ski schools are struggling: *ski instruction is too expensive.* It's a bad bargain. No....it is more than that; it is an obscene transaction. The $400 a day ski lesson is one pillar of the fence around the gated community of the modern American major ski resort.

In my opinion, the $400 a day ski lesson is not worth it to the student, the sport and industry of skiing or to the instructor.

It is not worth it to the student because the same fee is charged the customer for a wide spectrum of services provided whenever an instructor is assigned (off the desk) to a student. A client who knows his or her instructor can be assumed to know that instructor's value to them.

Whether that value is more in teaching or social skills is another affair, but it is their affair. (If truth be told, a substantial to a majority of all day private lessons are paid for not because the student is interested in polishing skiing skills, but so that lift lines can be cut. As such, the $400 a day lesson serves more as a high status escort service for wealthy clients than as an educational tool for skiers, and the instructor's primary job has little to do with teaching. And on powder days a number of instructors are hired as a means to get first tracks by getting on the lifts earlier than the general public.) However, a ski school assigning an instructor to a client is shuffling and balancing several factors....availability of instructor, quality of instructor, ski school politics, personalities, prejudices and, of course, the bottom line. American ski instructors work on a wildly fluctuating pay scale that, in my opinion, is shredding the quality of ski instruction found at most ski areas. The Aspen Ski and Snowboard School pays the most to its instructors of any that I am familiar with (more on that later), and even at this high profile, stylish hot spot of skiing, most instructors work the bars, restaurants, ski shops, art galleries, real estate offices and catering services in their off hours. Aspen has a sliding pay scale that rewards instructors according to their level of certification and the number of hours they work each season. An apprentice instructor who has worked less than 75 hours will make less than $9 an hour (or $54 for the six hour day). This is 12 percent of the price of the lesson, before taxes, and it gives the teacher who has worked all day not enough to live for that day anywhere in America, much less in Aspen, one of the most expensive places to live in the history of mankind. It gives the Aspen Skiing Company $395 and a gross profit of 88 percent for the instructor's day of work. Most of the student's money winds up in the pockets of the procurer, the ski school, not with the provider of service, the ski instructor. *That* is an obscene transaction. Even an insignificant squire whose mere presence costs seven times what he is paid for that attendance deserves a living wage.

The same lesson taught by an instructor with the highest level of certification will give the instructor about $20 an hours (or $120 for the day). This leaves $329 and a gross profit of 79 percent for the Aspen

Ski Company. Much later in the season, after this same fully certified instructor has worked more than 450 hours, he or she will earn nearly $35 an hour (or $210 for the six hour day), enough to live on for that day even in Aspen. It leaves $239 and a gross profit of 59 percent for the Aspen Skiing Company for the instructor's day of work.

In order to work 450 hours, a ski instructor must teach all day at least 75 days, and a small minority of instructors at any ski school work that much in a season. And the realities of time, both in a day and in a ski season, dictate that even the most devoted Aspen instructor will work minimum hours at the highest wage.

This is not to single out the all too often singled out Aspen to make a point about American skiing. It is not to be overly critical of the Aspen Skiing Company, which, after all, pays its instructors better than in the rest of the country. But it is to emphasize that instructors elsewhere make considerably less.

The complicated "Ski and Snowboard Schools of Aspen Compensation Grid" was developed at the beginning of the 1988-89 season to replace the somewhat more equitable bonus system that was previously in place. That system was put there by Aspen Ski School Director Curt Chase during his reign in the 1970s. Chase was (and is) a true friend to the sport and industry of skiing and to the instructors and students of the Aspen Ski School, and his legacy has been a great benefit to them all. The bonus was paid to each instructor at the end of the season, the size depending on how much money the instructor's efforts brought into the ski school. Hard working instructors had a sizable four figure stash to tide them over the difficult resort town off season between winter and summer. In accordance with the honest spirit and above board mechanics of capitalism this was only fitting, as the money was paid to the ski school for the instructor's knowledge and time and training. The student pays an additional fee for the right to ride lifts and ski on groomed runs. But in 1988 the Aspen Skiing company's aggressive new president envisioned other corporate uses....new hotels, lifts and the like.... for that money than giving it out as instructor bonuses at the end of the year. He also envisioned the public relations nightmare that would ensue if Aspen's high profile, opinionated, passionate and notoriously unabashed (and vocal) ski instructors suddenly had their salaries slashed between a fourth and a third. Aspen instructors have more than once raised the specter of a unionized ski school to go alongside the already unionized Aspen Ski Patrol. The ski patrol union has long been a thorn in the conservative side of the corporate administration of the Aspen Skiing Company, and the threat of unionizing is the one sound bargaining chip instructors and patrolmen have (and, for the most part, have not used) in the corporate world of American skiing. To replace Aspen Ski School bonuses, a complicated "compensation grid" was devised that first year which maintained salaries about the same as the previous year after bonuses were figured in. Since that time, Aspen Ski School rates have steadily risen about five percent each year. The obscure numbers of the compensation grid have not kept pace with the rising rates charged customers. Last year, for instance, the grid gave instructors about a 1.3 percent increase in wages. Each year the instructors get less and less a percentage of the money brought in by their efforts, precisely as was intended when the compensation grid was developed.

Most ski schools do not pay their instructors nearly as well as Aspen. Sun Valley, for instance, pays a plethora of their instructors $11 an hour while teaching their $415 a day students. And this hourly wage does not rise as the season progresses. This gives the instructor $66 a day, or 16 percent of the lesson price before taxes, and the Sun Valley Company $349 and a gross profit of 84 percent for the instructor's effort, skill, knowledge, training, and time. Some senior instructors make more, but few make even as much as 50%. Though Ketchum/Sun Valley is not quite in Aspen's league of high prices, it is catching up all too quickly; and $66 a day before taxes is not enough to live on, though $349 certainly is.

Every ski resort has its own system and pay scale and ski school rate, but these examples are indicative of the standard in America. Whatever the rate, it is not a fair value to the student because he is paying the same rate for what the ski area buys at very different rates. A $9 an hour teacher and a $30 an hour teacher are, like the difference between hamburger and filet mignon (assuming the meat came from non-mad cows), priced differently because of different values in the product. But the buyer of the lesson pays the same price no matter what the ski school determines is the value of the instructor's time. The student pays filet mignon rates for what the ski school itself values as hamburger. In addition, the student is paying the ski school, middle man an inordinate amount, for instance $239 or $349, not for the lesson but for access to the instructor. Not to put too fine a point on the vernacular, but the ski school student is being pimped as well as ripped off.

The price of ski lessons is not worth it to the sport and industry of skiing because it is a part of what is crippling them both. The number of skiers coming into the sport is dropping. The number of skiers dropping out of the sport is increasing. The number of skiers taking lessons is declining. The industry of skiing has managed to make the sport of skiing financially inaccessible to most Americans. The corporate ski school has managed to make ski instruction inaccessible to most skiers. Grooming has not made skiing too easy either to do or to learn, and technology has not replaced the human pleasure and satisfaction of acquiring and mastering a skill, nor will it ever. Taking ski lessons is not socially uncool, as has been suggested as a reason for diminishing ski school business. Calling a teacher or instructor 'coach,' 'personal trainer' or 'guide,' or denoting lessons as clinics or seminars does not change the ancient and basic dynamic of transferring knowledge and developing skills, and no one with $400 and the intelligence and motor skills to step into a binding will use such convoluted thinking either to decide not to buy a lesson or to purchase a seminar. I believe the issue is far simpler: ski instruction is too expensive. To paraphrase a well known political adage of a couple of campaigns ago, "It's the price, stupid." A ski lesson is not worth $400 a day, nor need it cost that much.

The expense of a ski lesson would be worth it to the ski instructor if his or her salary was in accordance with the amount the student pays, but 12 or 16 percent is not that amount. Ski instructors' labor produces an inordinate surplus of capital in which the people who earn it do not share. It is an old scenario most famously explicated in the 19th century by Karl Marx. Professionalism suffers because good professionals cannot afford to remain professional skiers, and professionalism suffers because a poorly paid worker is a disgruntled worker anywhere in the world, no matter what the job. Disgruntlement in a ski instructor does not lend itself to an enthusiastic attitude about either teaching skiing or encouraging skiers to take more lessons. The ski instructor's organizing body, 'The Professional Ski Instructor's of America' (PSIA), would be more accurately named 'The Professional Ski Schools of America' (PSSA). While the PSIA has done American skiing a conspicuous service by standardizing instruction techniques across the country and developing consistent teaching methods, it does nothing to strengthen the monetary affairs of the working instructor. The PSIA, despite its name and the flurry of activity it perpetually generates among its members, serves as an arm of the industry of skiing and does not represent the economic interests of working ski instructors. If it did, the profession of ski instruction and the industry of skiing would be far healthier than they are.

As it is, both are limping along like two corrupt if charming old geezers who have clogged the arteries of what once were healthy hearts, and atrophied the synapses in every part of their brains except that minuscule allotment devoted to the lowest common denominator of the bottom line, by a lethal mixture of greed's high living, neglect's mean spirit and hubris' shallowness. That high, mean lack of care is paid for from the lives of underpaid ski instructors, the pocketbooks of overcharged students, and a declining quality of the relationship between the two.

A well run ski school can pay for administration, advertising, marketing and all its other expenses, as well as make a suitable profit, on about 30 percent of the gross. On 50 percent of the gross a ski school makes a killing. On 80 percent it is a massacre. Among the casualties are ethics, decency, quality, soul and, of course, an exodus of many of the best ski instructors to the ranks of recreational skier.

All extravagances of greed and social and economic injustice—and the cultural illnesses they generate—can be alleviated, rectified or, on occasion, buried by addressing their causes. In complete awareness that the privileged world of a ski instructor does not carry an equivalent importance to that of a public (or private) school teacher, but without disregarding certain parallels between them, I suggest that the profession of American ski instruction is in dire need of some drastic changes. In the spirit of a long overdue, constructive revolution I propose the following:

Ski instructors need to get organized and united. Collective bargaining beats working for $9 an hour all day and waiting tables every night. Probably the first step would be to start a professional ski instructors association.

Instructors need to demand and get *at least* 50 percent of the price of the lessons they teach. It's their labor producing the income. Of course, such demands are worthless if done individually, but instructors themselves need to answer the question: Is a day's work as a teacher worth a living wage?

Ski Schools need to cut the price of lessons *at least* 50 percent. For instance, using the example of the $400 a day lesson, a $200 a day private lesson (between $100 and $140 of it being paid to the instructor) would likely more than double the number of skiers taking ski instruction. In a competitive market, ski lesson prices would likely be cut even more, to the benefit of student, industry, instructor and sport of skiing. Along with lower prices, ski schools need to promote means for entry and lower level skiers to learn how to ski through learn to ski weeks and rental packages which include a free day of beginner ski lessons and the like. Though some short sighted ski area executives and owners will not embrace this idea, it is proposed as a badly needed remedy to a faltering profession and industry that badly needs to help itself.

The U.S. Forest Service needs to reevaluate its policy of creating ski school monopolies at ski areas operating on public lands. In the beginning, the land use permit was given to ski areas to conduct business on U.S. Forest Service land with the intention that the permit holder could run a profitable business while providing a recreational (and instructional) service to the American public at a reasonable cost. From the standpoint of a recreation industry on public lands, the entire business, including the ski school, was much more a public service than a means for big business to take advantage of federal lands for private profit. The industry of skiing in America has abused that intention, to put it mildly, and if it is necessary to break up monopolies and open up ski instruction to true capitalist competition in order to help ski areas regain their sense of responsibility—so be it.

Other changes are both necessary and possible, but these will do to point the direction that American ski instruction needs to go. Until it does, qualified ski instructors will continue to abandon and thereby diminish the quality of the profession because their profession will not support them, skiers who would benefit from ski instruction will continue to stay away from ski schools because ski schools are prohibitively (and unnecessarily) expensive, and the general public will continue to find other things to do with its recreational time.

There are a few ski areas in America that show signs of addressing these problems—Winter Park and the Summit County ski areas of Colorado, Bogus Basin in Idaho, and Mt. Shasta Ski Bowl in California, among others, have made some small steps toward making skiing more available to the general public by discounting season passes to an affordable price—but the profession of ski instruction in America is not keeping pace with even these tiny steps.

Skiing is more than an industry and ski instruction is more than a cash cow for ski areas, but that is not how the industry and the ski areas are treating them. An industry-wide discussion is in order right now.

CHAPTER SIX

In Pursuit of Pure Speed

This essay is composed of three sections taken from "The Straight Course," a book I wrote in the late summer and fall of 1969 while recovering from an injury. The book is about the three years I was a speed skier in Portillo, Chile and Cervinia, Italy and has never been published. I made these sections into an essay in the early 1970s.

PORTILLO, SEPTEMBER 1963: THE RECORD

The process of detachment—of viewing myself abstractly—had reached an astonishingly intricate, fragile state. I was in an incredible state of mind. Fear, desire, frustration, the scope of our attempt, and pure physical and mental exhaustion had combined to wind me up so tight, so fast, that the contest was not as much with time as whether the record or the human mechanism would fall first.

The next day, the twenty-ninth, was the last day Portillo would be open, the last possible chance for the record. Accordingly, we decided to go up early in the morning and run while the track was still ice. We were sure ice would make the difference. With one day, perhaps only one run left in us, it was necessary to extend ourselves. Sleep the night of the twenty-eighth was restless and unfulfilling. Fatigue sleep of a job undone.

We rose early, ate, and were out on the hill while most of the hotel slept. It was cold and clear. The shaded track was rock hard. Springtime frozen corn; it would remain firm for several hours. We had prepared the track perfectly at the end of the previous day. For the first time, every condition was in our favor.

We took a practice run to test the timing from 20 yards above the measured area. We averaged more than 100 kilometers per hour, and I knew in the center of my spine our track was as ready as we. I would not allow the thought that it was more ready. I remembered what Reddish had told me many months before.

The sun began to climb the track. C. B. Vaughan and I went with it. Because of the steepness, 400 meters takes great amounts of time and energy, and I was very tired. We climbed slowly, planning to reach the top before the sun exposed the entire track. I felt C. B. had more energy than I, but that may have been hypersensitivity to my own state.

We talked and joked, but the next day we could not remember any of it. When we got to the top the sun was on the track. Portillo was awake. Far below—an impassable distance—people came out to watch. On the hotel porch many had binoculars. Skiers came down the plateau and stood off to one side near the bottom of the track. Spectators of a play in which the actors had not learned their parts, an audience removed, but only on the surface of action. They feared and hoped as did we. Difficult to realize at that moment, but we needed and used their positive energy, for it is true that each is a part of the main.

In that critical state and time, reality was C. B., the gigantic track below, the feeling of vertigo, and the hard knowledge that the next few minutes were the culmination of all that was behind, the determinant of much of what lay ahead. Funk, Purcell, the timers, other racers and many friends were down there watching with varying degrees of interest and involvement; our friends; warm human beings with whom we had formed close and not so close relationships, laughed, danced, drank, gotten angry, forgave and were forgiven; our immediate companions in eating, sleeping, working, relaxing—life; but at the top of the Portillo speed track those people might as well have been on another planet. All living, except my reality, was suspended. They could not really understand the high degree of control we had made from the chaos of our feelings, nor our predicament, nor the mind which equates self-abstraction with being near God. They could only see us as tiny figures on a white wall of snow, but the least thoughtful could not help but realize our commitment.

I was nearly sick with vertigo and fear. We did warm-up exercises (a delicate task on a slope of 80 percent steepness), and in those last minutes I discovered a bit of the structure of action. The months of discipline, work, self-abstraction and the winding-up process, honed to a fine, sharp edge by the last run on the last day under the iciest, most difficult, most perfect conditions enabled me to see myself marvelously clear.

I nearly laughed and would have but for physical fear. A great calm and confidence (not in *success,* but in my *self*) filled me. "Duped again," I would say in a later time. I was at the precipice of the fastest skiing ever done, the fastest a human body had moved without free-falling or mechanical aids, hanging on the side of a snow-blasted cliff, stinking with fear and the stubbornness not to be beaten by it, when I saw the absurdity of my position. Many things had put me up to where I was—whatever it was in my inherent personality that caused me to recognize skiing as my form of expression when a young boy had put me there, and a racing potential which eluded my best efforts. And a public school education with its accent on grade rather than content. And the power of the great yellow lie called journalism which warps the world's mind with its pretension and shallowness. And the Hollywood ethic upon which I was weaned, an ethic preaching that what matters is coming through in the end—a barely disguised belief in a better life after death which makes light-headed excuses for lifetimes of misery. And people like Number 7 who wage war on the past with inverted minds. And all the sweet experiences that had gone to hell. And Beattie with his clumsy feet and blind assurance. And all the teams I and others would never make. And all the old racer friends like Marvin Moriarity and Gardner Smith and Jim Gaddis who had been caught by the sharp, sly, double-edged axe of politics, wielded by the universal soldiers of my particular way of life; but there was also the strength that learning about those kinds of things gives. And there were the good examples of how a man should be; I had once categorized them according to three fine competitors—Werner, Miller, and Buek. There was Funk down there taking pictures; broken leg and all his hopes. There was Marcelle, dying the hard way. And Barnes, Lieder, and Tiger, already gone. And my parents, who never understood but took pleasure when it reached newsprint. There was the good life and people of La Parva. And there were all the friends right there at Portillo. Somewhere in the world was a guy I didn't know named Plangger, and he had something I wanted. And with me was my comrade, C. B. Vaughan. All the people and times and places I had known, and all the shades of emotions I had ever felt, and all the work I had ever accomplished came with me to Portillo. Pushed, pulled, or just came along as disinterested observers. Hard to know, but assuredly there.

And every one of them copped out at the last minute, leaving me entirely, flat alone. Duped again. Abandoned by my own illusions, leaving *just* me to do whatever was necessary.

The essential education.

The territory my mind had chosen as its battling ground—my place to wage war on all the inequity, hypocrisy, stupidity, and frustration I had ever known; and my time to justify myself for Marcelle, Ken, Tiger, Brett, Brunetto, Funk, Lewellen, and to my particular friends in Reno, Ron the Mustache, and Joan the Potter, and to a few others for their faith, friendship, and a smile at the right time-was an icy precipitous piece of snow on the side of an Andean mountain, useful in nature only for the tiny bit of water it would hold a little longer. Absurd. Pathetic in its attempt. Yet, something would be saved. Something communicated all around. Duped again, but not entirely for nothing.

I could have laughed.

Inside, where action begins, I was peaceful, confident, and supremely happy. Calm, because preparation gives self-control, and I had come prepared. Confident, because confidence is the only possible state of mind under such circumstances; to be where we were without believing in ourselves would be suicidal, and, while life *is* richer and more poignant when it is risked (an effect carrying over and preceding the act of risking), it is so through a deep desire to go on living. And happy, supremely so, to discover in that structure mentioned earlier, that life was okay, and so was I; the important thing was commitment, and I found in myself the ability to give everything, to lay the whole show on the line. In that ability is hidden happiness, and all men have it, lurking somewhere amidst neuroses, education, experience and belief, centered in the heart. Success, while certainly not unimportant, is a problematical (mathematical?) afterthought.

While in that delicate, beautiful state, I adjusted my goggles one more time and signaled my readiness to the timers, feeling more than usual action in the center of things. Far below *(like looking through the wrong end of a telescope)* the signal pole waggled back and forth. I wished C. B. luck, said I'd see him at the bottom. I felt a sentimental reluctance to leave the big redhead up there alone.

"Good luck, Boy," he said. C. B. called his friends "Boy."

I planted my left pole below and to the back of my skis, the right one above and to the front, executed a quick jump turn, pulled my poles out in midair, and landed in a full tuck, headin' down.

Acceleration like a rocket launched in the wrong direction. The sound of endless cannons, moving closer. Irreversible commitment.

The soles of my feet said this was the one. My eyes saw the transition and peaceful flat, far, far away. My body, appalled at the danger in which it had been placed, acted automatically, reluctantly perhaps, but with an instinct and precision that preceded the mind which put it there. My naked mind had finally gotten hold of the big one that had always gotten away.

Jesus, it is fast.

After 100 meters I estimate the speed at over 150 kph. That left 200 meters to the timing and 100 meters in the trap before the longed for landing. Never have I wanted more to be finished with something. A few seconds—less than ten—a long way, more than time can record. More than anything, I wanted not to fall. Probably there is little difference in the end result of a fall at 150 kph and one at 170 kph, but the ice that morning accentuated everything that was happening. Acceleration. Sound. The beating against the legs. The texture feeling. The thin line of error.

In big speeds the skis make peculiar movements. On ice they make them faster, harder. Tremendous air pressure pushes the tips up; the skis want to become airborne. You push forward with everything you have. The air pushes up the tips; you push forward; there is a continuous change of pressure from tip to tail of the skis. Continuous and violent. On a good run your body absorbs both change and violence. On a bad run your body demonstrates them. The tips tend to make a curious, fish-tail motion, which, combined with the tip to tail pressure change, cause the ski to pivot slightly underneath the foot. These things are happening to the skis you are riding. Happening as fast as a vibration and with as much power as the speed you are carrying.

While this is happening at the feet the rest of the body is trying to hold a stable, compact, tuck position. Air pressure tries to push you over backward with a continuous, ever mounting force. If you break the tuck the pressure tries to rip your arm off. If you stood up at those speeds, your back would hit the snow before the thought could come of what a mistake you had just made.

About a hundred yards above the trap, my right arm, as it had the previous day, flew out to the side for some inexplicable reason of balance. It is tremendously unsettling. (The next time you are ripping along one of America's scenic highways at 100 miles per hour, stick an arm out the window.) I jammed both hands forward and down-a high-speed version of what, in another age, was known as the "Sailer crouch," the stablest position in skiing-and rocketed through the trap and into the transition.

Each mile per hour after 95 feels like a difference of 10 miles per hour at half that speed. When I reached the transition I felt more like a Ferrari than a human, and I knew before the timers that no one had skied that fast before. The run-out was easy—gradually extending the arms and raising the body for air drag, and a long left turn entered at about 60 mph until I was able to stop. It took a couple of hundred more feet than any previous run.

I stopped. I took off my helmet and goggles. I was alive. The most alive I had been in my twenty-four years. I felt the sun and saw the beauty of Portillo in the Andes as never before. My spirit was clean. My mind could rest content. I had discovered my own structure of action, and I had acted. For the time, the illusions had been stripped away, and I was completely alive. Also, successful.

I walked back around the corner and halfway up the flat. Up on the hill, Funk was jumping up and down with his cast like a club-foot chimpanzee.

"One-seven-one," he yelled. "Wahoooo," hopping about like mad, arms waving.

I stood in the flat waiting for C. B. The calm joy I was experiencing was tempered by anxiety for the big redhead. I was safe in a giant, flat expanse of snow; I was alive; I was happy; I was tuned to a very high plane; but it wasn't over until C. B. was safely down, so I waited a little longer.

Despite fatigue, the aftereffects of hyperadrenalation, anxiety and realization of the world record with all its attendant hoopla, those few minutes were the most peaceful, satisfying moments I had ever known. I knew they would be few, and I knew they were enough.

In ten minutes, the diplomatic "Bobby" Muller and Chalo Dominquez, the timers, had reset the watches. The pole waved for "Ceb." He came in his yellow-black racing tights like a tiger falling off a white cliff. The sound—skis rattling against ice, wind rippling skin-tight clothes, and the impact of a body moving through air at 100 mph—carried clear to the flat; a unique sound impossible to forget, and not a reassuring one. C. B. rode a tight but high tuck. Twice his arms broke position, flashing out to his sides and immediately returned. Then, quite literally, he thundered into the transition and past me on the flat and around the corner to a stop.

It was all over.

I stood within my peace wondering about C. B.'s time and looking to see if it was in me to go up again that day, in case his time was faster than mine. Almost two years later I was to remember that moment; I remembered it because it took that long to understand what that moment, that question, that impetus in myself was. As luck would have, it was a catechism I was not to face that day.

C. B. was still around the corner, experiencing, discovering, and questioning on his own when Tito Beladone, the Grand Ambassador of Chilean skiing and friend of several years, skied down the outrun to me. "You and C. B. have the same time," he said. The moment was inordinately formal to Tito's vision of skiing, but he gave me a hug, a pat on the back, a kiss on the check, Chilean fashion, and his congratulations. He was elated and proud; I felt humble to have a part in giving him that moment.

I thanked Tito and skied down to C. B. I told him what had happened and we had a few minutes together. During those minutes we knew what we had accomplished, and it was a fine time.

Then the backwash of success arrived. The friends, the ones with faith, the interested, the incredulous, and even the cynical and weak doubters, came to say what we already knew. And it was wonderful to hear.

CERVINIA, 1964: THE WRECK

The Cervinia speed run is both objectively and subjectively different from Portillo's. The Chilean track measures 400 meters to the transition and up to 80 percent steepness. Italy's is a kilometer long and 62 percent at the steepest point. It starts nearly flat and falls off to about 20 percent for 400 meters On a good run the competitor is traveling about 60-70 mph at the end of this relative flat, then the contour changes abruptly and drastically and the rest of the track is a consistent 60 percent. This contour change coincides with a crevasse which is boarded over and covered with snow to allow a crossing. It is impossible to resist being thrown in the air where the track changes. Depending on the individual run, conditions of the track, and, of course, the competitor, seekers of speed fly anywhere from 20 to 120 feet. How the racer masters that obstacle will have an appreciable effect on his time. As in downhill racing, it is faster to be in the air 20 feet than 100 feet; but the most important factor is one's ability to hold the extremely low, tight, body position before the bump, in flight and after landing. Opening the arms slightly for balance will cost you the race. A serious alienation from the thread of balance at this point results in one of those struggling runs that bring awareness of the depth of the will to survive, a realization that casts a glow of understanding on the terror and struggle of rising from the swamp to open air. After landing, the big speeds commence. Up to then, speed is acquired gradually; the racer has time to get into a comfortable, compact position, time to get accustomed to speed, time to get acquainted with the muscles he will need, time to think. In elapsed time, measured in seconds, the racer is on the Cervinia track three to four times longer than in Portillo; they are tracks of different temperaments arriving at the same conclusion. Commitment. Concentration. Freedom. Or the struggle of terror.

There is another crucial difference between Cervinia and Portillo: the transition, in terms of safety the most important part of a speed run. In the transition, speed begins to diminish. The transition is like the first touchdown of a jet, except this jet lands at full speed. It is where the potency of speed, the consequence of commitment, the gyroscope of balance shows their hands. It is where gravity, always tiptoeing in your shadow, adds its weight to your passing. As if to see that your legs are as strong as you have committed them to be.

The transition in Portillo goes from a 52 percent slope to a 15 percent slope. You must accept and adapt to a 37 percent change in grade. Gravity does not hit you very hard; it tiptoes slightly behind.

In Cervinia the transition holds you the way a jet taking off forces you into your seats; except this jet reaches top speed much faster. The transition is from a 60 percent slope to a 15 yard flat to a 12 percent slope, but the 12 percent is in the other direction. Uphill. You are confronted with a 72 percent change at over 100 mph. It is a transition that would like to suck you down and break you into a million pieces and spit them out in China. Gravity romps upon your head.

There is a difference between Cervinia and Portillo which manifests itself more in psychology than objective reality. After the racer in Cervinia has gone 200 meters he disappears from the vision of the competitors on top. More than thirty seconds pass before an impersonal loudspeaker on a post at the start announces the racer's time and *"La piste e libera,"* the track is free. Sometimes the track is not free. This can mean several things, including a fallen racer. But you do not know because you cannot see; and the starters, in radio contact with the bottom, are arbitrary about what they tell you. Aside from his announced time, you do not know how it went for the previous racer. This can weigh heavy upon the mind.

July 15, 1964. A day I must always remember. A day that expanded the horizons of my experience, showing me something of myself that only such a day could reveal.

Good weather. The best track we had seen. C. B. had a good run the day before and was hungry for more. I, too, had banished my discouragement and felt confident. I remember, distinctly, abundant happiness; to be in Cervinia doing this was, as I told the Peace Corps girl, the *best* thing I could do with myself. Nothing was so important to my progress as a man than getting my body down a mountain on a pair of skis, just as fast as I could go. I don't know why, but I know it was so.

But that superb bitch, Fate, had a fickle lesson I hadn't learned. We were all at the top. The first run began. The timing was not functioning perfectly, and the times of several racers had been missed. C. B. was growling about the timers not missing him. Alberti and I posed for photographs. DiMarco had an early starting number; mine was several numbers later; he went, but I was not watching. Bruno and I were talking when the starters and the speaker on a post simultaneously silenced us and changed the mood of the day.

DiMarco had gone 173.493 kph. The record was his, once again.

I felt empty; I did not want to talk or look anyone in the eye. It was a private moment. I think it was a private moment for every competitor who was consciously and seriously ready to win. The others, the Italians, cheered and shouted for their countryman's success; it was not a good position for the Americans.

I went to C. B. We encouraged each other and readied ourselves to get the record back. He had served his apprenticeship, and when he went a few minutes later he was prepared. He went 168.145, a run beaten only by DiMarco, Plangger, and he and I in all of skiing history, but far short of what was necessary.

Then came my turn. I moved out to the track, acutely aware of that interpersonal pressure I have always hated. What had once been an attempt on my part was now expected of me. That was my feeling, as if a heavier load than I ever intended to carry was, suddenly, mine. But I knew the work well, and I had faith in my will.

"La piste e libera."

I began. In relative terms, it does not seem much to build up to 20-30-40 and 50 mph when, in a few seconds, you will be hurtling along at more than 100 mph. But you must pay close attention at those relatively slow speeds; your mind is absorbed in technical details, and there can be no abstract thoughts like records or the game. Your attention must be total.

Perhaps, on that run, my attention was strained.

I rolled my body into the most aerodynamic cone I knew how to make, working the terrain changes with a flat ski to get every wave of speed before the jumps and the steep hill, velocity at the jumps helping determine the eventual speed through the timing trap. I focused down, doing my best.

I flew off the jump but held position and landed with no problem. The big speeds rolled in upon me and I aimed along the right side, the fastest line.

About a hundred yards above the trap, the inexpressible happened. That thing you must never dwell upon, that point in space and time to which Perillat referred—"You must not think too much"—had coincided with my run. The thread of balance had broken. It was apparent and inescapable that I was going to fall. I was convinced. There was no fear, only a clinical, sure knowledge. All the time I was trying to avoid the inevitable fall, and all the while I was falling there was no fear. Only a (detached?) cool observation of the fastest flow of events I had ever witnessed. There is an infinitely fragile line of balance at 100 mph because you are more like a projectile than a skier, and once that line is broken it does not mend easily. About 200 yards remained to the transition;

it takes slightly over four seconds to travel that far that fast. It seemed like five minutes, and I tried every conceivable adaptation to regain balance—and the line is so thin that spectators didn't know I was in trouble until I actually fell. Even C. B., watching closely, didn't know, but only a forgiving God could have saved me and the forgiving gods were busy elsewhere that day. I knew it would expose me defenselessly once I fell, but I was not scared. I tried a hundred positions and a thousand thoughts, but I would not be forgiven inattention. Experience breeds a slight contempt for the forces in speed. When I reached the transition it sucked me down just like I knew it would, but I thought I'd try for Iraq in two or three pieces rather than China in a million. As I went down I tried to get on my back and bottom. Perhaps I could ride it out in a long skid. I'd seen ski jumpers do that. Now I know that strange things happen to your body when it meets the snow at 100 mph, no matter what the position. In the twinkling of hitting the snow I regained a proper respect for speed. If you are inattentive, as well as somewhat stupid, you may breed a contempt for big speeds, forgetting respect through the grace of being atop your skis each run. No one on his back at 100 mph will ever after have contempt for speed. Something caught—a hand, perhaps— and then came one of those falls skiers have bad dreams about. Eighty yards up that hill rising out of the transition, in every conceivable body position, including upside down and backward and 5 feet off the snow. A memorable fall. Visually a blur of snow and sky and an occasional form moving faster than focus. Too fast for the eye, but not for the mind. The films of the fall pass much more quickly than the memory impression left with my mind, for the mind registers feelings, the eye only illusion. The left ski went away as the binding meant it to, and was last seen on the way to Zermatt. The right ski loyally stayed, and halfway through the fall the leg broke. The fall and I finished our relationship and it left me in a pile. Alone. I hurt everywhere and I began to review my scant knowledge of physiology. Not until then did I fear (*feel* fear) that I may have destroyed my body. I once broke a leg that took two years to put back in shape. I flashed on those years. Bad years. I knew my good leg was broken, and my body was a pulsing pain. I undid the binding, which meant

I would move, and fear gave way to the objective mind. My fall deposited me apart from people, and it took a little time for them to arrive. My left ski, poles, gloves, goggles, and glasses were no longer with me, and the sleeves of the ultra tight Japanese speed suit were somehow shoved up and over my elbows in a wad. C. B. was the first person to reach me. I was happy for that and grateful that he came so fast. He supervised the first-aid men and I was touched by his concern.

Italians are really prepared for accidents; I was fascinated by the first air splint I had seen, used on my own leg. People were swarming around, and by then it was decided that in the relative world of injuries I was all right. There were the smiles and relief of the silence of disaster giving way to the movement of life.

There was no fear, only a clinical, sure knowledge ... all the time I was trying to avoid the inevitable fall, and all the time I was falling there was no fear. Only a (detached?) cool observation of the fastest flow of events I had ever witnessed.

A few years later I came to realize what it is to have your mind and the rest of your existence so far out of harmony. It is one thing to be intelligent, objective, aware, hip to your surroundings. It is something else entirely to observe your own impending destruction with the clinical eye of a research technologist in his laboratory, with no more feeling than the scalpel of a Dachau bone surgeon.

The mind was designed to keep body and soul (and mind) together. It was not intended to be so powerful as to block out the natural emotion of fear. If the mind can obliterate fear when there is every reason to feel fear then what can the mind not obliterate? Love? Compassion? The sight of blood? If you are not afraid when you *should be* afraid then you stand accused of stupidity. Your mind has sold you down a stream flowing nowhere.

In time, that fall gave to me a fear—not fear of broken bones or the impact after speed stops or even death, for you accept those possibilities in the act of commitment. No, not that, but fear of a mind so delighted with its own capabilities and power that it has neglected the basics of doing what it is supposed to do—keeping body and soul and mind together.

My mind failed in allowing no fear to me as I was falling up a hill at 100 mph, but valuable lessons are locked up within your failures. I learned that my natural feelings are friends, not enemies to be crushed and avoided and suppressed by a mind gone mad with power. I learned that from my fall, but I didn't learn immediately.

1965: SECOND YEAR AT CERVINIA: THE DEATH

From my journal

The morning of July twenty-sixth the track was ice down to the blue disc (the one Gasperl hit), about 100 meters above the trap. Solid, wind-blown ice. Below that, the track was covered with soft, new snow, about 8 inches deep, blown there by the laws of terrain and wind. Those in charge prepared it in the same, masterly fashion. We were two days without skiing and this day was added to the schedule; it was an extension of our time. We went up to the Plateau Rosa early. The weather was beautiful, a slight bit cold.

At the top we joked, wished each other luck, did warm-up exercises, adjusted equipment—just like always. I was completely absorbed in what had to be done. The two days off skis were noticeable.

Mussner went first. His time came back up as 172.084. I was really excited when I heard that. The first time over 170 this year! The record was in sight! I ran fifth or sixth and held my position. It was a wonderful, free run; but I felt the change going off the ice onto soft snow. My time was 170.373, but I, and everyone else on the outrun, thought they announced 173. I hurried back up thinking I had the best run of the round, and I was full of getting the record back. I don't know what it is about that bloody record.

When I got to the top Ninni told me I was fourth behind Mussner, Siorpaes, and Leitner. That seemed logical because I had been surprised to hear my time as 173. It hadn't felt so fast. The slight disappointment filled me even more with desire for the record. I kept saying to myself—"I'm gonna get that bastard back." I talked a little with Mussner and congratulated him for his fine first run. I spoke to Siorpaes. I observed the rituals. I remember grinning because I was sure Mussner and Siorpaes were as full of the record as I.

Then there came a time when no one wanted to go. There was no particular reason. One hadn't finished waxing. Another was cold. Still another was tuning his mind. I was still tired from climbing up too fast. Mussner appeared ready, but he didn't want to go. I don't know why—nerves probably. (I'm sure now that he had a premonition.) I jumped into the breach and said I was ready. Actually I was still tired, but I was so excited and anxious about finally breaking into the 170s that it didn't matter. I went anyway, and I held my position over both jumps. I put my head down just before the soft part of the track and immediately pulled it back up. The track was a monstrous mess. It hadn't even been side slipped between rounds. I lost my position. It was like driving a car across a furrowed field at 100 mph.

I didn't know how fast I was, but I knew it wasn't very good. Now I know that my time was 168.539 kph. I was mad about the track and I skied to a stop in front of Egon. I said, "The track is really bad, Egon, why don't they work on it?" He knew what I meant and felt just about like I did, and he said something like, "I don't know, you can't talk to these fucking Italians." Then I said, quote, "Well, someone's going to get hurt up there." Unquote.

Egon took my skis and began waxing them. A few were still getting into the 170s, and I was full of—with luck—the record.

Then Mussner came.

On Sunday night, the twenty fifth, Mussner saw a photo of Luigi taken on the first day. In this photograph Luigi's head is completely down and all you can see is the top of his helmet. It is the most fantastic Lanciato photo I've seen. Walter studied the photograph for a few minutes. "Tomorrow I will do that," he told Luigi. Luigi grinned, as any champion will whose disciples are trying to imitate him. It is the grin of pride and of being flattered, but it is also a grin of awareness of the difficulties in the refinements of any champion's technique, the refinements which all disciples try for and hardly any ever achieve. In this case, the refinement of putting one's head between one's knees and skiing blind at more than 105 mph.

Mussner came and his head was down. I have the impression that when I was on top and Walter didn't want to go he was forcing himself to be able to put his head down. (Perhaps also fighting a premonition.) This is what I think, but there is no way to know. Later, Franca told me that Mussner nearly didn't go again; I don't know why, nor does anybody. Then he said something like, "Well, there's still the record." And he left the top.

He came and I saw him from above the blue disc, just before where the track was bad. His head was already down, his position was good, and he held it like that all the way. Many things went into the sequence of what happened then, and no one will ever know exactly what they were, but this is what I think:

At the top of the timing area he began to veer right. I saw immediately that he was on his way off the track. A cold electric shock passed through me like a tidal wave of fear. My heart went numb and my blood disappeared. Walter went off the track just at the end of the timing, just missing the electric eye pillar. He went through a little post and that ridiculous net they had fanned out on each side. When he hit that post the world changed.

At that speed many things could cause a slight deviation of direction. It is impossible to have more than an opinion as to why he went off the course. It was obvious from watching how he held this position and from what he said afterward that he was unaware he was off course until he had already fallen. I believe two things killed Walter Mussner, not one more than the other. I think the bad track caused him to veer to one side against the natural slope of the track, and I think Walter's head being down made him unaware of what was happening, and, therefore, unable to correct it. I think if the track had been properly groomed he wouldn't have veered off course, and if he had kept his head up he would have known what was happening and he would have been able to correct it. But—and Walter Mussner is dead.

What happened when Walter hit that post and fell is something I don't think I will forget as long as I live; and it will be more than a few days before the image leaves my mind, allowing me easy sleep at night and to write and read and be naturally of this life the rest of the time. He clocked a time of 170.132 kph just as he fell; but to the naked eye, it appears that the racers in the last 30 meters of the 100-meter trap accelerate to a much greater speed.

I would not be surprised if the racer who clocks 170 for 100 meters is traveling at 190 for the last 10 or 20 meters. Right there, where there is that little boost of acceleration that anyone can observe, Walter fell. With incredible force and speed he went end over end, feet and then head hitting the snow, and each turn wrenching his body unbelievably. Afterwards, eleven holes were counted in the snow, feet, head, feet, head, feet, head, and, at the end, everything. It was difficult to believe it was a human body undergoing such gyrations, such speed, such force. The only thing I have ever seen like it were movies of Bill Vukovich's car at Indianapolis when he was killed in 1955. It was similar to that.

For a few seconds that seemed like minutes after he stopped in a motionless pile in the transition, everyone was frozen still with astonishment and fear. There was—I am sure in everyone because it was there in me—the hope of a miracle that Walter Mussner would get up and that no one would have to go pick him up. At the same time, I don't think there was a doubt in anyone's mind that he wasn't going to move by himself. I have seen some bad falls, and I have even had a few myself; but this wasn't like a skiing fall anyone had ever seen before. No one has ever fallen like that.

Then Rico was screaming over the loudspeaker. That snapped people out of their trance. Dozens of people were suddenly all around Walter, about 30 yards from where I stood. I started to go, but instinct told me not to; and I am glad I didn't. Ivo (Mahlknecht) and Felice (DeNicolo) were there, and they were closer comrades than I; so he wasn't alone when he shouldn't be alone.

It took about half an hour to get him off the hill. During that time not one person even side slipped the track, though competition was obviously to continue as soon as possible. I was mad and sick with the knowledgeable suspicion that if Walter wasn't dead he was an agonizing pile of broken bones. Egon was furious the way the German temperament gets furious when unhappy.

I stared at the group around Walter. Egon finished waxing my skis. I was, however, finished psychologically and spiritually, and I knew it. I told Egon I would run again if the track began to be fast enough for a record. I would go up and wait and listen to the times. If they got close I would go; if not, not. Egon said it was finished, but I went up and waited anyway; but I never came down on the track.

Just before I went up to wait, Hans Berger broke away from the group around Walter and came my way. Hans, who lives in Kufstein, is small, with tiny, delicate features and an expressive face. He usually looks about eighteen years old, though he is thirty. When he came up to me, he looked a hundred years old and there were tears in his eyes.

"Ist es schlecht?" I asked.

"Ja," he said in a strange way.

"Sehr schlecht?"

"Sehr schlecht" he answered in a way that made me know it was.

I went up to the top and waited with that in the pit of my stomach. Probably, it was best the track never got fast enough to make me think a record was possible.

They took Walter to Aosta and he lived a little more, than five hours. Unfortunately, he was conscious most of that time. He fractured his skull, broke two vertebrae in his neck, pulverized his entire pelvic region, broke one femur and tore loose the femoral artery, and he tore himself open from the anus to the navel. He had acute hemorrhages of the brain, stomach, and leg. Toward the end he went blind. If he had lived he would have lost one leg, he wouldn't have been a man any longer, and he probably would have been paralyzed. Kiki went with him to Aosta and held his hand until he died. She is only twenty and has never seen a dead person before, and she was still in shock and sometimes hysterics the next night when she and her mother told me about it.

The Italian and Swiss papers are full of stupid things about it. The people of Cervinia all say that the track was "perfetto," and they put the whole blame on a mistake of Walter's. They've gone on at some length why it's not the fault of the Lanciato committee, the organization, or anyone s. That is not quite true. Some say there is nothing dangerous about the Lanciato. That, too, is not quite true. Others call the Lanciato stupidly insane. Nor is that true. If I uttered to the press what I think about the track, they would interpret it as blaming those responsible for track maintenance for Walter's death. That, also, is not the truth; and it would do infinitely more harm than good. And it would not help Walter. There is no prevention (except abstention, which is ridiculous) for such accidents, and there is no blame. It is part of skiing that fast.

I was the only one competing that day who saw Walter fall, and I returned to the top with a different perspective on our endeavors. The racers and officials asked about the delay. Why was the track closed so long? I said Walter had a bad fall that tore up the track a bit; the delay was necessary for repairs. I had neither desire nor right to elaborate. I sat at the top for a long time. Some racers got in six runs, nearly everyone got four or five. Only Mussner and I ran just twice. Visions of his fall tumbled through my brain. I could not make them leave. (They entered my dreams and woke me in the night for the next two years.) It was the same clear day, but a grainy, colorless filter had descended on the world.

Leitner, leading with 172.744, decided not to run again unless his time was beaten. It never was. My time dropped from fourth best to eighth. Luigi, suffering badly from a strep throat and cold, took five runs before breaking into the first ten. My place on the result sheets, the race itself, winning or losing no longer mattered. What importance has the race alongside life itself? What game do we play in which the loser forfeits life? What type of men play this game? For it was obvious from the beginning that one of us would die because of some human failing, neglecting for a billionth of eternity the rules of the game. Is human failure cause to die? If it is, are we not playing with the rules and stakes of Neanderthal man? I never meant to play a game in which one of the players would inevitably, through mathematical laws as sure as those governing Russian roulette, smash his body beyond repair; yet I played and watched it happen and I felt deep in my innards that I had always known it was going to happen. I remembered waiting for C. B. at the bottom of Portillo's track, wondering about the game's next move if he beat my time. The questions would not disappear. I had no answers.

My friend Franca Simondetti gave Leitner and me some Sangria. We drank it over small talk and silence. Strange to drink the sweet Sangria, to feel its wonderful vapors fill your body and your brain, exploding your taste buds as you sit in the sun—sweet Sangria—all the while trapped with death in a vision of the boyish face of Walter Mussner and a fall unlike any other. Strange to sit like that with Ludwig Leitner, the big German who exudes toughness and confidence and plays the game hard, drinking and healthy. Life's mysteries unfold through everyday functions.

Tiring of Sangria, small talk, and waiting for a run I neither wanted nor would ever make, I skied down alongside the track. Racers were still coming, about one a minute. As a competitor, I was allowed to stand close to the track, and I watched the big speeds from about 30 feet away. For the first time in three years of playing with eternity, I viewed it with a new realization of flesh and blood men, mere mortals, at play with the forces of the universe; it was wondrous that we dared, but never again would I view another man as a rival whose mistakes or refinements I must note and use to my advantage. I could hardly believe what I saw. I knew these men. We had joked, laughed, eaten, drunk, and skied together. We had entered into freedom and struggled with terror, and together we had ignored our common reality. Walter Mussner reminded us of our negligence. I watched my friends like children in a play yard; proud, arrogant, innocent. We had accomplished great things, but, when all was done and spoken, we were just men; probably we could be better men, for we had not put away childish things.

When I got down to Cervinia, the word was around that Mussner was badly hurt. Only those who saw him fall had any idea what that meant. Most of the racers didn't think that Walter would not be back with them. I returned to my hotel, changed clothes, and packed my ski bag for Egon to take to Kufstein. Walter was in Aosta and I had heard he was alive when he reached the hospital; that is usually a good sign for the chances of survival. I put my thoughts with Walter Mussner and packed my bag.

After, I was carrying the heavy bag of skis up the street to Egon's hotel when something happened I cannot define but only describe. It came in what I have come to know as a "flash." Suddenly I knew Walter Mussner was dead. It was sure; it was something I *knew*. Walter was dead, and I no longer felt the hard sadness that had been with me since the fall. What I felt was something like intense peace and joy and relief, all together. I do not know if that feeling arose because Waller was out of his suffering, or because what had happened had happened to him and not to me, or if there was another reason. I set down my big, red Kneissl ski bag and rested. I did not question the fact of his death nor the quality or means of my knowledge, but I wasn't *supposed* to feel what I felt. For I felt better and more alive than I had since Walter began veering right. An hour later Kalevi told me Walter Mussner was dead.

Diary, July 4, 1965

  From now on every man who tries seriously and truly for a record carries death in his hind pocket. I think that this year everyone will make it, but after this it will get too fast, too tough, and eventually someone will buy the farm no one ever wants but everyone gets.

CHAPTER SEVEN

The Harriman Cup

DURING THE MIDDLE THIRD OF THE 20ᵀᴴ CENTURY there was no more prestigious ski race in America than Sun Valley's Harriman Cup. From 1937 until 1965 this downhill/slalom combined race consistently attracted the finest ski racers in the world. The downhill courses used in the Harriman were the stuff of legends, always respected, often feared, and never taken lightly. The Harriman, as it was known among ski racers, was Sun Valley's premier international event, and it was defined by its downhills. So long as Averell Harriman's Union Pacific Railroad owned Sun Valley, it was a mainstay of the competitive, advertising and even cultural ambiance of Sun Valley and American ski racing.

When Harriman opened Sun Valley in the fall of 1936 he decided to have a ski race which including the best Europeans he could entice to Idaho. He did it for the sake of ski racing and skiing, and, of course, for the publicity it would bring to his new resort. The event was called the Sun Valley International Open. The first year was also the U.S. National Alpine Championships, which guaranteed the best Americans would participate. The "open" category, in that seemingly more innocent time when professional (i.e. ski instructors) and amateur athletes were segregated, accommodated the professionals, most of them European mountain boys who had fled Europe to escape the Third Reich. Only amateurs could compete in the National Championships, but everyone could compete for the Open. Harriman gave the Harriman Cup to the winner of the downhill/slalom combined in the open category, and eventually the Sun Valley International Open name was dropped in favor of the Harriman Cup.

The first race was held on an unnamed peak north of Sun Valley in the Boulder Mountains. It took competitors from the U.S., Canada, Europe and Scandinavia three hours to hike up the downhill course and just over five minutes for the winner to ski down. Among the racers in that first Harriman who have significant places in the history of American skiing are Robert Livermore, Joseph Benedicter, Charles Proctor, Sigmund Ruud, Jack Durrance, Hans Hauser, Hjalmar Hvam, Don Fraser, Alf Engen, Don Amick, Andre Roch and Alexander Bright. Before the race, no one except the eventual winner had any hope that an American could win, but U.S. National and collegiate champion, Dick Durrance, beat his closest competitor, ex-world champion Walter Prager, by more than 20 seconds. He then followed this up the next day by winning the slalom by three seconds. Durrance was America's first great ski racer, and his win at the first Harriman changed his life and the course of American skiing. Harriman was so pleased with Durrance that he named the mountain where the race was held Durrance Mountain. (Today Durrance Mountain is a favorite with local back country skiers. During his presidential bid in 2004 John Kerry, a 2nd home owner and frequent visitor to Sun Valley, climbed up Durrance with his snowboard in two and a half hours and boarded back down in the company of secret service men, a ski instructor, a few photographers, journalists and other local back country skiers in far more time than five minutes.) Harriman also launched Durrance on his photography career, buying him the best camera, supplying him with mentors, and hiring him to be the Sun Valley staff photographer. And he awarded Durrance a replica of the Harriman Cup to take home. The original was to stay in Sun Valley until someone won it three times.

The cup itself is a silver Revere style bowl, seven and a half inches high with a diameter of 14 inches. It appears to be larger than it is. The first name engraved on the side is "Dick Durrance, 1937; the last are "Ingemar Stenmark 1977" and Lise-Marie Morerod 1977." There were generations of Harriman Cup ski racing between those years, and a thousand stirring stories.

Suzi Harmon Gillis McLeod, who placed 4th in downhill and 5th in slalom in 1952, wrote of the Harriman Cup, "Grown men have shed surreptitious tears losing it and women have cried winning it."

Indeed, by 1938 the Harriman was expanded to include both genders. The first women's winner was Grace Lindley, who wrote of this race, "The first Sun Valley Open races for women have set a precedent and a high standard for future ladies' competitions in this country. For the first time, the heretofore 'Short Subjects' on the big racing programs have now attained equal significance and attention. We were ready for the difficulties of the first schuss, having seen all the men come down—many in the first flight fighting for balance and vorlage—the angle being extremely deceptive in the bad light and heavy snowfall....As Arnold Lunn would say, 'She was running with great skill and courage—well up in the first ten, when she took three double somersaults in the transition of the schuss in the big gully!' Kathleen Starrett's collision with the finishing post, the only accident of the day, unfortunately put her out of the slalom. We all appreciated the prompt, warm transportation to the Inn. We were cold and wet, having been out all day." A young Washington girl, Gretchen Kunigk, took third in the downhill and fourth in the slalom. Ten years later, Gretchen Kunigk Fraser would win the Olympic slalom in St. Moritz, the first American to win an Olympic medal in alpine skiing. Though he lost the downhill to Ulli Beutter of Bavaria and the slalom to his old rival Prager, Durrance won the combined again in 1938.

In 1939 the races were moved to the Warm Springs side of Bald Mountain, the downhill being run on a course Durrance scouted, designed and helped cut. Racers again spent several hours climbing up the steep and narrow course, considered the toughest in America at the time. Today's Sun Valley skiers who ski Warm Springs via International ski this course regularly, though it is much wider and far better groomed than it was in 1939. Despite all the work and time he put into designing the downhill, or, perhaps, because of it, Durrance won neither the downhill, slalom or combined in the third Harriman. Toni Matt won the downhill, Friedl Pfeifer the slalom, and Peter Radacher the combined. Erna Steuri won all the women's events.

By 1940 Durrance was finished with college, living full time in Sun Valley and very serious about winning the Harriman a third time. He trained hard all winter on Bald Mountain, as the first chair lift had been put up on the River Run side of the mountain, an amenity for which Harriman Cup racers were very grateful. "I realized if I didn't win it this time I probably never would," he said. The 1940 Harriman downhill, particularly Durrance's run, raised the standard of American ski racing. In every ski race, and certainly in every Harriman ever held, there has been drama, excitement and the unfolding and expansion of human skill and character, but some races provide the setting for new standards, great stories, and the inspiration that comes to us all from those who push limits the furthest. The 1940 Harriman was such a race because of Durrance. There is a fine and exciting description of this race in "The Man on the Medal," Dick's wonderful memoir written with John Jerome. He took the Warm Springs Steilhang (now known as International) straight and describes the moment, "I was heading straight down. At that point I do remember the fear of God sweeping over me, and I started talking to myself; Whoa, this is too fast. I was cussing in German and English. This is bad, I'm in trouble. But there was no choice; I had to take it straight." He came off the Steilhang with too much speed to hold his line. He swung wide into a grove of small trees, knocking one of them down and himself too; but he managed to get back up without losing speed. He said of that moment, "At that point I says, Himmel, you're a lucky son-of-a-gun. I was amazed—I must have been going pretty fast through those trees—and I said to myself, 'You'll never be so lucky again, so you might as well let 'er go from here.' I didn't slow down at all but rode it straight every bit of the way...." Durrance fell at the bottom of Warm Springs, losing much time as he walked across the finish, but he still won the race over his old rival Prager by more than three seconds. Motion pictures of Dick after he "let 'er go" show that he was moving very fast, probably in the 60 to 70 mph range, extreme velocity for the equipment of the time. (A few years later, when he was general manager of the Aspen Ski Company, Durrance cut all the runs on Ajax Mountain wider than any other runs in America so that "people could choose their own line down." It is not too much to imagine that his 1940 Harriman downhill run contributed to his championing the double wide ski run. Nor is it out of the question that Dick's "let 'er go" attitude set a tone for American ski racing that has influenced such diverse racers as Bode Miller, Andy Mill, Bud Werner, Dick Buek, Jim Barrows, Susie Corrock, Rip McManus, Kristin Krone, Bill Johnson, Ralph Miller and others.) Friedl Pfeifer beat Dick in the slalom, but Durrance won the combined for the third time. It was his last big win as a ski racer. Only one other skier, the great Austrian Christian Pravda, was ever able to win the Harriman three times, in 1953, 1956 and 1959. Grace Lindley won the 1940 downhill, Nancy Reynolds Cooke the slalom, and Marilyn Shaw, who was only 15 years old, the combined.

In 1941 the men's downhill was won by Sigi Engl and the slalom and downhill by Friedl Pfeifer. Gretchen Fraser (nee Kunigk) won the downhill and combined, and Nancy Reynolds Cooke won the slalom.

The downhill in 1942 was moved to the other side of Bald Mountain and came down Canyon to River Run. This was far more convenient as the lifts were on the River Run side of Baldy. The slalom races over the years were held in different locations, Ruud Mountain, Dollar Mountain and on Christmas Ridge on Bald Mountain. Barney McLean won the downhill and the combined in 1942, while Gordon Wren won the slalom. (Six years later Wren placed 5th in the Olympic jumping competition in St. Moritz, the best jumping performance by an American in Olympic competition until Lars Haugen was retroactively awarded a bronze medal for the 1928 Olympics when an error in tabulating the judging was discovered many years after the fact.) Catherine Henck won the downhill and Clarita Heath won the slalom and combined.

The Harriman Cup was one of millions of minor casualties of World War II and was not held between 1942 and 1947. Sun Valley was used as a military hospital and recuperation center during that war.

By 1947 the Harriman, along with many other aspects of American life, was able to be "joyously revived," in the words of Suzi McLeod, with a fine field of pre-war veterans and new blood. The race was moved back to the original Warm Springs course. The downhill was won by Barney McLean, the slalom and combined by the Swiss World Champion Edy Rominger. The great French racer Georgette Thioliere (4th 1948 Olympic slalom, 3rd 1950 FIS World Championship downhill) won the downhill by five seconds and the slalom by one second, just ahead of Gretchen Fraser. Fifteen year old Andrea Mead placed 5th in downhill, 7th in slalom and 6th in the combined. Among others competing that year were Rhona Wurtele, Suzi Harris, Brynhild Grasmoen, Toni Matt, Paul Valar, Bob Blatt, Karl Molitor, Steve Knowlton, Jack Reddish, George Macomber, Dick Movitz, Gordon Wren, Dev Jennings, Harvey Clifford, Karl Stingl, Don Goodman, Chris Schwarzenbach, Alex Bright and Don Amick.

1948 was Jack Reddish's year. Reddish, one of the finest ski racers in American history, won a difficult downhill by finishing more than five seconds ahead of the gregarious Canadian Yves Latreille. He followed up by winning the slalom by more than three seconds over Barney McLean. That was the first of five times Reddish placed among the first three in Harriman Cup races, though he never won the combined again. Only one other racer, Jannette Burr Johnson, placed in five Harrimans. Burr won the 1948 Harriman downhill by more than six seconds. Ann Winn won the slalom. Suzi Harris, who was third in both events, won the combined.

The 1949 races were moved back to the river Run side of the mountain, going down Olympic Run's tricky variations of terrain. Henri Oreiller, who had won two gold and one bronze medal in the previous year's Olympics, won the downhill, slalom and combined in a field that included Toni Matt, Jim Griffith, Ernie McCulloch, Dean Perkins, Yves Latreille, Dave Lawrence, Barney McLean, George Macomber, Dick Buek, Leon Goodman, Gale Spence, Harvey Clifford, Yvan Tache, Pierre Jalbert, Steve Knowlton, Jack Reddish, Jerry Hiatt, Amos "Doc" Little, Jr., Pete Seibert, Mel Dalebout, Darrell Robison, Karl Stingl and Gene Gillis, a veritable "who's who" of post WWII North American skiing. French ski team member Lucienne Couttet-Schmitt also won the downhill, slalom and combined, beating such racers as Paula Kann, Jannette

Burr, Andrea Mead, Katy Rodolph, Suzy Harris, Sally Neidlinger and Rhona Gillis.

1950 was a landmark year for the Harriman, setting the stage for the rest of its fifteen year existence. It was held right after the 1950 FIS World Championships in Aspen and hosted a superbly strong field. The men's course was changed to go from the top of Baldy down Ridge, Rock Garden, Exhibition and Lower River Run, the classic route it would follow thereafter and considered to be one of the most difficult downhills in America. The Women's course started at Round House and went down Olympic. Hans Nogler, an Austrian ski instructor in Sun Valley, scored one of the biggest upsets in Harriman history by defeating World and Olympic champion Zeno Colo in the downhill. Francois Baud won the slalom, but Nogler won the combined and the cup. Andrea Mead won the downhill, slalom and combined, the youngest woman to ever win the Harriman.

A pair of Canadians, Ernie McCullogh and Rhona Wurtele Eaves, won the Harriman combined in 1951. Verne Goodwin won the men's downhill, beating out McCullogh and the young Californian Dick Buek. The next finishers are an interesting list of the history of American ski racing: Guttrom Berge, Yvan Tache, a four way tie for 6th between Jack Nagel, Toni Matt, Brooks Dodge and Jim Murphy, followed by Jack Reddish, Darrell Robison, Bill Beck, Yves Lattreille, Jim Griffith and a teen-age Ralph Miller from Hanover High School. Jack Reddish won the slalom, but the great McCullogh was rewarded for his consistency. Eaves won the downhill and Sandre Tomlinson won the slalom in the women's division over a young Skeeter Werner.

The twelfth Harriman Cup in 1952 was again won by McCullogh who dominated the downhill, winning by more than six seconds over Guttrom Berge, followed by a tie between Otto Von Allmen and Phil Puchner. Von Allmen and Nogler tied for first in the slalom ahead of third place McCullogh. Though Von Allmen tried to tie things up, he was forced to take second to McCullogh's consistency. Rhona Gillis won the women's downhill, finishing 10 seconds ahead of Elaine Holmstad and Lois Woodworth. Mary Jane Griffith Marin beat Charlotte

Zumstein and Woodworth in the slalom (all three were within eight tents of a second), but the consistent Canadian Woodworth won the combined. That night at the banquet in the Sun Valley Lodge, Mary Jane Marin presented the first Jim Griffith Award to Jack Reddish. Jim Griffith, Mary Jane's brother, was a member of the 1952 Olympic team and was Sun Valley's favorite native son. An enormously popular and talented racer, he died from complications after hitting a tree while training for the Olympics in Alta. The award in his name was given thereafter at each Harriman to a Sun Valley racer for sportsmanship and contribution to ski racing. The award that year was accepted by Nelson Bennett for Reddish, who had remained in Europe to race after the Olympics.

The infamous 1953 Harriman Cup was a race of superlatives. The fastest. The most dangerous. The worst weather. The most injuries. The least visibility. The toughest field. The downhill was run in a driving blizzard down the standard course, with fewer gates than usual on Exhibition. Christian Pravda, arguably the best of all ski racers, won this very difficult race, followed by Dick Buek, Ralph Miller, Othmar Schneider, Jack Reddish and Otto Von Allmen. There were many falls and serious injuries that day, and the great Toni Matt broke his leg badly enough that he never raced again. Though it was likely Buek's finest ski race and a portent of what might have come, he was seriously injured in a motorcycle wreck a couple of months later and never regained peak form, to put it mildly. A 16 year old boy from Steamboat Springs, Colorado, Bud Werner, tied with Darrell Robison for 8th in his first Harriman Cup downhill. Andrea Mead Lawrence (by then married to American racer Dave Lawrence) won the downhill, beating Jannette Burr, Sally Neidlinger, Skeeter Werner and Mary Litchfield. The slalom the next day was held on Ruud Mountain in perfect weather. It was won by the incomparable Olympic and World Champion Stein Eriksen, followed by the previous year's Olympic slalom champion Othmar Schneider, and then Jack Reddish, Christian Pravda, Franz Gabl, Otto Von Allmen, and a tie for seventh between Buek and Bill Tibbits. Neidlinger beat Mead Lawrence for the slalom title, followed by a third place tie between Jannette Burr and Joanne Newson, and then Skeeter Werner, Lucille Wheeler and Mary

Litchfield. Pravda won the first of his three Harriman combined, ahead of Schneider, Reddish and Buek. Mead Lawrence won the second of her two Harriman combined, ahead of Burr, Neidlinger and Werner.

Six years after he had swept the Harriman field in 1948, Jack Reddish won the 1954 downhill. He was primed to win the combined again, but Dartmouth's Tom Corcoran won the slalom and the combined that year. Jannette Burr won both the downhill and slalom to take the women's combined, the only time one of America's least recognized great ski racers won the Harriman.

Contingents of the best European racers were on the North American ski circuit in 1955, and they completely dominated the Harriman. Austria's Martin Strolz (who made one of the best and most popular ski boots in the next decades) won the men's downhill. Martin Julen of Switzerland won the slalom. And the "Blitz from Kitz," the dashing Andrl Molterer won the combined. The women's downhill and combined was won by Madeline Berthod, who a year later would win Olympic gold in downhill for Switzerland. The slalom was won by Austria's Thea Hochleitner.

1956 was almost the year of the Americans at the Harriman Cup. Except for one Austrian male and one Norwegian male, every competitor that year was an American. However, the Austrian was Christian Pravda who won both the downhill and the slalom events by seven seconds over his closest competitor, Tom Corcoran; and of course they placed one-two in the combined. The races were held in splendid weather in spring conditions, contributing to the fact that 18 men finished the downhill and 11 did not. Gardner Smith from the Reno Ski Club took third in the downhill by a unique and controversial tactic. In those days gates were not numbered. After the schuss down Ridge there were always a few gates on Rock Garden to slow racers so they could make it off Rock Garden and under the Exhibition lift and onto the cat track leading to Round House Slope. In that race the first two gates on Rock Garden were set in such a way that the racer had to go left and turn back right to the second gate and then turn hard left back to a third gate, thus keeping velocity in check. It was a wise configuration, but course setter Sigi

Engl had set the first two gates in a perfect square. Though Engl's intention was obvious, one could be forgiven for reading the course as if the upper flags of each gate formed one gate, and the lower flags another, thus allowing a racer to eliminate the two hard turns and go straight through to the third gate. That's what Gardner did. He was disqualified, of course, but he protested and the jury ruled in his favor. Engl was, to put it mildly, angry and indignant, but Gardner, an eccentric, talented and popular racer, won his bronze Harriman pin and the applause of fellow competitors for his cunning. Sally Deaver, who two years later would place second in the FIS World Championship giant slalom, won the downhill by nearly five seconds over Jeannette Burr and more than seven seconds over third place Madi Springer-Miller. Jack Reddish came out of retirement to place third in the slalom, thus earning his fifth top three Harriman placing and a diamond Harriman pin. Deaver won the slalom by more than three seconds over Rhona Gillis. Pravda, Corcoran and Reddish were the first three in combined for men, and Deaver, Linda Meyers and Phyllis Simon were the top women.

Between 1955 and 1958 Toni Sailer won most races in which he was entered, no matter whether it was downhill, slalom or giant slalom. Between his three gold medal performance in the 1956 Olympics and his two golds and one silver medal domination of the 1958 FIS World Championships he won everything in the 1957 Harriman Cup against a strong field of Europeans. Freida Daenzer of Switzerland won the women's downhill, Norway's Inge Bjornbakken won the slalom, and France's Therese Le Duc won the combined.

The 1959 Harriman was anticipated to be a great contest between Pravda and America's finest skier, Bud Werner. A few weeks before the Harriman Werner had become the first American to win the prestigious Hahnenkahm downhill in Kitzbuehl, Austria. Werner famously said, "There are only two places in a race, first and last." After his Hahnenkahm downhill victory he fell in the slalom in pursuit of this ethic, causing Hahnenkahm combined winner Anderl Molterer to quip, "I didn't win the Hahnenkahm, Buddy lost it." As is the case in so much of human affairs, Werner's strength was also his weakness. Though he has been termed America's favorite hard luck ski racer, it is fair to consider that much of Bud's hard luck was self-induced by an inflexible if admirable ethic. As expected, Werner was out to win the 1959 Harriman, but he took a line off Round House slope onto the top of Exhibition that he could not hold. He fell, assuring Pravda the win. After this race Pravda said, "If Buddy knew what I know, no one could beat him." In the same year on different continents, two great Austrians accurately described America's best ski racer with precision, respect and deep affection. Pravda won the slalom the next day to cinch his third Harriman combined and retire the cup. (After Pravda died, Christian's son, Chris Pravda, brought the cup back to Sun Valley, and it is on display in the Sun Valley Lodge. The other retired cup, Dick Durrance's, is on display at Dave Durrance's ski shop at Aspen Highlands.) Austria's Putzi Frandl won the women's downhill and combined in 1959, while Linda Meyers won the slalom.

After the 1960 Olympics in Squaw Valley, there was a special running of the Harriman which drew most of the teams. The Sun Valley downhill was praised by most racers as a much better test than the Olympic downhill in Squaw. 1960 was certainly one of the strongest fields ever to race in the Harriman. Among the field were Willy Forrer, Guy Perillat, Bruno Alberti, Fritz Wagnerberger, Carlo Senoner, Hans Peter Lanig, Adrien Duvillard, Willy Bogner, Roger Staub, Francois Bonlieu, Jim Barrier, Charles Bozon, Egon Zimmerman, Mathias Leitner, Gerhard Nenning, Pepi Stiegler, Felice DeNicolo, Chuck Ferries, Karl Schranz, Jean Vuarnet, Georges Schneider (ten years after winning the FIS World Championship slalom title) and Max Marolt, on anyone's list of the best of the day. The downhill was won by Switzerland's Willy Forrer who finished two tenths of a second ahead of Guy Perillat and Bruno Alberti in a tie for second. Mathias Leitner beat Pepi Stiegler by two tenths of a second in a one-run slalom; but the great French skier Adrien Duvillard was first in the combined, ahead of Germany's Fritz Wagnerberger and Italy's Carlo Senoner, who, six years later would win the FIS World Championship slalom title. The women's field was also very strong, including Putzi Frandl, Yvonne Reugg, Marianne Jahn, Bev

Anderson, Pia Riva, Therese Leduc, Traudll Hecher, Nancy Greene and Betsy Snite. Frandl won the downhill, Hecker the slalom and Jahn the combined, for a complete Austrian sweep of this Harriman.

Bud Werner finally got a Harriman win in 1961, winning the downhill over a mostly American field, an important triumph for Werner in his comeback year after breaking his leg shortly before the 1960 Olympics. The Harriman that year was a portent of things to come. Eighteen year old Bill Kidd won the slalom and eighteen year old Jimmy Heuga won the combined. Three years later Kidd and Heuga became the first American men to win medals in Olympic alpine skiing, Barbara Ferries, younger sister of Chuck, won everything for the women in 1961, and a year later she placed third in the 1962 FIS World Championship downhill.

The 19th Harriman Cup in 1963 was mostly an American event with a couple of Canadians, a German and two Swiss; but one of the Canadians was Nancy Greene, the German was Barbi Henneberger, and the Swiss were Jos Minsch and Willy Favre, all among the best in the world. Werner finally had his well deserved day at the Harriman, beating Minsch, Favre and Ferries in the downhill and beating Minsch and Bill Marolt in the slalom to win his first Harriman combined. Suzi McLeod wrote of this event, "He (Werner) won the first run of slalom and with the cup all but in the bag went all out to win the second run. It was to be the first and last Harriman victory for America's most beloved ski racer." She did not mention that Werner was true to his ethic to the end. After the downhill Werner remarked, "This was a big win for me." It was his last big win. Jean Saubert beat Henneberger and Margo Walters to win the women's downhill, and won the slalom by eleven seconds over Linda Meyers to take the combined. There was a special giant slalom run in conjunction with the 1963 Harriman, but it did not count toward the combined. Minsch edged out Jimmy Heuga by three tenths of a second to win the men's, and Henneberger beat Saubert by nearly three seconds to win the women's giant slalom. A little over a year later, Werner and Henneberger were killed in an avalanche in Switzerland while making a film for Henneberger's fiancé, Willy Bogner.

There were only 20 true Harriman Cup competitions, and the last was held in 1965. It was fitting that the great Austrian, Karl Schranz, and the great French skier Marielle Goitschel won the last Harriman in 1965. Schranz, certainly among the finest downhill racers in history, proclaimed the Harriman downhill "the most difficult downhill in the U.S." That would seem a fitting epitaph to one of America's most superb ski races and ski racing traditions. Sadly, those traditions, like the Roche Cup, Snow Cup, Silver Dollar Derby, Silver Belt and other races have been abandoned by American skiing.

A faux Harriman Cup was held in 1975 and 1977, but each consisted of a giant slalom and slalom held on Greyhawk on the Warm Springs side of Bald Mountain. Not surprisingly, the great Ingemar Stenmark, who dominated the world in slalom and giant slalom but who did not run downhill, won both times and his name is inscribed on the cup for both those years. The women's winners those two years were Hanni Wenzel in 1975 and Lise-Marie Morerod in 1977. But the true Harriman Cup died a natural if unfortunate death in 1965, and the most difficult downhill in the U.S. has not been run since.

CHAPTER EIGHT

A Speed Skiing History

THE FIRST RECORDED SPEED SKIING RECORD was set in 1867 in La Porte, California by a woman with the provocative name of Lottie Joy, who traveled 48.9 mph/79.003 kph. The length of her run and the method of timing are unknown, making hers one of several unofficial but significant world speed skiing records. The second was also in La Porte by Tommy Todd who traveled down a 1230 foot track in an average speed of 87.7 mph/141.001kph in 1874. If Todd's timing was anywhere near accurate, it is not unreasonable to speculate that he was traveling near 100 mph during that last part of his run. Joy and Todd were part of sizeable ski crowd in northern California in the 19th century, many of them Norwegian gold miners who introduced skiing to the area and who passed the long Sierra winters organizing social and competitive events around skiing. They used hand crafted wooden skis up to 12 feet long and one long pole for balance. Each racer's secret formula for wax in these races was closely guarded, but persistent reports indicated that human sperm was a key ingredient of the best recipes. These concoctions were called "dope."

It needs mentioning that while Joy was the first speed queen and Todd the first speed king, they are only the first we know about. People have been skiing for thousands of years, and it is inconceivable that they have not *always* pursued pure speed for the sake of the speed. It is in the nature of man to do so, and that we do not have speed skiing records prior to 1867 only indicates the relative and incomplete scope of recorded history itself. It is not too much to imagine that buried in some obscure ancient Scandinavian piece of writing is a description of skiers schussing the steepest, longest hill hundreds, perhaps thousands of years ago, just to see how fast they could go; their 'time' perhaps measured by some method we have forgotten.

As it is, the first *official* speed skiing record was set by Gustav Lantschner in 1930 in St. Moritz. He was timed at 65.588 mph/105.675 kph. The following year Leo Gasperl moved the speed up considerably by going 84.692 mph/136.600 kph also in St. Moritz. Gasperl accomplished this by attaching hay hooks to the front of his skis which he held onto with his hands and having a rudimentary aerodynamic cone strapped to his butt.

Gasperl's record held until 1947 when the great Italian skier, Zeno Colo, who would be World and Olympic champion in the next few years, went 98.761 mph/159.292 kph in Cervinia. This record maintained until 1959 when Edoardo Agraiter went 99.307 mph/160.174 kph in Sestriere.

In between these two records, a significant, seminal and extremely bold speed skiing event took place in Portillo, Chile. Under the guidance of Emile Allais, and with the participation of American racers Ron Funk (who fell at nearly 100 mph with bear trap bindings and long thongs and was seriously injured), Bud Werner and Marvin Melville, the American Ralph Miller went 108.7 mph/175.402 kph. Miller was timed by Allais over 50 meters with a hand held stop watch. At 100 mph a tenth of a second difference over 50 meters is about 18 mph, and anyone who has ever used a hand stop watch knows that two timers timing the same thing will always have a tenth of a second or more difference. For that reason Miller's run is considered unofficial. He may have only gone 99 mph, but it is just as likely he went 112 mph. People who have raced on the Portillo track and know where he started tend to believe Miller was the first to go over 100 mph.

But officially that distinction goes to Luigi DiMarco who in 1960 traveled 101.224 mph/163.265 kph in Cervinia. DiMarco, the dominant speedster of the early '60s, set another record of 108.349 mph/174.757 kph in 1964, also in Cervinia. In between, however, in July 1963 Alfred

Plangger went 104.298 mph/168.224 kph in Cervinia, and two months later Americans C.B.Vaughan and Dick Dorworth tied for a record of 106.520 mph/171.428 kph in Portillo in an event organized by Ron Funk.

The '60s saw the first real technological breaks (and breakthroughs) from those of traditional downhill skiing, starting an evolution of speed skiing technology and techniques that continues to this day. Some of these found their way back into traditional ski racing. The first bent ski poles designed to fit around the body of a skier in a tuck were bent to form in a Cervinia blacksmith shop. The first non-porous speed suits were developed; these suits are now made of polyurethane coated polypropylene, a long way from Lottie Joy's woolen skirts. The first silver dollar size ski pole baskets and the first low profile, flat tip skis were made. Cervinia's annual Kilometro Lanciato was the premier speed event in the world which produced most of the world records from the early '60 until the late '70 when it was discontinued because it was held on a glacier on the Plateau Rosa and its crevasses grew too large to safely bridge.

Eighty nine years after Lottie Joy raced in California, the first official women's record was set by Emanuel Spreafico in 1963 in Cervinia at 78.82 mph/127.138 kph. The following year Kristl Staffner pushed it up to 88.802 mph/143.230 kph, also in Cervinia.

Japan's first speed skier, Yuichiro Miura, competed in the KL in 1964. He had trained for the event on Mt. Fuji, using a parachute to slow down in place of the run out Mt. Fuji lacks. Though he never held the speed record, Miura finished seventh with 172.084 kph, more than respectable. He fell eight times that week while traveling over 100 mph and walked away from every fall, bruised but unbowed. The experience inspired him to go to Mt. Everest a few years later to take advantage of less air resistance at higher altitudes and attempt a world speed record on the tallest mountain on earth. Though finding terrain and building a track on Mt. Everest suitable for skiing over 100 mph is unreasonable and the actual skiing he accomplished there was minimal, Miura did make a name for himself as "The Man Who Skied Down Everest," and the documentary film of that expedition won an Academy Award. In 2002 Miura, at the age of 70, became the oldest man to climb Mt.

Everest. He accomplished this in the company of his son, the first father/son team to climb the tallest peak.

On a more somber note, the first (but not the last) speed skiing death occurred in 1965 when Walter Mussner skied off the Cervinia track at 105 mph. The helmets of that time were the same ones used by downhillers, and the most aerodynamic position using them was to put the head down and essentially to ski almost blind. One element in Mussner's fatal accident was that he had put his head down and was unaware his line was taking him off the prepared track.

Within a few years a big revolution in helmets, poles, fairings, speed suits and skis was occurring in the world of speed skiing. Helmets were both more aerodynamic and allowed better visibility. The ski equipment manufacturing companies, working with the best speed skiers, began developing drastically new and better equipment. Tuck positions and equipment were tested and adapted in wind tunnels used by automobile and airplane manufacturers. In time, a few racers (notably Sean Cridland, Kalevi Hakkinen and Kirsten Culver) mounted their skis on the tops of cars and practiced their tuck positions at over 150 mph on the roads of Finland and the Salt Flats of Utah. Techniques improved and racers' expectations of themselves and of the boundaries of the possible continued to expand. By 1970 speed skiing was ready to begin a rapid push into velocities that would have been unimaginable only a few years earlier.

In 1970 the Japanese skier Morishita Masaru broke DiMarco's six year old record by a hefty margin, traveling 113.703 mph/183.392 kph in Cervinia on a pair of Yamaha skis and beginning a remarkable decade in speed skiing history. Cathy Breyton became the first woman to ski over 100 mph when she went 103.300 mph/165.000 kph in Portillo in 1978. That decade was dominated by the American Steve McKinney who set four world speed records on three different tracks (Cervinia, Portillo and Les Arcs) and was the first skier to travel over 200 kph. McKinney was the leader of an era of speed skiing and was instrumental in several significant changes in the sport. One of them was the formation of International Speed Skiing (ISS) the organizing body of the first professional speed skiing circuit which for a few years in the early 1980s staged professional races all over North America. The most significant of these races were in Silverton, Colorado where in 1982 and 1983 Franz Weber set two records, the latter at 129.017 mph/208.029 kph, and Marti Martin-Kuntz set a woman's record of 111.114 mph/179.104 kph.

By the late '80s the professional circuit had come unraveled and the FIS was sanctioning speed races in preparation for speed skiing to be a demo event at the 1992 Olympics in France. That event was a huge success, with Michel Prufer setting a record of 142.165 mph/229.299 kph for men and Torja Mulari going 135.931 mph/219.245 for a women's record. However, a Swiss speed skier was killed the morning of the final race while warming up. He was free skiing and was not on the track when he collided with a snow machine and died. This tragedy which was not connected to speed skiing contributed to the IOC's decision to not include speed skiing in the Olympics.

Whether or not speed skiing is included in the Olympics, it continues to evolve and grow in response to the natural human curiosity about the question every skier asks: "How fast can I go?" A modern speed skier needs some special equipment the normal recreation skier does not have. In addition to a polyurethane coated suit, racers use aerodynamic helmets that look like something from a Star Wars film, 240 cm skis, the narrowest boots available and foam fairings to fit them, bent poles filled with lead, gloves that are leather on the inside and rubber on the outside, and a fire retardant high density foam back protector to cut down on burn injuries in a 140 mph fall. Also, speed tracks are groomed to near perfection by winch cats guided by lasers to make a nearly impeccably smooth surface.

At this writing (April 2010) the fastest skiers in history are an Italian man and a Swedish woman who set their records in Les Arcs in 2006. Simone Origone has gone 251.410 kph, and Sanna Tidstrand has traveled 242.590 kph. The fastest American male is Ross Anderson who went 247.930 kph in Les Arcs and is the 9th fastest skier in history. The quickest American female is Tracie Sachs, 3rd on the all time fastest list, who traveled 238.570 kph also in Les Arcs in 2006. Michael Milton of

Australia holds the record for one-legged skiers at 213.650 kph. While these speeds seem to be close to the limits of the possible, that is how it has seemed since the days of Lottie Joy and Tommy Todd. More than 300 skiers have traveled faster than 200 kph. It is impossible (and thankless) to predict the limits of the possible in skiing (or, for that matter, anything else), but one thing Tidstrand's speed makes clear is that women are closing the gap on men in the world of speed skiing.

CHAPTER NINE

Avalanche

A survival story

MOUNTAIN PEOPLE HAVE THEIR OWN WAY of dealing with each other and of coping with the harsh realities of an unforgiving environment. Mountains, like oceans, like people, like rivers through the land can change from placid and lovely to tempestuous and deadly with little warning. Mountains are indifferent to the activities and aspirations of humanity, and humanity, in response, has learned to depend upon its members for survival.

The Sierra Nevada is probably the most benign range of mountains on earth. The Lake Tahoe area is the most densely populated in the Sierra and its inhabitants are familiar with the ways of snow. Nevertheless, big snow storms come in from the wet Pacific Ocean with the subtlety of an invading army. Locals tend to curtail activity and stay by the fire in intelligent recognition of the inconvenience and menace of large storms. Tourists try to get the hell out before it's too late, not always successfully.

On Saturday, March 27, 1982 the snow began to fall with a heavy steadiness that quickly bogged down the Sierra. Lake Tahoe was particularly hard hit. Most weekend skiers managed to get out of the Sierra and below snowline by Sunday afternoon. After that, for the next ten days major highways were open only sporadically. Few locals could remember a bigger storm. Frustration was palpable among locals who could not get to work and tourist trapped on the wrong side of the Sierra crest from their homes. Among those whose business it is to know mountains and snow and the unpredictable avalanche, there was an undercurrent of perilousness, perhaps akin to that felt by Albert Einstein and a few other sages in the 1930's.

Alpine Meadows Ski Resort was closed on March 30th. By the 31st, a Wednesday, 12 1/2 feet of new snow had fallen and 2 inches an hour continued to pile up. Most highways were closed. At 7:20 a.m. Bernie Kingery, 11 years the Mountain Manager of Alpine Meadows, and Howard Carnell, General Manager, decided to keep the area closed. Only a few years before, three skiers had been killed by an avalanche at Alpine. Kingery, 50, was one of the best avalanche men in the area, and he knew the avalanche danger was out of hand. Despite Alpine's state of the art avalanche control, there are limits to man's influence on nature's indifferent patterns of continuous change. Avalanche control is described by Casey Jones, Alpine Meadows ski patrolman, "It is an on-going learning process. The more you learn the more you realize you don't know anything about it. It's not guessing; it's drawing on past experiences, making estimations. It's a very educated guess. You use CYA (cover your ass) in all circumstances. Allow yourself plenty of time and fully assess the situation. We do it in teams."

Avalanche danger had been high and more than one residence in the area had been hit that winter. The Alpine Meadows road is highly susceptible to avalanche, but it had been cleared twice before noon on the 31st. At 3 p.m. there were 23 employees at Alpine.

Anna Conrad, 22, was a lift operator at Alpine. Her boyfriend, Frank Yeatman, 22, a student, was visiting during spring break. Anna wasn't working that day, but she and Frank decided to cross-country from her house up to Alpine Meadows to get some things from her locker in the Summit Lift Building. This 3 story A-frame building was situated about 150 feet above the main lodge. By 3:30 p.m. most people were sitting out the storm, shoveling to keep abreast of the snowfall, hanging out at home or in the bars and restaurants, or (a minority) trying to get somewhere in an automobile. There was one avalanche dog named Mariah and seven people in the Summit Building. Kingery found out that Conrad and Yeatman had skied up the road under some dangerous avalanche conditions. While Yeatman waited in the lift operations office, Kingery chastised Anna for her carelessness. It is easy to imagine Kingery's experienced solicitude for Anna's mountain innocence. Anna walked into the lift operations locker room. Kingery had sent Jake Smith, 27, a trail crew worker, to get a snowmobile ready for use in closing the Alpine Meadows road so avalanche control work could begin. With Kingery in Base 4 Headquarters room were Beth Morrow, 22; Randy Buck, 23; Tad Defelice, 24; and Jeff Skover, 23. They were helping Kingery and waiting for Smith to radio that the road was clear to begin avalanche control bombing.

David "Cadillac" Scott had worked all day clearing snow from the lodge deck. At 3:30 Scott's friend, Marty Marchese, convinced Scott to take a coffee break. They went inside and joined some other employees. Howard Carnell radioed that the road had slid and was blocked a mile below the lodge.

Dr. Leroy Nelson, 39, an orthopedic surgeon, and his 11 year old daughter, Laura, were walking in the parking lot. David Hahn, 46, was also walking there. John Riley, 74, the founder of Alpine Meadows was in his motor home where he lived in the parking lot.

When it snows several feet in a short time avalanches are likely, anywhere in the world. Man is at worst helpless and at best limited in the face of such manifestations of nature's power. Jake Smith was the first to know, the last thing this popular young man ever knew. At 3:45 p.m. a garbled radio transmission was picked up from Jake. Kingery and the others head the word "avalanche." Inside the lodge the words "slide" and "help" and a scream were heard. Kingery asked for Jake's location. There was no answer.

Five seconds later the avalanche pounded into the Summit Building. One of three simultaneous slides that started about 700 vertical feet above the lodge hit the building. The area had long been known as "Bernie's Chute," now a name of grim irony, and 11 avalanche control shots from a Howitzer had gone in there that morning. The avalanche's air blast literally blew the summit Building apart. The slide roared over the lodge deck and through some of the front windows. Other tongues of the slide buried the parking lot.

In ten seconds it was over. Scott, whose life had been spared by a well timed coffee break at a friend's instigation, said, "It was dead silence." Randy Buck was lucky. After being buffeted back and forth he wound up with head and shoulders above the snow, a broken rib and a vertebra broken in two places. He said, "As soon as I got out I realized that Tad was right next to me and his head and shoulders were out. I was still in the room I had been in, but there were no walls. I wiggled out, asked Tad if he was OK...Any pain? He said no. So I said I would dig him out later and search for other people. I couldn't see anyone else. I started digging right around where I was. People started arriving 2-3 minutes later."

Those people, Scott, Marchese and the others in the lodge, saw Jeff Skover's hand sticking out of the snow and dug him out. He had minor head injuries. There were no signs of Kingery, Morrow, Yeatman or Conrad. In the parking lot Dr. Nelson, Laura Nelson, David Hahn and Jake Smith were all buried. John Riley was uninjured in his motor home. Three snow grooming machines had been smashed. One was described as looking like a "pretzel."

Within minutes 25 people, survivors of the avalanche and nearby residents, were probing for victims. It was a major disaster during the biggest storm in 40 years, the "main road was blocked, and most of Alpine's avalanche rescue equipment had been in the now destroyed Summit Building. Large trees and power poles were snapped off like tooth picks. Debris from the Summit Building was spread 100-150 feet below the building remains.

Jake Smith, who was wearing a Skadi, was the first to be found: He was under 10-15 feet of snow. Despite CPR work done on him even before he was free of the hole he was dead. Dr. Nelson and Hahn were found that afternoon, but they, too, were dead.

The storm continued to howl. Darkness and avalanche danger caused the search to be called off at 8 p.m. Five people were still missing. That day in nearby Squaw Valley two expensive houses were demolished by avalanches, including the one that had been hit earlier in the year. (Interestingly enough, the owner built a new house in the same spot.) Hundreds of people were evacuated from their homes.

The following day, April 1st, the storm broke for several hours. Major search efforts were started. Every neighboring ski area and the community as a whole gave Alpine Meadows complete support...this included avalanche rescue equipment, snow plows, personnel, facilities for the press, etc. (Squaw Valley set up press conferences in their lodge, causing TV and newspapers alike to use Squaw Valley dateline, causing many people all over the world to think the avalanche had occurred in Squaw Valley.) Alpine Meadows season passes were honored at local ski resorts until Alpine re-opened.

Laura Nelson's body was found almost immediately. Later, Frank Yeatman's body was found in the ruins of the Summit Building. Beth Morrow's body was dug up 100 feet from where she had been sitting when the avalanche struck. Whining was heard in the Summit Building. Jim Plehn, Alpine Meadows' avalanche forecaster, owned Mariah. Two days earlier Plehn had been partially buried in an avalanche. Plehn stuck his hand through an opening in the snow and found his dog. Mariah sniffed his hand, licked it and then chomped on it and wouldn't let go until rescuers dug her out. Mariah was dehydrated but otherwise OK. The search was halted at dark.

The weather deteriorated on April 2. Forty Alpine Meadows homes were evacuated. The road was filled with snow and trees. Avalanche danger was awesome. A decision was reached by avalanche specialists, ski patrol and the sheriff's department that the situation was critical and the search must be curtailed. This difficult decision was particularly frustrating for Roberta Huber who raises and trains avalanche dogs. Roberta and Bridgette, a German Shepherd, had gone into the Summit Building area before other searchers could pollute the smell. Bridgette dug into the locker room area and came back to her owner. Roberta and a friend yelled. No response. Bridgette repeated her performance. Huber knew someone was in the building, but "we couldn't search through because the avalanche crew was blasting and we all had to leave."

No one was allowed into Alpine Meadows on April 3. The storm raged. On the 4th some avalanche control work was started, but the weather deteriorated and all search efforts were stopped.

It was clear on the 5th. By noon more than 150 people were searching in the area where Anna Conrad and Bernie Kingery were still buried. Roberta Huber and Bridgette were among them. Bridgette went straight to the same spot from where she had been pulled three days earlier. 12 people went to work in that immediate area. At 1:20 p.m. two ski patrolmen saw a hand sticking out of the snow. It belonged to Anna Conrad who was reaching up for another handful of snow, all she had eaten for the five days she had been buried. The hand disappeared.

"Anna, is that you?"

"Yes, it's me."

"Anna, we love you. We are coming to get you."

"OK, I'm hanging on."

Anna's parents, Gene and Joan, had come from their Riverside, California home to await word of their daughter's fate. They have "faith in God," and Mr. Conrad believes part of Anna's survival is due to all the people who prayed for her. "We had faith," he said, "but we also felt that five days, four days, three days is an awful long time for someone to survive under those kind of conditions. The longer it went the less convinced we became." On April 5th the Conrads were waiting at a sheriff's substation in Tahoe City. The call came in. A sheriff's officer asked Gene Conrad, "Your daughter's name is Anna, isn't it?" "Yes," Conrad replied. "They found her," the officer said, and then he hesitated, "she's alive." "What did you say?" Anna Conrad's father replied.

Anna Conrad was miraculously still alive. She had heard Huber and others yelling for her three days earlier. She yelled back and kicked the lockers which had fallen around her and kept her from being crushed, but she was not heard. A high elation ran through the searchers and the community as word of her rescue spread. Anna was the first 'live find' by an avalanche dog in North America. Anna was far from unscathed, mentally, emotionally, or physically, eventually losing her right leg below the knee and part of her left foot to frostbite. But she survived.

Joy turned to sorrow two and a half hours later when Bernie Kingery's body was found a few feet from where Beth Morrow was discovered.

On one level the Alpine Meadows avalanche was over, but, of course, such things are never entirely finished. The resort will carry on. Families and friends of the seven who died will mourn their loved ones and re-establish their lives without those people. Avalanche professionals will glean what they can from the tragedy. Anna Conrad will learn to walk and will build a different life. So long as it snows there will be avalanches. So long as people live and play in the mountains there will be people caught in avalanches.

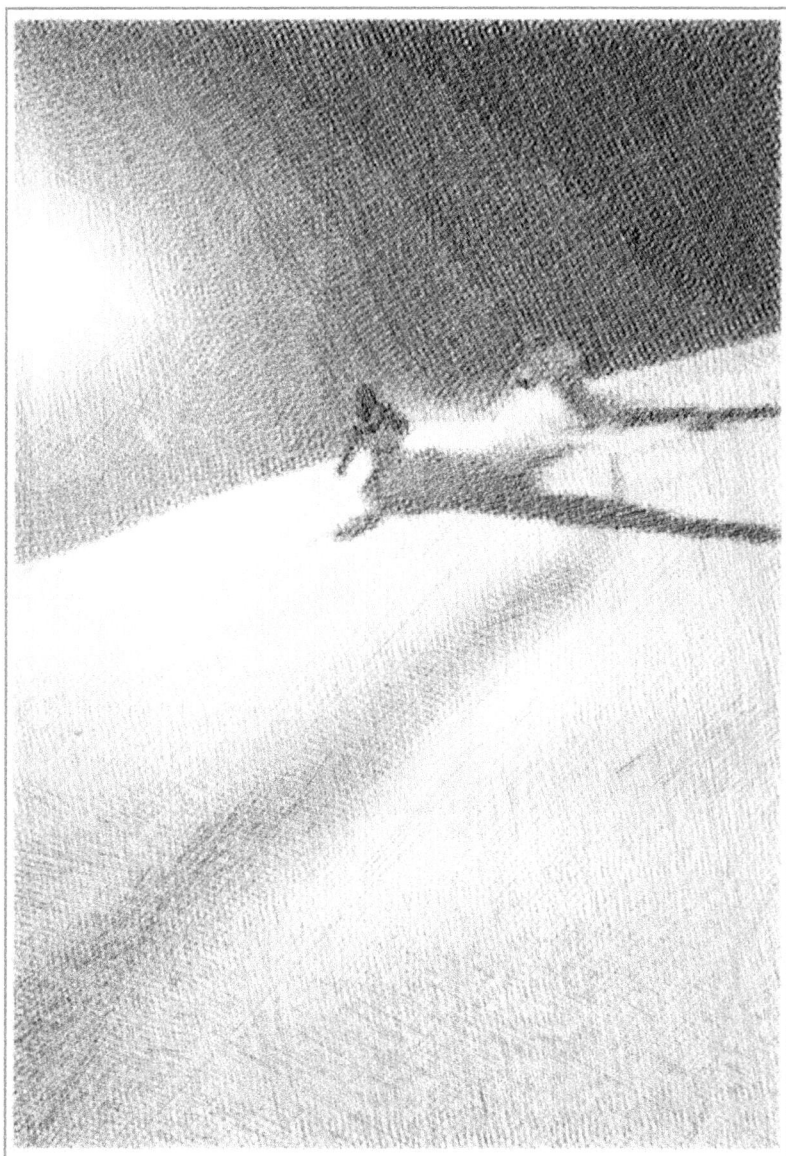

PART TWO

People

CHAPTER TEN

Steve McKinney

I FIRST MET STEVE MCKINNEY in the winter of 1953. He was in his bassinet on the porch of the Sky Tavern Lodge at the Sky Tavern/Mt. Rose Ski Area outside Reno, Nevada, and I was a 14 year old ski racer. His mother, Frances, was a ski instructor at Sky Tavern, who made sure all of her seven children were, literally, born to skiing. Frances was a graceful woman of refined intelligence who loved life and her children with an intense passion which she passed on to each of them.

The last time I saw Steve McKinney was in October 1990 at the Squeeze Inn in Truckee, California. Steve and his son, Stephan, and me and my son, Jason, had breakfast together at the Squeeze and talked about our climbing expedition to Bhutan that had collapsed suddenly and unexpectedly a couple of weeks earlier. We exiled disappointment about not going to Bhutan through plans for future expeditions and adventures and with discussion about our present good fortune to be able to have breakfast together in a favorite restaurant with our sons. Steve McKinney loved his life and his son and family and friends with an intense passion that touched everyone who knew him.

A month later, November 1990, Steve was driving alone from southern California to meet his sister, Tamara, and attend a U.S. Ski Team fund raising function in San Francisco. It grew late and Steve was tired and he pulled his small Volkswagen off the side of the freeway and crawled into the back seat to sleep. While he slept a drunk driver veered off the highway and crashed into the car and Steve was killed. Had we gone to Bhutan, he wouldn't have been in that car by the freeway in the middle of the night.

But Steve was the sort of man who believed that when his time here was up it would not matter whether he was in California or Bhutan, and his time was up.

Between his birth in 1953 and his death in 1990 Steve McKinney lived a full life because he was the rare man who followed his passion. I was a friend to his family and we were all in the world of skiing, and so I followed his junior ski racing career and was aware of his extraordinary talent and athletic ability. By the early 1970s he was among the most promising young downhill racers in America. He was skilled, smart, strong and courageous. He was also ambitious and loved the game of competition. A fine athletic career as a downhill skier for the U.S. Ski Team was easily his for the taking, and many thought that would be his path. But Steve was restless and independent, and he was definitely wary of the kind of authoritarian politics that inescapably plague conventional organizations like the U.S. Ski Team. To some, Steve was considered a rebel, but, in my opinion, Steve was not so much rebellious as he was independent and proud. He had and knew the value of personal integrity.

In the spring of 1973 he bowed out of some World Cup races in California and went to Alaska in search of new adventures. Most young people who have spent their formative years in junior ski racing do not willingly pass up the opportunity to participate in World Cup races; but, as indicated, McKinney was unique and independent, restless and curious, always on the prowl for new horizons. When he returned from Alaska he showed up unexpectedly in Yosemite Valley where I was living and climbing. He was in the company of ex-U.S. Ski Team downhill racer and rock climber Craig Shanholtzer. Steve had decided to take up speed skiing and rock climbing at the same time, and with typical enthusiasm and intensity he committed himself to learning the basics of both. He planned on going to the Kilometro Lanciato in Cervinia the following month, and we talked at length about what he needed to do and know in order to be prepared.

Before that could happen, Steve returned to Tahoe and took a hundred foot leader fall attempting to climb a route beyond his novice experience called "Rated X" on Donner Summit's Black Wall. He wound up in a body cast from his neck to his hips. Never one to let a broken back keep him down, Steve went to Cervinia anyway and skied in his cast and observed the speed skiers and what they were doing. Later that summer, he and I went climbing for the first time since his accident. After a couple of easier climbs we did "Rated X." Steve did not lead it but he climbed it, and afterwards he was both mentally and physically back on track. He spent the winter thinking about what he had seen in Cervinia and getting ready.

The next summer, 1974, Steve and Tom Simons went to Cervinia. Steve was ready and won the KL competition, setting the first of his several world records. The world of speed skiing would never be the same. Steve was the right person in the right place at the right time to attract the media's attention and give speed skiing a public profile it had never before known. Steve exemplified that elusive term "charisma." He had the 6'4" 190 pound physique of a Viking warrior, the long blonde hair and good looks of a rock star, the confidence of a King, the personality of a fun loving sage, and he was THE MAN in an endeavor that answers a question that occurs to every person who has ever put on a pair of skis, even to those who do not wish to find out the answer: how fast can I go?

For the next ten years McKinney either held the world speed record or was very close to it. He either won every big speed race or he was one of the favorites. He was the first person to ski over 120 mph and the first to break 200 kph. He was instrumental in starting the first professional speed skiing circuit, and he was a principal in International Speed Skiing, the organizing body of that tour. More, he was the pace setter, the leader, the example and the inspiration for a generation of speed skiers. And despite the effects of age, numerous serious injuries and personal traumas, and the natural evolution of his sport which always leaves yesterday's heroes behind, he invariably came through. He tried very hard to do his best and he inspired others to do the same.

Steve became a serious and accomplished mountaineer in the 1980s.

He climbed 24,785 Mustagh Ata in the Chinese Pamir Mountains. After returning from the summit he turned around and climbed it again to help a British double amputee (both legs below the knee) accomplish his goal of reaching the peak. Steve was on two expeditions to Mt. Everest. On the first one he was instrumental in saving the life of John Roskelley, one of America's greatest climbers who came down with pulmonary edema at 25,000 feet and was practically carried off the mountain by McKinney. On his second expedition he flew a hang glider off the West Ridge of Mt. Everest from 22,000 feet despite an earlier crash at a lower elevation on a trial flight.

Steve McKinney was my friend. He is known primarily as a speed skier, as well he should be; but he was also a talented writer, musician, horseman and climber; and he was a philosopher and thinker and seeker of the truth. Steve was generous, forgiving, funny and honest, and he was very easy to be with. We had a lot of fun together on skis, in the mountains, traveling, climbing and, yes, partying, all the while discussing the endless mysteries, impasses, challenges and ideas of what it is to be a human being. Like many others, I am grateful to have known him, but I miss his presence in this life. In my mind, Steve McKinney was a great speed skier because he was a great human being, not vice-versa.

CHAPTER ELEVEN

Skiing with Ted Kennedy

DURING CHRISTMAS 1983 I was teaching skiing for the Sun Valley Ski School. At the time it was a great job that paid reasonably well, kept me on skis, and introduced me to many fascinating and memorable people, experiences and realizations. During that particular holiday season I wound up skiing with U.S. Senator Ted Kennedy and several members of his immediate and extended family. As a group the Kennedys were all decent to excellent recreational skiers, intelligent and fearless conversationalists and a great deal of fun. They approached skiing with the same engaging, competitive and determined enthusiasm that marks the public lives of their more public members. Ted Jr., who had lost a leg to cancer, was an outstanding one legged skier. Skiing with the Kennedys was a great gig for a ski instructor, and it was a holiday season I both cherish and will always remember for several reasons.

It was Sun Valley Christmas cold, Bald Mountain was covered with snow, skiing was excellent, and we skied hard. Each morning I met the group at River run and we organized the day and went up the mountain. The practicalities of cutting lift lines and ski school rules involving money dictated that instructors never ski with more than four in a private lesson, but the Kennedys have always been champions of democracy, well known warriors in the battles against dictatorships of all kinds. In theory, each day began with a plan of which members of the group I would ski with for how many hours and where and when we would meet up to change groups. But, as Emerson wrote, "The astonishment of life is the absence of any appearances of reconciliation between the theory and the practice of life."

Needless to say, Ted Kennedy in a Sun Valley lift line in 1983 was a highly visible presence. That and a familial gregariousness enhanced by being on Christmas vacation contributed to a unique (in my experience) ski lesson phenomenon: we collected people as the day progressed, usually but not always other members of the family who wanted to ski together. Among the non-family people collected was ex-Senator and Congressman John Tunney of California, son of the great heavyweight boxer Gene Tunney. We always started out with four in the group, but it never lasted. I was not nearly as obsessed with ski school protocols and rules as Ski School Director Rainer Kolb would have preferred (to say the least), but even so my powers of lift line and public diplomacy were stretched, stressed, challenged and put into debt to some very cool lift operators when I consistently showed up in ski school lines with a private lesson for ten.

Fortunately for all of us, it was Christmas, skiing was excellent, and most people were in a good mood and understood at least instinctively that I was not of a mind or in a position to treat Senator Kennedy and his family like the normal millionaires, celebrities and icons of American life that frequent Sun Valley. I wasn't going to or particularly wanted to do that.

My favorite of the group was Jean Kennedy Smith, who, a few years later would become U.S. Ambassador to Ireland. For whatever reasons I wound up riding the lifts and talking with her more than to anyone else, and she was bright, curious, concerned about the world and about individual people, and, it seemed to me, a model of engaged compassion and intelligence. Her husband, Stephen, handled the money for the group and was a very generous tipper, which, naturally, insured my devotion to helping them having the most enjoyable Christmas vacation possible.

What I most clearly remember about that Christmas was Ted Kennedy's last run. We were having lunch at Round House when the Senator asked me if I would be kind enough to ski down with him and then return to pick up the rest of the group. Of course, I said, "Of course."

Senator Kennedy was and is, in my opinion, one of the great Senators and defenders of the people in all American history. He and his family have paid dearly in the coin of grief for their service to America, and Ted Kennedy worked exceedingly hard and effectively to keep care of its citizens. I for one, have always have been grateful to and for him because of his work in the Senate. Unfortunately, at least in those days, he had not worked equally as hard to keep care of himself, and it showed. Though he was a very good intermediate skier, he was overweight, out of shape, thousands of feet higher than where he normally lived, and obviously not at the top of his game. We took a leisurely run down Round House Slope and Olympic Lane. It was snowing lightly, the light was flat and it was cold, probably about zero degrees Fahrenheit. We were the only skiers on the run. All went well until we were about a hundred yards from the end of Olympic where it joins River Run. The Senator was following me and he fell down. I stopped about 30 feet below him, expecting him to get up and continue as he was obviously not hurt and he had fallen before and always gotten up by himself. He didn't move. I asked if he was alright and he said "Yes." I waited. He didn't move. I waited. Finally he asked if I could climb up and help him. I did. When I got to him I saw that despite the cold and the fact that he was not wearing a hat, Senator Kennedy was sweating copiously and breathing as if he had just crossed the finish line of a four minute mile.

Heart attack was my first thought. All the signs were there.

This was not good, not good at all, not a good Christmas omen, not good for Ted, not good for Dick.

The second thought of a moderately compassionate, engaged, intelligent, caring, responsible person and professional ski instructor should have been something like "What can I do? How can I make this better? What will make him comfortable? How can I get the best help the fastest?"

Alas, I must admit those were, at best, my third or fourth thoughts.

I was momentarily paralyzed by my second thought that I very badly did not want to be present and involved in the demise of the third Kennedy, the younger brother of John and Bobby. Fame is a double edged blade. Anyone of my generation knows exactly where they were when they heard about the assassinations of John and Bobby, 20 and 15 years before, and what they meant to America and the world. I suddenly did not feel very good or imbued with Christmas cheer and was thinking more of John and Bobby than of Ted. It took a moment to realize that the Senator felt a lot worse than me and to bring myself back to the present. The next few minutes took a couple of years to pass, and I'm sure for Ted Kennedy they took a couple of decades. After an indeterminate time, (probably 10 minutes), to my great relief and his comfort, his breathing leveled out and he felt better and got back up on his feet under his own power. We skied down to River run and I walked the senator to the Sun Valley bus and he got on and the bus drove away.

Seeing Ted Kennedy on that bus was one of the fine Christmas gifts of my life. I rode the lift back up to Round House with a sense of concern for the senator's health, and a huge sense of relief that my first thought after he fell was erroneous. It was, after all, a Merry Sun Valley Christmas, but I have always been troubled with myself about my second thought not having been, perhaps, my tenth, and the incident caused me to more closely examine my own priorities and concerns in the present moment.

Two days later Senator Kennedy was checked into Walter Reed Hospital in Washington, D.C. suffering from exhaustion and other unspecified ailments.

Ted Kennedy, in my mind, was an unflinching friend to America, a vital force in and one of the best servants of the public in the U.S. Senate, among the best there has ever been. He seemed to take better care of himself in subsequent years, perhaps in some part because of his last run on Baldy.

CHAPTER TWELVE

Ed Scott

SEVERAL YEARS AGO I WAS DINING WITH A FRIEND at Smoky Mountain Pizza in Ketchum, Idaho. We were in the back room by the old stone fireplace and the window looking out on Sun Valley Road. A large, battered, brown 1976 Dodge Coronet station wagon pulled up and began arduously maneuvering into the lone parking place in front. It was a painstakingly slow process to observe, and it was not hard to imagine how the vehicle had earned its wounds. Both automobile and driver were Ketchum icons; and, since the history and present substance of both skiing and Ketchum have been profoundly enriched by the driver, I watched with interest and affection the careful changing of angles and inching forward and backwards until the car was parked. It took a long time. Then 84-year-old Ed Scott and his wife Barbara got out of the car and Ed, Barbara at his side, maneuvered himself with tiny, shuffling steps into Smoky Mountain Pizza as slowly, carefully and painfully as he had parked the car. In his last years, Ed suffered from Parkinson's Disease and low blood pressure and was a marvel of concentration and tenacity in performing the mundane rituals of life, like walking. He and Barbara sat down across the room. We exchanged greetings. Scotty swept the room with his hand. "Do you remember, Dick, do you remember?" he asked. Indeed, I did. I could only imagine Scotty's poignant memories of that room where he opened his ski shop in 1949 and worked for the next 20 years. In that room, he had repaired the skis and equipment of thousands of skiers and revolutionized the ski pole. The Scott pole changed the ski pole industry more swiftly and completely than any other equipment breakthrough in skiing history. Scott's life itself is testimony to the force one man can exert on history, in this case, ski history.

Edward Lawrence Scott was born July 11, 1914 in Philadelphia to Louis and Francis Scott. He grew up in Bell Rose, Long Island and was known as "Ned," although the ski world called him "Scotty." When he was ten years old his father made him a pair of pine skis from plans published in The Boy Mechanic. That he and his father shared something as magical as making a pair of skis from scratch speaks to Scotty's lifelong passion for making, fixing, tinkering and inventing "things." Along with skiing, those passions would determine his life's path.

When he was thirteen Scott met aviator Charles Lindbergh, whose chauffeur lived next to the Scotts on Long Island. The morning of Lindbergh's historical first solo nonstop flight across the Atlantic in 1927, Scott rode to the airport with Lindbergh and watched him take off. It is not hard to imagine that when Lindbergh actually reached Paris Scott learned a deep lesson in character, perseverance, independence and courage.

Scott entered MIT in 1932. That first college Christmas his parents gave him a pair of eight-foot Northland pine skis with a simple toe strap through a mortised slot in the skis. There were no metal edges. Scott described what he did with those skis: "Wearing galoshes, we'd walk up a hill, set the skis down pointed down the fall line, kick our toes into the straps, and run straight down the hill, balancing with our hands like a tightrope walker (no poles, of course)."

Scotty also attended Amherst, but his downfall from academia to an unconventional lifestyle began at Thanksgiving 1935 when he took a vacation job in Macy's ski department in New York City.

"After Christmas," he wrote, "I switched to Alex Taylor & Co., New York City's leading ski shop at that time. They operated New York's first snow trains, on weekends, running up into New England. We operated a rental ski shop in a converted baggage car. Once at the destination, the train parked all day and we employees got to ski too. I was hooked. Here was a new and interesting sport, in beautiful surroundings, and exclusive enough so that you could feel that you'd discovered a unique and private world."

The last two sentences could describe the experience of millions of skiers of every era. Scott discovered that he loved skiing and he loved to tinker around with ski equipment. For the next four years, Scott worked in New York City ski shops during vacations. In 1936, Union Pacific Railroad built America's first high mountain destination ski resort in Idaho. Twice Scott applied for jobs there and the second time, in 1939, he was successful, but just then his father died. He said, "I felt I should get into some permanent sort of work, so I resigned before ever seeing Sun Valley."

Scott went to work for Ford Motor Co. in an auto assembly plant. He then worked on aircraft engines for Pratt & Whitney and on tank engines for Ford before being drafted in 1942 at the beginning of World War II. Scott spent the next four years in Europe as a U.S. Army tank mechanic. He saw England, Scotland, Belgium, Germany, Czechoslovakia and, his favorite, France.

"France was much more interesting and different," he said. "And I studied a little French in high school, so I could speak some of it." Scott fell in love with a Frenchwoman. Photos from WWII France show Scotty with a woman and her two children, too old to have been Scotty's. After the half-track on which he was riding detonated a mine he was hospitalized in France. At the end of the war, he returned to the U.S. and in 1946 he went to San Francisco where his sister Marian lived, and took a job in a machine shop. By now he was a consummate mechanic, but work alone could not make him happy the way skiing could, so he looked for a second job in a ski shop in the Bay Area. He met Bill Klein, ski school director and ski shop owner both in Berkeley and at Sugar Bowl, the only ski area in California with a chair lift. Scotty quit his job and spent the winter in Sugar Bowl. It was a turning point in his life. "Well," he wrote, "I found a paradise. I was in skier's heaven. I got to make a few runs nearly every afternoon when the shop wasn't busy, and on more of a mountain than I'd ever seen in the east. I enjoyed the people and was filling a real need. I decided that I'd spend the rest of my life at a ski resort, and that if I did it might as well be the biggest and best one."

He drove to Sun Valley, got a job at Pete Lane's Ski Shop in the Challenger Inn. He worked on the Sun Valley chair lifts and put his roots down in the locale where he would spend the rest of his life. Here Scotty would become "the conscience of the community."

He enjoyed the people, he definitely filled a need, and he always demanded the best from himself. He could be intolerant of less than that in others.

Warren Miller recalls that Scott quit his job, furious that Lane had made a disparaging remark about a girl friend of Scott's. It was not a casual move. In those days at Union Pacific's Sun Valley, room and board was included for workers, and without a job Scotty was on the street. He wound up paying fifty cents a night for sleeping bag space on the floor of the unheated garage where Miller lived.

In 1949 Scott scraped together enough money to open his own ski repair shop in Ketchum, breaking Pete Lane's monopoly on Sun Valley ski repair. His clients came to include many of the best racers in the world. He made friends of many of those skiers, and he put off a few of them, too. Ed Scott, who did brilliant work with his hands, also wielded a razor sharp tongue and wicked pen. And on occasion those hands turned to fists on the ends of long arms attached to a big, strong body. He had the testy wit and moral courage to use tongue, pen and fist whenever and however he saw fit. Jim Harris, an old friend and longtime employee of Scott's had this to say: "He was so outspoken. He was just a tough-minded guy and heavily opinionated and it got him into some brawls. I loved working for him. He was wild and crazy and a renegade."

A local Scott legend has it that he and friends were partying at a hot pool, when a tricycle standing at one end inspired the partygoers to a wager against anyone being able to ride the tricycle the length of the pool. No one could until Ed Scott pedaled triumphantly end to end underwater.

He surely had a wild streak, but Scotty was essentially a working man, and he wrote of his ski shop endeavor: "A couple of years showed no profit so I began adding unique and better items to retail (foreign skis, boots and bindings when the other shops offered mostly domestic brands.)"

What he couldn't sell because it didn't exist was a really good ski pole. The standard tonkin bamboo pole was a menace, shattering easily and seldom lasting an entire season. The shards of a broken bamboo pole could be deadly. Frank Springer-Miller, writing in the 1953 American Ski Annual, noted that "I am dead set against the tonkin pole unless they are wound with cord: once I broke one into a dozen murderous stilettos which, fortunately, attacked a tree instead of this scared beaver."

"I looked for a good metal pole," Scotty said, "but none were being made. All were too heavy and too flexible." Ed Scott, the man who rode the tricycle the length of the pool underwater, thought there should be a better product.

To use a veteran phrase, the rest is history.

In Scotty's own words: "So I bought light steel shafts from Kroydon, a golf shaft specialist who'd ventured into ski poles. I had Dartmouth Ski Co. make their children's size rings out of adult-quality materials, and thus had a small light ring. I bought Vibram molded rubber grips with integral adjustable leather straps, and thus assembled a distinctive and better pole. I sold maybe 50 to 100 pairs per year. One fall I ordered a bunch of shafts from Kroydon and was told they'd quit making them and had sold their tooling to Sigmund Werner Co. I wrote them and was told that they wouldn[1]t sell shafts to a potential competitor.

"I'd seen a thin, tapered, light aluminum shaft on poles made by the Dale Boison Co. in Los Angeles several years earlier, and asked Warren Miller to locate the source for these shafts (Boison had quit the pole business). He did, and I bought maybe 100 duplicates from the tube-tapering specialist, Le Fiell Mfg. Co.

"Someone would buy a pair, go skiing, and come back with a friend that afternoon who had to have a pair too. They sold on 'feel' alone. Next year I had them use larger diameter tubing with thinner walls, which obviously would make a stiffer yet lighter shaft. These sold even faster.

"Well, I knew I had a hot item on my hands. If I didn't do something with it, sooner or later one of the larger firms in the ski industry would see a pair that I'd sold, realize the potential, and start making them. I had absolutely no capital or facilities or experience in running such a business. What to do? Just bend my head down and start moving ahead.

"I took a couple of sample poles and a list of Head Ski dealers, and drove all over the West taking orders. I'd go in a shop and ask 'What's the best pole that you carry?' Invariably it would be Eckel, a nicely-finished steel pole with a slender, buggy whip-like shaft that was as heavy as a croquet mallet. I'd ask them to hold two of our poles in one hand and one Eckel in the other, and flick them back and forth. Their eyes would bug out. 'Two of yours weight less than one Eckel.' It wasn't quite true, but it seemed so. Then I'd ask them to put one hand half-way down the shaft and flex each one. 'And yours are twice as stiff' (true). So I'd say 'OK, how many do you want?'

"It was literally that easy. I came home with initial orders for one or two thousand pairs, and figured I had it made. Went to the pawn shop that passed for a bank, and showed them the stack of orders. Was told 'That's just a stack of paper. We can't loan on it.'

"Managed to borrow a little, stretch credit to the limit, make and ship the poles. Couldn't keep up with the reorders. It was an overnight sensation, partly because all other poles were designed stupidly and unimaginatively. (What could be simpler than using aluminum tubing of larger diameter and thinner wall? Why hadn't anyone stumbled on it?)"

Coincidentally (synchronistical?), this was the year Wedeln hit the U.S.: short, quick, linked turns initiated by a pole plant. A light-swingweight pole was the only way it could be done easily. The new Scott pole was a sensation and a revolution. Skiers took their poles to lunch with them so they wouldn't get stolen. Ski lodge cafeterias were festooned with Scott poles leaning against chairs and tables and walls within their owner's sight.

"In 1960," Scott wrote, "our first winter in the pole business, I ran a free ski repair shop for all racers at the Squaw Valley Olympics. The loose rules under which we operated forbade giving away free equipment (though all mechanical work was free) to the racers, so we had to charge them for our poles. Exceptions: We had given free poles to the U.S. & Canadian teams a month earlier. Nevertheless, many top racers put aside the free poles they had, bought and raced with ours. Word of this usage of a brand new product from an unknown manufacturer spread pretty quickly, and helped us a lot."

But Scott was an inventor, tinkerer, repairman, worker, not an industrial businessman. He wrote of these first years: "Made no profit on 16,000 gross. Next year I raised the price from $17.95 to $19.95 (retail), sold 32,000 worth and still no profit. Next year $21.95, 83,000 gross, still no profit. Next year $24.95, 125,000 gross, still no profit. Next year 252,000 gross and still no profit."

In 1961 Scotty struck a blow for the little guy. As reported by John Jerome years later in Skiing: The only West Coast trade shows were held by the Western Winter Sports Representative Association, an organization of sales reps. They barred manufacturers from the shows. Scotty could not show, because he handled all his sales personally and had no reps, the WWSRA told him.

Nonsense thought Scott and headed for the trade show at Seattle. He reserved himself a room across from the show and set up a display. There was pandemonium. The director of the show called the hotel manager. The manager tired to remove Scotty. He refused to be budged. The hotel put up a screen around his door and posted a bellhop to make sure no ski retailers visited the room. That was enough for Scotty, champion of justice and defender of the little guy, in this case himself. Never let it be said that Ed Scott didn't recognize restraint of trade when he saw it. He hopped a plane to San Francisco, brought a case in federal court, which ruled in Scotty's favor. From then on Scott poles were exhibited at every WWSRA show.

Scott writes: "At the 1962 Chamonix FIS our poles were used by 13 of the 18 medal winners and almost 3/4 of all the entrants. At Innsbruck in '64, under the watchful eyes of pole manufacturers who had paid thousands of dollars to racers for using their poles, we didn't do quite that well but still had well over half of all entrants.

"In Portillo at the 1966 FIS, far from the watchful eyes of their patrons, the racers were free to use what they pleased and we hit an incredible 5 out of 6 of the entrants.

'From then on it was all downhill, as the fees paid per racer by other firms became so high and the competition between pole manufacturers so keen (one U.S. manufacturer paid an Austrian $5,000 just before the Chamonix downhill to switch poles; and another U.S. manufacturer offered the Austrian team $5,000 for anyone who'd win a gold medal using his poles) that our 'no payola' policy reduced our statistics considerably. We were spending about 10 percent of gross on advertising and giving away almost 200 pairs to racers in each FIS and Olympics, which made the poles the best-known and most in demand in the world very quickly but it wiped out any profits."

But so long as Ed Scott was in control of his company he maintained a policy of never paying racers for using his product. As the ski industry boomed during the 1960s, this was viewed as a quaint, puritanical ethic in what Scott viewed as a libertine business culture. Scott continues: "In 1965, Tom Corcoran, one of the best U.S. racers and a Harvard MBA, asked me how we were doing, and when I told him he bought out Stan Mullin, our largest stockholder (including myself), arranged a large working capital loan, and took an active and enlightened interest in the business. Wholesaling poles up through 1968, we had an accumulated net loss of $5,000. Finally, we made $30,000 in 1968-69.

"Meanwhile, the conglomerate fever of the late 1960s reached a high pitch and many firms were interested in acquiring firms in the ski industry. Outsiders have always thought the ski business was bigger and more profitable than it was, but it was growing rapidly. Eighteen firms approached us at varying levels of seriousness about acquisition. True Temper's ski division, Shakespeare reels, Outdoor Sports Industries (Gerry), Browning Arms, Sea & Ski, Garcia, O.M. Scott (grass seed), Wilson Sporting Goods, Unitec Industries, etc., etc. I told all of them we'd sell, but not until we could have a big enough year to command a good price. I set this at $1,000,000 first, and they all shook their heads. As interest heated up (I leaked the info about suitors to the trade press), I jumped it to $2,000,000. Finally in 1970, Kingsford Charcoal offered

$1,200,000 down and another $1,300,000 if profits could be increased over a five-year period. Down payment alone was fifty times our accumulated earnings over the ten years we'd been in business and forty times our best year's earnings, so it was too good to turn down. After I sold, I ran the company on contract for awhile.

"We had 50 percent of the field at Val Gardena in 1970, my last year of racer promotion. In all that period we never paid a cent to any racer, coach, or team, and only twice were ever asked to. The racers respected our policy.

"In October 1971, I was fired when I sued Kingsford for some added stock they owed me and were withholding, but by that time I think that no other ski product has ever dominated its segment of the industry so totally and for so long a period, and I find considerable satisfaction in having built it up without racer payola."

Though Scott is generally credited with inventing the aluminum ski pole in 1959, it is not true and he never made that claim. What he did do was find the right thickness, right tapering, right diameter, right weight and right strength aluminum shaft. He wrote, "I did not pioneer or invent the aluminum pole. Light, well-balanced (low swing-weight) poles would have been stumbled upon by others very soon after I did it, anyway." This is neither false nor true modesty on Scott's part. It is a quintessential example of the innate honesty Miller and many others honored in Scott.

"Ed Scott always said it like it was, no matter what," Miller says. "He couldn't be bought, and neither money nor praise had much effect on him. He simply wasn't for sale. Scotty knew what he wanted to do and he did it, and I very much admired his ability to be his own man. He could be an irascible SOB, but he was morally clean and there aren't enough people like him anymore."

Ed Scott loved ski racing, for itself. Scotty racing is an image to bring smiles to those who knew Scotty in later years. He was tall, lanky, and balding, with sloped shoulders and thick glasses. He was a less-than-gifted athlete who never mastered the subtleties of skiing technique, though he raced with a reckless enthusiasm and the commitment of a champion. His ski racing falls were the stuff of Sun Valley legend.

In Scott's mind, his main contribution to skiing was not the lightweight ski pole. It was the ski boot re-shaping press he designed. In 1986 he wrote, "The contribution that helped and benefited more skiers than the pole, by far, was the ski boot re-shaping press that I designed and which still is in use in most good ski shops. It was first produced in the mid-sixties about when the craze for 'cast-iron' boots began (both leather and plastic). It made it possible for people to ski fairly comfortably in boots that were impossibly painful before the pressure points had been re-shaped. Without it, hundreds of thousands would have quit the sport, and other hundreds of thousands would never have taken it up."

Scott hated to see skiers in pain. At the 1960 Olympics, the great Russian Nordic skier, Maria Gusakova, brought her too small, ill-fitting boots to Scott and showed him her bruised feet. Scott invented on the spot a boot press that stretched this particular pair. After Gusakova won gold in the 10-km race, she returned to give Scott a thank you kiss.

After selling the pole business in 1971, Scott was retired until 1975 when the old itch to make things better than anyone else took hold again. He saw that bicycle brakes were as unsatisfactory as ski poles had been, and he went to work on a solution. Scotty began making superior bicycle brake shoes, which he did for the rest of his working life.

He also helped design and manufacture a state of the art snow making gun in the late 1980s. In 1986 he wrote of his involvement in skiing: "I was in the ski industry in the period that I think was the most fun, and think I got out at about the right time. I doubt I could function in the ski business today."

He did, however, function quite well as the conscience of his community of the Wood River Valley of central Idaho.

In one letter that appeared in the Idaho Mountain Express Scott chided the pretensions of a local seminar on The American Hero. Scott wrote, "The implication that there's some connection between heroism and the West is in itself a joke, a pathetic offshoot of the kind of local thinking that equates manhood with a pickup truck equipped with oversized tires and a rifle rack, or that leads grown men to wear cowboy boots and ten gallon hats while wandering from bar to bar."

He was still at it in 1998 when he wrote a deriding letter of those who objected to affordable housing in the Sun Valley area. He asked, "Is Ketchum simply for sale? How many Taj Mahals crowded side by side would it take to become bad taste?"

Longtime Ketchum resident, writer and Olympic skier, Betty Weir Bell, wrote, "Scotty's our public conscience, our watchdog, and though sometimes I cringe at his bluntness, I envy him his clarity of view and his courage to state it. Edward L. Scott's a local treasure."

When Ed Scott died in March 2001 at the age of 86, the community of Ketchum, the community of skiers and the industry of skiing lost one of its original innovative (and free) thinkers and ethical lodestars. In a time when, for example, skis made with a thin aluminum alloy layer containing approximately .04 percent of titanium are marketed as titanium skis, he is remembered as having been ethically true to himself while never making much money from his endeavors. His life is, perhaps, an object lesson for members of the ski industry. He was a pillar of the Ketchum community and a true friend to skiing throughout the world. Ed Scott was an honest man, and honesty is not marketable.

He made local history as a political and environmental activist, letter-writer to the local papers and speaker at public meetings. Mary Jane Conger (nee Griffith), ex-ski racer and third generation Ketchumite said, "He cared about his community. He attended meetings regularly and tried to make Ketchum a better place." She remembers him as a 'realist,' concerned about "growth issues and the environment because they reflected deep values about why people came here in the first place. He definitely made a mark on this community."

Ruth Lieder, ex-mayor of Sun Valley, said, "He was famous for writing letters to the newspapers." She recalled that it could be hard to take if the letter was critical of her. "But with him," she said, "it was always okay because it was always very factual and well researched. He never just shot from the hip."

His concept of patriotism was formed as a soldier in World War II, while mine was formed as a member of the counter-culture during the

Vietnam War. As a consequence, I became the target of one of his letters in criticism of something I'd written in opposition to a proposed U.S. Air Force bombing range in southern Idaho. Like Lieder, I didn't enjoy the criticism, partly because of my respect and admiration for the writer; but it was okay because it wasn't a personal attack; it was factual, respectful of me even if I disagreed with him, and, of course, he didn't shoot from the hip. But he shot straight.

Scott was a private man who kept his personal life secluded from his professional one. He was married twice and had one daughter and four step-children, and no one who knew him would disagree with this description from his obituary in the Idaho Mountain Express. "Scotty was well known as an iconoclast, albeit a reserved and taciturn gentleman of the old school, characterized by his witty humor, his tenacity, fierce loyalty to his friends and deep love for his family."

Scotty's sense of skepticism and innocence squandered was expressed very firmly in his poem Epitaph For Man, written during the Cold War:

We were but guests upon this earth,
Who'd so abused her hospitality that best begone.
Begone! And when we were, no living thing did shed a tear,
Or even know or care.

We split the atom, trod the moon, but could not live in peace.
Our best and brightest strove only to destroy,
And in the end they did.
Oh, earth! Forgive us if you can.

CHAPTER THIRTEEN

Dick Barrymore

IN THE FALL OF 1962 I was carrying a full load of classes in my last semester of undergraduate work at the University of Nevada in Reno, working a half time job, training for the upcoming Olympic tryouts, and trying to put aside enough money to travel to all those tryouts. I was broke and maxed and felt like a juggler with one ball too many in the air.

My friends and fellow ski racers Ron Funk and Don McKinnon knew about my situation and they also knew that their friend Dick Barrymore was looking for someone in Reno to organize a showing of his ski film. I'd never met Dick or seen his films, but I knew about him and about his filming trip with Funk to New Zealand the year before. Ron and Don put Dick and me in touch and we signed a contract that fulfilled both our needs. Barrymore would get introduced to the Reno ski crowd and I would make enough money to race on that winter. I had to guarantee Dick a certain amount of money to come to Reno, but we were assured the film would be shown to a sell-out crowd. After all, Dick was a great if relatively unknown ski filmmaker, and I would spare no efforts to promote the man and his film to a town filled with skiers.

What could be better?

Dick showed up the afternoon of the showing after a long drive from Los Angeles. He took a nap, showered and we went to the State Building Auditorium which I'd rented for the film. It was, to put it mildly, not a full house, but Dick, as always, put on a show to remember. It was the best ski film and narration the few of us present had ever seen and heard. I was amazed and inspired as well as filled with the dread of financial disaster, for the night's receipts were far less than I had agreed to pay Barrymore, not to mention the costs I'd already incurred. When the film was over and it was time to settle accounts, Dick said, "Let's go have a drink." We took the cash box and went across the street to the bar of the old Riverside Hotel. We ordered a drink and Dick asked how much it had cost me to put on the film. I told him. He took that much out of the box and gave it to me. Then he told me what he thought it cost him to come to Reno from L.A. He took that out of the box for himself. And then he said we should split the profits, which came to something like $30 each, saving me a financial/personal debacle and a huge amount of stress while giving me something far more valuable than the money involved.

That was Dick Barrymore and the beginning of a friendship that lasted until his death on August 1, 2008.

During the 30 years of his ski filmmaking until the late 1980s Dick made a huge contribution to the world and business of skiing, to the culture of skiing and to the legacy of ski films. I'll leave it to others more knowledgeable to analyze and praise that contribution. Suffice it to say that his work was full of happiness and fun, inspiration and beauty, good fellowship and wit, and his films honored skiing, skiers, the mountains and the lives and lifestyles that revolved around them.

In 1969 New York Times film critic Roger Greenspun had this to say about what was perhaps Dick's best known film, "The Last of the Ski Bums," starring Ron Funk, Mike Zeutell and Ed Ricks, (Greenspun and the Times misspelled Funk's name as Fink, an hilarious aside): "'The Last of the Ski Bums'...succeeds surprisingly well—surprisingly at least for me, because I have never been on skis in my life, have never wanted to ski, and in general have embraced indolence with a passion most men reserve for their mistresses...'The Last of the ski Bums'...knows that skiing is a more serious occupation than, say, working, and that like sailing, climbing, and all the lonely ways of wasting time—it is a form of contemplation."

I've never known a more riveting storyteller or person happier in front of or better able to hold an audience than Dick Barrymore.

He was, however, a terrible poker player. In Portillo in 1963 he couldn't resist playing poker with the truly poker-faced Monty Atwater, and Dick consistently lost. His natural ability to tell a story worked against him at poker, for his expressive face revealed the quality of his hand. When it was bad Dick looked like the woman of his dreams had just walked out the door; when his hand was good his face lit up like she had just walked back in unbuttoning her blouse. Dick was an easy read at poker.

Skiing for his camera was, at least in my experience, always a pleasure, never an ordeal or a job. I still remember a day in Bariloche when Ken Corrock and I skied powder for Dick and his camera and because of Dick's presence and personality we had more fun than if we had been only skiing for ourselves, and that's why I remember it. It was a few years before I saw the footage taken that day and it was obvious that Ken and I were having a great time. Part of Dick Barrymore the ski photographer was that he wanted everyone to have as much fun as he was having.

He was a superb pilot and though I am generally quite uncomfortable in small planes, I always had confidence in Dick's piloting skills and attention to detail. He liked to tell the story of how he would fly from Sun Valley to Dana Point to work on the editing of his films and of how he would read the Sunday paper during the long, lonely early morning flight across the emptiness of Nevada. One day while reading his paper he noticed another small plane flying below and left of him and Dick could see the pilot of that plane was also reading the paper. Dick never read the paper again while flying. He picked me up once in Driggs, Idaho to fly me to Boise and we followed the freeway rather than take the shorter path across Craters of the Moon Monument with its expanse of jagged lava flows because "...there's no place to put a plane down there." That was Dick Barrymore the pilot.

During the mid-80s Dick and I were living in Ketchum and we both were wrestling with unruly relationship issues. During that time we had a weekly dinner conference to commiserate, confer, confide, advise and laugh at each other and ourselves over our follies and adventures within the biggest adventure of them all—love. No one told a story on himself as well as Dick Barrymore, and his material was almost unbelievable except that his friends knew it was true. Mine was pretty good as well and we were never at a loss for words, stories or lessons, some of which we learned. Those weekly dinners were salvation and tonic, completely enjoyable, and will always be remembered for, among other things, the attitude about and perspective on the life and lifestyle Dick embodied and we had both chosen and lived in slightly different ways. He summed up that attitude and perspective in his book, *Breaking Even*: "I wouldn't trade one moonrise over the Aiguilles in Chamonix, one sunrise from the summit of the Matterhorn, or one choking powder run in the Monashees for a basket full of General Motors blue-chip stock certificates."

The last time I saw Dick he was at his mother Blanche's condo in Ketchum a couple of weeks before he died. He had endured a brutal several months of surgery for brain cancer, after which he opted out of traditional western medicine chemo and radiation therapy in the U.S. and went for a Hail Mary shot at alternative treatment in Mexico, and he was wrapped up in a blanket on a recliner chair watching TV when David Stelling and I arrived for a short visit. He turned off the TV and we talked mostly about old friends, including Funk and McKinnon. Since we were there Blanche announced she would leave for a short time and go to the post office. I said that I hoped she had some good mail waiting for her. The 96 year old Blanche Barrymore, who had buried her other child, Dick's brother Doug, 21 years earlier and who was now nursing her remaining child through his last days, looked at me with a charming, roguish smile and said, "Well, I probably won't be receiving any love letters, but maybe I'll get a nice package."

It was an insight into where Dick got his sense of humor, his love of life, his gratitude for powder snow, moonrises and sunrises.

The last thing Dick Barrymore said to me as David and I were leaving was, "Dick, you're looking very healthy."

"Yes," I replied, "I'm feeling pretty good."

That's good," he said, "that's good."

So was Dick Barrymore.

PART THREE

The Backcountry

CHAPTER FOURTEEN

No Es Malo; Es Diferente

SOMETIME BETWEEN TEN AND THIRTY THOUSAND YEARS AGO, during the higher Paleolithic age, man first appeared in the wild, mountainous, lake filled, forested and desert land we know as Patagonia, the southern part of Argentina where winter runs from June through September. Around the lake called Lago Nahuel Huapi (Tiger Island Lake) at least three different indigenous tribes lived in peaceful co-existence for thousands of years until the 17th century when the Mapuche or Araucanos people were forced out of Chile to the west by the relentless, brutal, gold seeking Spanish invaders. The Araucanos absorbed the native cultures around Nahuel Huapi and lived without undue influence from the outside world until about 1860 when White Man, the European, arrived. As happened throughout the Americas, Europeans quickly took over the land and devastated the cultures of the aboriginal peoples. Everything continuously changes, people age and die, peoples and cultures come and go. History takes no prisoners.

In 1895 Carlos Wietherholdt, a German trader, built the first buildings on what would become the city of San Carlos de Bariloche. He began a trading business with Puerto Montt in Chile to the west. By 1897 there were 14 settlers around the shores of Lago Nahuel Huapi, most of them German and North American, though in 1901 a group of Swiss immigrants arrived. On May 3, 1902 the city was officially founded, named Carlos after Mr. Wietherholdt and Bariloche from the Indian term Vuriloche. The first tourists arrived later that year, setting the stage for its main industry ever since. The first road was completed in 1913 so that U.S. President Theodore Roosevelt could visit the area.

A hundred years after its founding Bariloche is a booming, sprawling resort Mecca of some 100,000 permanent and semi-permanent souls and many thousands of rotating tourists there for skiing, climbing and hiking, fishing, lovely mountain scenery, shopping, night life and the action. The entire area, with the exception of towns like Bariloche and a few others is a huge National Park and nature preserve. What might it be in a hundred years? We were there for the 1st Open International de esqui de Montana of Bariloche (what is known as a randonnee ski race), for an extended ski tour through the mountain huts to the west, for a few lift accessed turns at the Cerro Catedral Ski Area, and for the fine Argentine dining. We were four Norte Americanos, Kris Erikson, his wife, Cloe, Jeannie Wall and me, and we found a lean snow year on our arrival in early September 2004.

Wall, of Bozeman, Montana, was the best female randonnee competitor in North America and a contender for the first three on the World Cup circuit. One of the best known endurance athletes in America, winning Wisconsin's prestigious Birkebiner cross country ski race before retiring from Nordic skiing to concentrate on randonee racing, she has an impressive rock climbing and mountaineering resume and was one of Outside Magazine's 25 "Sports and Adventure Goddesses Who Rule." (See Outside December 2003) While pursuing all these endeavors she managed to maintain a job with the Patagonia clothing company for nearly 15 years. She is known as a fierce competitor who lives her life in a multi-tasking spinning swirl of dizzying complexity and movement. A good friend once said, "There are not enough hours in the day to keep up with Jeannie's whirling dervish of a life." But during the grueling hours of endurance athletics, whether competitive or not, she becomes focused and absorbed in the endorphin fueled moment at hand.

Kris had only been in a few randonnee races, but his climbing and ski mountaineering background is deep and extensive and in each race his results get better. On October 1, 2002 be became the second person to have skied from the summit of Tibet's 26,906 foot Cho Oyu and the second American to have skied from the top of any of the world's 8000 meter peaks. Though mountains do not require or recognize them, his mountain credentials are impeccable, and his humility about his accomplishments is as refreshing as his vision is clear. "Skiing an 8000 meter peak isn't about powder," he says of Cho Oyu. "I could only link seven or eight turns before collapsing into what felt like cardiac arrest." He makes his living as one of the best mountain photographers in the business. He lives in Livingston, Montana.

Cloe, like Kris, smiles a lot and puts people at ease and is a Montana native who grew up in a cabin in the woods heated by a wood burning stove with no running water. She has a Master of Architecture degree and her own business, has traveled extensively in Europe, lived and studied Arabic in Morocco and has been to the Antarctic with Kris. She writes about local Montana issues with an emphasis on historic preservation, sustainable architecture, growth and planning and land preservation. A rock climber, mountaineer and alpine skier, Cloe had done very little back country skiing when we arrived in Bariloche.

I was the support team for Kris and Wall, the two person Norte Americano contingent in the 1st Open International, and I saw a very unorthodox randonnee ski race. Most randonnee competitions involve racers in a Le Mans start where competitors run to their skis at the start, get in their bindings, climb up a few thousand feet with skins on their skis, tear off the skins, ski down a few thousand feet, put skins back on, skin up a few thousand feet and repeat, depending on terrain and length of race. Sometimes there is a section that requires booting up while carrying skis, on occasion using crampons. A typical race takes between two and three hours and involves some 6000 feet of climbing. A storm moved in the day before this race (September 4) and the ski area, Cerro Catedral, was closed. The top of the mountain was swept with 140 kph winds, and there was only snow on top of the mountain. Not wanting to postpone or cancel the race, the organizers staged a race like no other.

The race began at 10 a.m. in the mire at the bottom of the Cerro Catedral in a driving rain storm. Forty two competitors ran up muddy trails and roads through the lengua tree and bamboo forest until reaching snowline, carrying skis and boots on their backs. The best competitors reached that point in a little less than half an hour, the slowest in well over an hour. There, just where the falling rain turned to wet snow, they changed into ski boots and skis and skinned up another thousand feet where drier snow fell horizontally in a driving wind, skied down to the same point in soft, bottomless slush that collapsed in unexpected places and ways. There were many falls. At this first changeover occurred a demonstration of sportsmanship, comradeship and the sense of community that seems to prevail among ski mountaineers, even the competitive ones. Wall arrived at this point a few seconds ahead of Spain's Emma Roca. Wall was unable to unclip the uphill mode binding release from her boot and was essentially stuck on her ski in the downhill mode. She struggled with it for a bit and then pleaded, "Help me." Roca did just that, stopping her changeover efforts to open Wall's boot release before returning to her own race. Wall eventually won the women's race in one hour twelve minutes and nine seconds, fourteen seconds ahead of Roca. They placed, respectively, fifth and sixth overall, beaten only by the four man Spanish team. After a second climb up the competitors skied down a different route to the muck line, changed skis and boots from feet to back, donned tennis shoes and ran from snowline to finish in the mud at the bottom. The men's winner was Javier Martin de Villa of Spain, who is often among the first 15 in the world, in one hour one minute twenty-four seconds. On the last mud run section to the finish Kris was in fifth place when the skis on his back came undone and exploded into an unmanageable mess. He was trying to fix the situation when he was overtaken by Argentina's best randonnee racer, Leandro Martin Proverbio, who stopped to help. Kris insisted that the Argentine move on. Kris finished the mud run carrying skis and boots in his hands, finishing 6th among the men, 22 seconds behind the good sportsman Martin Proverbio. The slowest competitor took almost three hours to finish.

After this exercise in mud running with skis and pack under leaden skies, we retired to the banquet at El Tesoro Restaurant, a carnivorous feast of chorizo, blood sausage and veal. It was slim pickings for me, a vegetarian, and Wall, a carnivorous but notoriously discriminating eater. Kris polished off a gargantuan plate of meat, washed down with fine Argentine wine, and coined the motto of the day, the axiom of the race, the theme of our entire trip, a useful axiom for dealing with life's changes, and the title of this story: "*No es malo; es diferente,*" (It is not bad; it is different.), a perspective consistent with the attitude of the cheerful, optimistic and accomplished Erickson, though one that likely would not be shared by Bariloche's original, indigenous inhabitants.

By the time the banquet ended temperatures had dropped and snow was covering the mud at the bottom of the Cerro Catedral. That night it snowed at less than 2500 feet in town, more than 4700 feet lower than the top of the ski area. Cloe arrived from Buenos Aires the next day and joined us in waiting while it snowed steadily for three days and nights. When it stopped we went to Catedral for a day of outrageous lift accessed powder skiing clear to the bottom of the mountain which, just a few days before, was bare. It was a day of powder skiing to remember. We knew the back country had plenty of snow and that avalanche conditions might be worrisome, but we had confidence in our collective and individual mountain judgment, the snow was plentiful, the time now.

The next day, September 8, we headed out. By then we had hooked up with an acquaintance of Kris', James Bracken, an American semi-expatriate who lives most of the time in Bariloche and a few months of the year in Silverton, Colorado working construction to make enough money to live well in the depressed economy of Argentina. Bracken is a quintessential type of mountain dweller, living for the climbing, the skiing, the turn perfectly made where none has been made before, the alpenglow on snow covered ridges, the summits and the valleys, the north star and the southern cross at night, and the wildness coursing through those experiences and places, and with the people and lessons found only in exploring those mountains. The rest is just for the amenities and to keep James and his lovely Argentine girl friend sheltered, fed and happy. At heart, James is a gracious dirtbag with an engaging smile and the laid back demeanor of the mountain dreamer.

There are two routes usually taken into the Refugio Frey, a two story stone mountain hut built in 1957 less than four miles as the condor flies from the ski area; but mountaineers can only dream and be envious of flying condors. One route involves riding the ski lifts to the top and traversing exposed ridge lines far above tree line at the 7000 foot level, dropping down a couple thousand feet to Laguna Schmoll, bushwhacking through a valley of small lenguas trees and climbing a few thousand feet out and dropping down to the Frey at 5900 feet. Route finding is crucial and wind hammered new snow in unknown terrain made avalanche danger a concern. James recommended the normal, longer, contoured route on an avalanche free summertime trail completely in the woods until just below the Refugio. James suggested we could make the trip in two and a half hours, though the signs at the trailhead indicate four hours for the dry land summer hiker. In 1968 I had hiked into the Frey for a week of climbing, and even considering all the holes and warps within the tattered memories of my 65 years I suspected Bracken was being unrealistic.

He was. Mountain dreamers often are, and I write this with the personal experience of many years of mountain dreaming.

The five of us set out around noon from the ski area under blue sky and sunshine through the woods and a burned over section from the fires of a few years ago, across dozens of streams, around cliff bands with waterfalls and consequences for mistakes, the whole covered with enough snow to make skinning possible about ninety percent of the way. I took off skis to cross streams and rock bands probably fifteen times, and, despite my best efforts, by the end of the day my new Atomic skis and five year old beat up skins looked about the same age. We saw two sets of puma tracks and the signs of rabbits and other smaller animals, but the only wildlife we observed were birds. It was slow, tedious, frustrating going, breaking trail through not quite enough snow until we had gained perhaps a thousand of the more than two thousand vertical feet we had to go. We reached this point in about two and a half hours where the trail reaches the Arroyo Van Titter and becomes steeper and changes direction from southwest to northwest. By this time James had gone on ahead, Wall and Kris were patiently slowing their pace for Cloe and, especially, me; and it was evident that our packs were heavier and the day's exertions more rigorous than we had anticipated.

The woods in the Arroyo were denser and the warm temperatures became chilly in the shade. We passed the Refugio Piedritas, a small dwelling with a huge religious icon outside, mostly used by the Argentine Slovenian mountaineering community. Just before Piedritas a lone skier, dressed in ancient lace up boots, traditional sidecut skis from the past with old fixed bar Silveretta bindings and well worn clothes passed us at a brisk pace. His attire was a striking contrast to all the new, state of the art Patagonia gear we sported, but he was obviously fit. We later learned he was Pedro Fine, an Argentine mountain guide, a fine fellow of great enthusiasm for the mountains, a good climber still working on his skiing skills, and a singer prone to breaking into song at unexpected times for personal reasons. An electrician by trade, Pedro can make more money guiding tourists in the mountains than he can practicing his profession in the depressed economy of Argentina, and is as refreshing as he is irrepressible. It took James four, Kris, Cloe and Wall five, and me five and a half hours to reach the Refugio Frey, a most welcome sight.

Little had changed in the 36 years since I'd last visited. Though 50 can sleep there sardine style, two hut keepers, Pedro, another Argentine skier and the five of us were the only residents that night. Situated on a knoll above the frozen, snow covered Lago Tonchek in the bottom of a basin ringed with spectacular red granite spires, the highest, the Torre Principal, almost 8000 feet, the training ground of many of Argentina's leading rock and alpine climbers, the Refugio Frey would not look out of place in the German Alps. We were reminded of our friend, the Italian born Bariloche raised great climber Rolando "Rolo" Garibotti, who learned the basics of his impressive climbing skills on these lovely stones and who now, when he's not climbing somewhere in the world, lives in Boulder, Colorado. Rolo had left for the Rockies and we had come to the Andes, and I thought about how our circle of friends and acquaintances are largely mobile adventurers, travelers, curious continentals, cultural if not spiritual descendants of those original 17th century gold seeking Spanish explorer/invaders. Our civilization if not our persons has plundered the gold, taken all and decimated much of the land, and brutalized and in many cases drove to extinction the indigenous peoples. Still, our society and our persons push on. What is it we seek in exotic and new places and experiences that we do not have in our own back yards? That question deserves more attention than most of us are willing to give, as do the non-linear thoughts that every search is an escape, every gain a loss, each expansion a contraction and all new places and experiences a reminder of and return to something ancient, familiar, and as common as the earth on and from which we all live. The Spaniards didn't have enough gold they thought, and they never did find enough. (How could they?) But they discovered and built something different. A tiny part of that something is the Refugio Frey in a place no Araucano ever visited or wished to visit in winter, a place that a hundred and fifty years earlier would have been inconceivable. We visit searching for the pure gold adventure of good skiing in high mountains without asking whether there is ever enough or looking too closely at what will be built as a consequence of our explorations. It is unquestionable that something unforeseen will come of what we do. It always does.

Beer, wine, and home made Pizza are for sale at the Frey, but the energetic Ms Wall threw her considerable single burner camp stove gourmand cooking talents into creating a feast to fuel tired bodies and enhance the pleasures of eating. We thoroughly enjoyed and appreciated her efforts and cooking skills and went to bed with sated appetites and muscles grateful for rest.

I rose in the night to pee and the wind outside blew so hard it appeared to be snowing, but it was not. The Southern Cross marked the sky and it was completely clear and very beautiful. Except for that I slept like the proverbial baby.

We slept late and on arising determined that the wind blasted slopes would not be worth exploring, though the wind itself had ceased. We decided to move on to the Refugio Jakob (also called Refugio San Martin), a 7 or 8 hour push to the northwest where we hoped to find better snow. While we were drinking morning coffee and eating breakfast and (slowly) getting organized for the day's exertions, the hut keeper (also named Pedro) skinned up a sketchy looking south east facing couloir some 1200 to 1500 feet above and to the north west of Lago Tonchek. We watched his progress and skeptically noted places where he left no track and how he avoided steep pockets of drifted snow. We were pessimistically interested in what kinds of turns the snow would allow him to make and whether that snow would slough, slide or avalanche, and we were almost completely packed and ready to leave when Pedro made his descent.

He made beautiful, smooth turns on what was obviously superior and stable powder snow. It was a reminder of an old mountain lesson: the wind can blow like the Furies, but it can't and doesn't reach everywhere equally. We changed our plans on the spot and had what, for me, was the best day of the entire trip, a day that gave a deeper and different meaning to our motto, "*No es malo; es diferente.*"

We unloaded our packs and took day supplies and headed across the lake and up the big east facing bowl under the beautiful Torre Principal, the dominant rock spire to the west which I had climbed in 1968. James had teamed up with Pedro Fine and was ahead. The rest of us followed their zig-zag tracks, grateful for them breaking trail. At the top, on a tiny col beneath the main rock face of the Principal, we rested, snacked, drank water and took in the extravagant vista to the west, the glacier bound nearly 12,000 foot high Monte Tronador and, in the distance, the snow covered volcanoes of Chile, so reminiscent of Shasta, St. Helens, Adams and Rainier along the Pacific coast of North America.

Then Kris went to work. In addition to the same size and weight pack we all carry on our backs while ski mountaineering, Kris carries what he calls, his "angry child" on his chest, a 25 pound pack of camera gear. (The angry child was named by Hans Saari, Kris' favorite climbing/skiing friend/partner who referred to Kris as "the invisible man" because Kris was never in any of his photos. While skiing with Kris in 2001, Saari died in a fall down the Gervasutti Couloir on Mont Blanc du Tacul in Chamonix.) Kris spent the next several hours lugging around the angry child, setting up shots, and photographing us enjoying the best skiing of the trip. We skied the line we had climbed, more than a thousand feet of steep skiing in powder and corn on the same east exposure above the Refugio and the lake. It was lovely. Then we climbed back up and, while Kris, Cloe and Wall took another lap I continued up to a higher col on the south flank of the Principal, exploring new terrain. A hundred feet or so below the col I had to remove skis and kick steps in steep hard corn snow that turned to rock where I had to toss skis and poles ahead and figure out a few fifth class rock moves in ski boots. As I was doing this, Wall appeared below me. They had completed their lap far faster than I had anticipated, though Kris and Cloe were taking a different line to a lower spot on the same ridge.

When Wall joined me at the col we looked off the other side and could hardly believe what we saw—some 1200 vertical feet of south west exposure (the same as winter north east exposure in the mountains of Montana, Colorado or Idaho) of what I described in my journal that night as "perfect winter powder in the most outrageous beautiful landscape." None of it could be seen from the valley of the Frey, though Pedro and James and the hut keepers knew it was there. It was the kind of place and snow conditions and situation that enriches the lives of ski mountaineers and makes one grateful and appreciative of the path one has chosen in life.

"Waaaaahhhhoooooooo," waaaaahoooooed Kris when he reached the ridge a hundred meters below us and saw what we saw.

Kris set up and we took turns skiing for his cameras in the best snow of the year in either North or South America. It was worth the entire trip. Half way down we noticed James hiking up from the valley below. He had gained the ridge lower than Kris and Cloe and had skied a bold and impressive line through rocks with severe consequences for blowing a turn. Cloe and Wall continued straight down the slope toward James. Kris found a knob above a large cliff with a view of the entire valley. I skied a line for Kris in difficult (and, I think) photographically spectacular wind crusted snow to the east and under the cliff Kris was on. Kris skied down to me and then joined the others for another lap. I was tired and not up for another round. Instead, I skinned 45 minutes to the east and north to the lowest point of the ridge forming the valley we were in.

When I got there I could see the Refugio Frey, Lago Tonchek, the Cerro Principal and its many beautiful satellite spires, the dark forests below and my companions slowly working their way back up for another run. I took off my skis and sat on a large, dry rock and drank and ate and contemplated both the stunning scenery and the personal rewards and costs and implications of participating in mountain adventures with people thirty and more years younger than me, two of them world class athletes. So long as gravity is in my favor I am a passable partner in most groups of back country skiers, but overcoming gravity on the climbs is harder and slower each year for these ancient bones and muscles.

Unfortunately, most of my old skiing/climbing contemporaries are dead, or, in terms of hard physical activity, rotting away from ennui, alcoholism, old injuries, soft living, materialism, cancer, golf or giving maturation more respect than it warrants. While my younger companions are both kind and considerate about my slowness and fatigue, such human qualities, while ethical and admirable in all situations, are not the foundation of adventure, exploration or, even, safety in the mountains. It is clear that my back country and other options are shrinking, that solo adventuring is in my future but preferable to the couch, and that trips like this one are to be savored in the present moment, for they are rare and will not come again. Before leaving my rock and skiing down the north facing slope in corn snow to the Lago Tonchek and back to the Frey, I resolve to dig deeper and push harder and keep closer to the pace for the rest of this tour.

I arrived back at the Refugio just as a group of 15 Argentine mountain guides on a training/certification course arrived. A couple of Canadians and a party of Americans (including one from Bozeman who Kris and Cloe knew) also arrived within the hour. The quiet mountain hut became a flurry or activity, conversation, laughter, stories and human crowding. A very different mood and tempo greeted my companions when they returned. That night one of the guides in our bunk room snored. No matter how often or firmly he was poked awake and rolled over to a new position, a few minutes later he was contentedly snoring again. Sleep was less than completely restful that night, and we all awoke with the edge slightly dulled.

We got an early start in the morning for our next destination, the Refugio Jakob, also called the Refugio San Martin, five miles west and slightly north for a condor, nearly eight hours and two big climbs and two heavily wooded descents for the ski mountaineer. Bracken and the cheerful Pedro Fine joined us. Bracken had been to the Refugio in summer and was our guide, but, of course, winter and summer in the mountains are different worlds. On the first climb up from the Frey to Laguna Schmoll and on up to the highest ridge to the north we encountered ice, sastrugi, wind packed powder, breakable wind crust, rock and dirt. At one point we removed skis and kicked steps in hard, steep snow. In order to keep closer to the group's pace I pushed harder than was comfortable and by mid-day I was reminded of Oscar Wilde's quip, "Good resolutions are useless attempts to interfere with scientific laws." I wondered if there was honor, merit, meaning or redemption in foolish, unrequited resolution; and I thought of Don Quixote and of Spanish seekers of gold, and of gallant knights charging windmills. Pedro's weak skiing skills and old equipment, which kept coming off with each of his several downhill falls, gave me some (literal) breathing room in keeping the pace. I waited for him to make sure there wasn't too much distance between the six of us. Though there were at least 15 guides a few hours away, this lovely terrain would be an ugly place to be injured. After the first big climb of the day and the treacherous ski descent in corn (not much), glop and isometric snow to the upper part of the Arroyo Rucaco we were all ready for a break. The weather was spectacular and the scenery even better. Even without fine skiing we were happy ski mountaineers.

I headed out half an hour ahead of the others up the big, open, stream laced valley of isothermal snow toward the Paso de la Brecha Negra, some 2500 feet above the Lago and Refugio Jakob. I knew the others would easily catch up, and the solitude of breaking trail at my own pace in such a place on such a day was pleasant and nourishing to the soul. As the broad reaches of the upper Arroyo Rucaco rose up to tree line the terrain grew steeper and the route finding through potential avalanche possibilities required more attention. As expected, the others caught up and James and Pedro took the lead in breaking trail to the Brecha Negra. We rested on top of the ridge and considered our options getting down to the Refugio. All of them were steep and by that time of day the sun had cooked the snow into an inconsistent, bad casserole that looked worse as one got closer to it. James took his own route and the rest of us another down some 2500 feet of unfaithful skiing conditions best not remembered, especially at the bottom in the maze of young, willow-like lenguas. When Wall and I reached the bottom we found James resting by the stream draining Lago Jakob, a trademark goofy, endearing grin on his face, having found the better route down. James views the escalating problems and pressures of the world—over population, environmental degradation, war, famine, economic and social injustice, militarism, etc. —as unsolvable and out of control. In James' view, the only personal or social relief is to be found in escape, by which he means the mountains and personal freedom under the radar. He is more forthcoming about the selfishness of his attitude than most of us, but his smile and lack of pretension makes no excuses for how he is and what he thinks, and the world has much to learn from its James Brackens.

The others were a bit behind, but the three of us reached the Refugio in a few minutes to find all but a small section with a wood burning stove and a few beds and a table locked up. The expected hut keeper was not there. We took over the open room and made ourselves at home. Soon we were all there, tired, hungry and involved in the required rituals of getting water from the stream, cooking, drying wet skins, exploring the neighborhood and, since the summertime outhouse was shut down, finding appropriate facilities. We laughed and joked with the relief of rest after hard exertions. The day before Kris had somehow managed to drop and retrieve his headlamp from the single hole Frey outhouse, (don't ask) and we had some fun at Kris' expense about the incident, reminding him of the blue-armed airline passenger in Hunter Thompson's fine read, "The Curse of Lono." The eating orgy that ensued that evening was impressive, especially on James' part—bread, flat bread, Swiss cheese, Roquefort, tuna, wine (don't ask), pate, cookies; and when those hors d'oeurves were done we cooked dinner and ate and slept like weary travelers.

The next morning Wall, the Ericksons and Bracken set out to explore the terrain under and around the Cuervas del Diablo (Horns of the Devil) and Pedro and I stayed at the Refugio. Pedro said he wanted a "tranquillo" day. I was fatigued beyond what I should have been. I wrote in my journal and Pedro sang and we drank tea and talked about where we might go the next day. It was September 11, and I noted in my journal: "I am glad to be in this wild and isolated place instead of in the U.S. where this date has nearly replaced July 4th for the Uber Patriots and those who prefer hatred to understanding, tolerance and compassion..... To be here is a rare gift, a precious experience. As James points out, it is a selfish escape, but what one makes of that experience need not be selfish or escapism."

Pedro left to explore the terrain to the north, scouting out a possible route to the Refugio Italia. The maps indicated that this involved a steep climb of more than 2000 feet to gain a ridge, following that ridge for four or five hours and descending very steep terrain to the Refugio. Further north is the Refugio Lopez, and we had thought to go there as well.

When the others returned they reported good but not outstanding skiing and more lovely vistas. Cloe was tired and feeling a bit out of sorts, while Kris, Bracken and Wall were wired. Pedro returned to report a steep ascent to the ridge that would involve crampons and carrying skis in uncertain snow conditions. We had another fine evening of conversation and abundant eating, interspersed with bursts of Pedro's singing. We noted that our food was no longer abundant. That night was not a good one of sleep for me. A heavy chest/head cold took over my body and caused me to cough and nasal drain all night. It kept me awake, and, of course, everyone else as well. The same cold had leveled the entire Spanish randonnee team a few days earlier, and would strike Wall and the Ericksons a few days later. It never feels good to cough and have a nose running like a faucet, but, in the relative world of sickness and health, I was not that sick. I just didn't feel very good. *No es malo; es diferente.*

In the morning we rose early but spent three hours dithering over what we were doing. The dithering dynamics broke down like this: James was definitely going on to Refugio Italia, with a mind to continue on to the Lopez. Pedro was going with him. Though food supplies were dwindling, we all could manage with some adjustment. Kris and Wall definitely wanted to continue the tour to the Italia, a shorter day by at least three hours than going back out to the ski area, but it added another day before it was possible to get out. Cloe was tired and having her own health issues and was not psyched to continue. My health issues, fatigue and a cold that was not going to get better in the next few days, were obvious to everyone. Any way I went was going to going to cause my body a certain amount of suffering, but nothing that couldn't be handled. For me, there were a couple of more pressing concerns. We were not sure the Refugio Italia would even be open, as we had thought the Jakob would be completely open and with a hut-keeper, and we had no tents. There were two more alarming matters to my way of thinking about mountains: our less than perfect maps clearly indicated there was no way to the Italia that did not involve descending huge, steep, open slopes that we knew had new snow sitting on old; and some old instinct about James' infectious enthusiasm for terrain he'd never seen in winter raised red flags in my brain and nervous system. I've learned to pay attention to such instinctive, on occasion (not in this case) unreasonable, flags, though sometimes discussing them with others is a bit like talking about angels and ghosts, channeled teachers and the spirits of ancestors, LSD visions and psychics with, say, Bill O'Reilly or Dick Cheney. That is, it is not a rewarding conversation. After a couple of hours of frustrating negotiations I knew I was not going north. Neither was Cloe. Kris and Wall were not pleased, but they were good enough to acquiesce. So, at ten in the morning the four of us headed back up the 2500 feet to the Brecha Negra and James and Pedro headed north to the ridge running from Pico Jakob to the Cerro Navidad, which we should be able to see from the Negra.

Our route would involve some 10 to 12 miles as the skier skis and 5000 to 6000 vertical feet both up and down. A long day's journey into night, as it was. The first climb up through the lenguas forest was as fast as skiing down and no harder. Once we broke out of the trees it was straight forward, steep and mostly wet snow over ice and pretty good skinning. Wall broke trail. She later told me she was extremely anxious about my health and the consequences of me flaming out, and she was worried about avalanches. This caused her to be more manic and frenzied than usual, but she kept the pace moving which was the right thing to do. I knew I'd be slower, but I was not worried about making it, as was she. Avalanches, however, are always something to keep in mind in such conditions, and we all did. It took two hours to reach the Brecha Negra a bit ahead of Kris and Cloe. When they arrived we followed the ridge north and east to the 7000 foot Cerro Tres Reyes, 2500 feet above the heavily forested Arroyo Rucaco. That took an hour and a half and a bit of excellent route finding by Kris around some rock gendarmes on the ridge. It was steep off the ridge and the heavy powder snow sloughed off below us in rolling pinwheels that grew big enough to take a man down, but nothing slid. The weather was excellent, as were the views. We scoped the ridge north with binoculars, but we never saw James and Pedro where we thought they should be. We learned later that they made it as far as the ridge above the Refugio Italia but were unable to find a route down that didn't involve unacceptable avalanche risk. So they were forced to double back and descend into the Arroyo Casa de Piedra where they bushwhacked for 12 hours, until ten that night. They stopped and built a fire and bivouacked by the stream draining the Laguna Navidad. They talked and Pedro sang until dawn when they continued an epic bushwhack carrying skis. After eight hours they got out none the worse for wear with a fine adventure better in the telling than in the experiencing, one I'm glad to have missed. If we had gone with them, it would have likely taken me at least two 12 hour days to get out, probably more, and the experience would have violated the theme of our trip.

When we arrived at the Cerro Tres Reyes Wall said to me, "Don't look," referring to the spectacular view of the 2500 to 3000 drop into the Arroyo Rucaco and the equally spectacular but more daunting climb back out to the Punta Princesa at the top of the Cerro Catedral ski Area. I did look, of course, and my three companions agree that my face dropped, but I think they were seeing things that weren't there. Wall opined that it wasn't as bad or long as it looked. "*No es malo*," Kris intoned, "*es diferente.*"

We rested only a bit before skiing down a large open bowl in heavy powder verging on glop that turned to heavy, unskiable glop the lower we descended. It was okay until we got into the trees and bamboo. Wall and I broke trail and found a way through the trees and cliffs and streams in isometric snow that collapsed to the bottom with every step. It was difficult, energy draining and frustrating skiing. One could be forgiven for thinking "*Es malo y es diferente.*" At the bottom of the Arroyo Rucaco we had to remove skis and ford the stream at a junction with another stream on some rocks to the only nearby clearing free of snow. We had lunch there. The Ericksons soon arrived. Cloe was clearly hurting, not in her normal cheerful state of mind, and, when she slipped off a rock during the crossing and fell into the stream, close to tears. She had a hard day and, as a consequence, so did Kris. It was a quiet luncheon in the clearing.

We began the last climb of at least 2500 feet. After taking my crampons, ice ax, shoes, binoculars and books to lighten my load and increase hers, Wall broke trail straight up a narrow, steep couloir of glop, the only clear way to above snowline, an obvious avalanche gully. It was very hard going, but she was on a mission to get us out before dark and was impressively strong in leading the way. Toward the end of the gully, just before tree line, Kris caught up and took over the lead. Then Cloe, who had regained her normal cheerfulness and delightful smile, passed me. As we got higher the snow got better. We had some problems on the traverses with the lower track of new snow slipping out on the ice below. Each time it happened it consumed lots of energy and generated a like frustration. Half way up the face the wind arrived and the temperature dropped. It was, after all, late in the day, nearly five in the afternoon. I was slow and very tired. We took one break about two thirds of the way up, and it was clear that we were going to be okay and dine in a Bariloche restaurant that night, but the last hours of such days are often the hardest. These were.

The top of the ridge was blown bare by those 140 kph winds, and we walked on dirt and rock to the other side and the top of the ski resort. We took a break and looked down into the valley and the end of our tour. We still had some 3000 vertical feet over three miles to ski, but it was downhill on mostly groomed trails. The lifts were closed, the runs empty. We anticipated an easy and refreshing run in fading light. My companions started down before I was ready, expecting that I would easily catch them as I normally would in downhill skiing. But the exertions of the day and my sickness and, perhaps, a bit of dehydration caught up with me, and by the tenth turn both my thighs cramped with extreme prejudice, refused to respond to reason or a lifetime of skiing technique. They simply quit functioning in any meaningful sense of the word "function." They hurt like hell. It was a long, slow, painful descent with lots of side slipping and trying to ski with ram rod straight legs so I wouldn't have to use the muscles of my cramping thighs. It's challenging to ski without thigh muscles and I've never experienced anything quite like it, as if, after a lifetime with the same body, an alien corpse had infiltrated and taken over. It was the hardest part of a hard day. All of it was relieved and put behind and nearly forgotten later than night after we had shaved, showered and shampooed and were dining in our favorite Bariloche restaurant, La Marmite; but as I met up with the others near the bottom of the mountain at seven in the evening I was keenly aware that I had just gotten a glimpse of the future, and it didn't look good. "This is not good, Dorworth," I said to myself. "This is not good." But as I looked at the faces of my companions—seeing Kris' intensity and gracious good will and cheerfulness, Cloe's lovely smile and openness and intelligence, and Wall's anxiety driven resolve and focus which had gotten us out in nine hours instead of the eleven it might have taken, I was grateful and appreciative for their company and our experience together, and I was cheered by and found my own resolve for that future in the thought, "*No es malo; es diferente.*"

CHAPTER FIFTEEN
A Summer Outing on Mt. Shasta

"In the solitary, stony fastness among the mountains there is a strange market where you can barter the vortex of life for boundless bliss."
Fosco Maraini

IT IS A FINE AND BEAUTIFUL THING to climb up and ski down a mountain like Shasta with your children. Such experience is a gift from Ullr and the other mountain deities eternally watching the inner and outer landscapes of all skiers and mountaineers. Every cramponed step, each turn of the pressured ski is made in the solitude of the human condition, magnified by awareness of one's insignificance in the stony fastness, made meaningful by companionship, relationship, connection and empathy. My family life and, therefore, relationships with my children have been, ah....'eccentric' (as in overlapping circles with more than one center axis, though unconventional certainly applies) may be the kindest (to myself) way of putting it, but I am happy with who we are and where we have gotten to and with the love that exists between us. I have spent a fair piece of my life in that strange market Maraini describes, bartering for treasures that, at this stage of the process, seem a bargain at twice the cost. To say you are grateful for children, for mountains like Shasta, for skiing and climbing and for the boundless synthesis that brings us all together is somehow insufficient. But it is a start and I am grateful.

Mt. Shasta is a 14,162 foot dormant volcano rising 11,000 feet, base to summit, out of the clear-cut forests of Northern California. In total mass it is the largest volcanic peak in the continental U.S., the 2nd tallest mountain in the Cascade Range (Mt. Rainier is higher), the 2nd highest in California (Mt. Whitney is taller), and the most prominent landmark in that part of the world. It catches every storm coming out of the Pacific across Northern California, and it always has snow. There are five major and two smaller active glaciers on the mountain. Scientists estimate that it erupts roughly every 250 to 300 years and has been doing so for a million years. About 10,000 people live in towns—Weed, McCloud, Dunsmuir and Mt. Shasta—around its base, and all their lives would be endangered should it explode. Since it *will* erupt sometime between the next ten seconds and the next thousand years, it is best to climb and ski it while one is able. In good snow years, June is usually an enjoyable time.

Accordingly, in June 1995 we gathered at the home of my oldest son, Richard McFarland, in McCloud on the south flank of Shasta. Richard, 37, lives there with his wife, Erika, and two sons, Rio, 8, and, Dillon Denali, 1, my grandsons. They own and operate Jefferson Lumber Co. which recycles, remills and sells old lumber from the Pacific Northwest. Richard and Erika are river guides, ski instructors and ski patrolmen by inclination, interest, profession and passion; but the exigencies of a less eccentric family lifestyle brought them to fine recycled lumber as the right livelihood. They are salt of the earth people whose values begin with the earth and do not exclude.

Scott Markewitz, 34, the next son, drove in from his home in Salt Lake City two days after returning from France where he and his wife, Veronique, were visiting her family. Scott, master photographer, fine skier and climber, aerobic fiend of awesome capabilities, has made an enviable life and a quality reputation out of the mountains, the outdoors and the camera. Personal prejudice aside, he is the best action ski photographer I know. Personal relationship aside, he is a pleasure to work, ski, climb, have dinner and be with.

Jason Hajduk-Dorworth, 24, is the youngest. He, too, is a fine skier. He arrived in McCloud one chemistry final exam short of a solid year of being a full time paramedic, a full time pre-med student and a half time skier at South Shore Lake Tahoe. Somehow, he also manages to fit in an energetic social life suitable to his age. Needless to say, he was exhausted, though at 24 such distractions from the goals at hand as fatigue matter less than I remember or can sometimes believe. Jason is smart, responsible, funny and full of care for people and the world in which we live. Jason's friend, Patrick Carland, 25, came with him. Patrick, an energetic, intense adventure skier with a nasty looking 18 inch scar along his spine from an adventure skiing broken back incurred a year and a half before, shared Jason's impatience with the conditions of life, weather, snow and time as they are.

In short, my children (and grandchildren and daughters-in-law) are wonderful, full of their own lives and a joy and satisfaction in mine.

How my sons came to have names like McFarland and Markewitz are stories beyond the scope of this writing, perhaps more properly belonging in The Journal of Jungian Psychology.

The winter of 1994-95 in the mountains of Western America was unusual. It started in October and the following June when we gathered at Shasta it was still in full force, despite a small break for spring in February. Snow. Rain. Wind. Cold. Avalanche. Discomfort and danger and exactly the opposite conditions we had hoped to find on Mt. Shasta in June. I arrived a week before the others at Richard's, and most of that time the mountain was hidden in clouds dropping rain on the lowlands and snow up high. During clear spots in the atmospheric action I watched through binoculars huge snow plumes blowing off the summit and the ridges, moving the snow around, loading the leeward slopes with potential avalanches.

Jason and Patrick arrived a couple of days early. Jason had been on Shasta before, but Patrick had never seen the mountain. The weather allowed barely a glimpse. Richard and Erika took them on a rainy raft ride down the Sacramento River in full wet suit regalia to relieve their impatience for ACTION right NOW.

We had agreed on June 19-20 as the time frame when all of our varied if not always variable schedules could coincide. Jason, for instance, planned to come off the mountain the evening of the 20th, drive 4 hours (5 hours for me) back to Tahoe, study all night and take his chemistry final at 10 a.m. on the 21st. We had chosen the standard route up Shasta. It is called 'Avalanche Gulch,' though basin better describes its geography. We planned to get as high as Helen Lake, at the bottom of the basin, the first day, camp overnight and continue to the top on the second. Many years earlier a friend died in an avalanche in Avalanche Gulch, and I appreciate why early students of the mountain chose the name.

From my journal of July 18: *"McCloud. Evening. Raining. Jason and Patrick discouraged. Richard up. Jason is not comfortable with this mountain. (He had badly injured an ankle two years earlier on Shasta.) Patrick is young, energetic, bright and restless. Scott coming in the morning.*

"Weather might clear. Zanger (Michael Zanger runs a guide service on Shasta and has written an excellent book about the history, legends and lore of the mountain) says there are 1 to 2 feet of new snow at Helen Lake. Much will depend on whether others went up today and if they made a trail. It looks poor right now."

From my journal later that night: *"The sky is clear. The mountain is visible. Probably some serious avalanches as soon as it warms up. We are considering alternate routes. It will probably take more than two days, and it is probable that Jason and Patrick will take off tomorrow after some hiking and a little skiing. Scott phoned from Lovelock and is on the way."*

The morning of the 19th dawned clear and cold with wind up high. Scott had not arrived, so I went into town (Mt. Shasta) on last minute errands. Before I got back clouds began forming, Scott arrived, and Jason decided his time would be better spent studying chemistry and that he and Patrick would leave. Erika's brother, Chris Carpenter, was going to go with us, but at the last moment he, too, decided against it. That left Scott, Richard and me. At Zanger's suggestion, we decided to climb the more difficult but less avalanche prone Casaval Ridge, to the north of Avalanche Gulch.

The usual last minute expedition organizational chaos caused a late start. It was four in the afternoon by the time we actually began moving up the west side of the mountain from the end of the road at Bunny Flat at 6800 feet. We all elected to use alpine ski boots and skis with mountaineering heel lift binding adapters and skins for climbing. This system worked perfectly and gave us the best tools for skiing down, but alpine boots are not built for climbing or carrying loads. We had to accept the inevitable consequences of sore feet, blisters and more pain than usual. We were there mostly for the ski down, and when the skiing is good the additional pain is part of the price for the privilege of bartering in that strange mountain market. For climbers, there can be bliss in the climb, with its subsequent satisfaction, followed by the fatigue filled descent of the post-climax. For the climber/skier, the descent heightens the bliss, prolongs the climax and considerably shortens the time of descent. When moving in the mountains, time increases fatigue and fatigue clouds judgment, impairing both skill and strength, so skiing off big mountains can be the safest way to descend. The trade off is the extra weight of the skis going up. The limiting factor is one's confidence in being able to ski steep, variable terrain with a pack on snow that has not been groomed. Both trade off and factor are considerations to be taken seriously.

Eight minutes after we began skinning up, long before our bodies adapted to their efforts, large, wet snowflakes began falling out of a windless, leaden sky. We followed a well beaten ski and foot trail to the Sierra Club Hut, known as the Shasta Alpine Lodge, a stone/wood edifice built in 1923. For a small fee one can enjoy the comforts of the lodge. Two middle-aged women on cross-country skis passed us on the way down. They were flushed and giggling and obviously enjoying a great day, having gone no higher than the lodge. A couple of snow-hikers descended as well, their exertions more, their enjoyment less than that of the ladies on skis, and they said so. Two climbers on foot going up with big packs passed us with a few words of cheer and encouragement.

The Shasta Alpine Lodge was completely buried by snow, the chimney sticking up and a tunnel dug down to the entrance. Without the beaten trail to its entrance, one could easily pass by without knowing it existed. On June 19th new snow continued to fall upon the old.

At the lodge we left the path and cut north to gain the lower section of the Casaval Ridge, taking turns breaking trail. As expected, Scott, an endorphin connoisseur, soon forged ahead. I followed and Richard lagged behind, and I worried about his conditioning. For me, the first couple hours of hauling heavy loads are as difficult as the last. Only in between does it seem a reasonable, meaningful activity. The mind and body rebel against such labor, such mindless drudgery, such......work. Only after giving in to the task at hand do they join forces to be efficient, skillful and smart about moving with precision up the mountain. Only then is there joy in the labor, satisfaction in each step up of the well placed, skinned ski. Then the bartering begins.

Surroundings come into focus. The mountain comes alive. Trees reveal their personalities. Every move, thought and perception are the familiar ones of a householder in his own home, seeing unimaginable beauty in the tiniest detail, in the light on a crystal of snow. At the same time, one needs the alertness of a warrior in enemy territory, surrounded by hidden treachery and the constant possibility of ambush.

After an hour and a half my feet began to hurt, the blistering began, but the rest of my body settled into the rhythms and movements of the climb with somewhat the same mental state as an office worker at midmorning on Monday. The slope grew steeper as we ascended and by seven that evening we had gained some 2000 feet elevation and were nearly above treeline on the Casaval Ridge. We found a reasonably flat spot, shoveled it as smooth as the mattress of dreams, and set up my old, well traveled three man VE24 dome tent and settled in.

Richard took charge of cooking, and very soon his MSR stove had produced boiling water and hot food to replenish our tired bodies. Scott took photos. I jotted in my journal. From the comfort of a warm sleeping bag within a tent, I relished the pleasant sensation of rest and food and hot drink after exertion. The view from our tent platform was spectacular...rolling clouds and mist and an occasional glimpse of the land below, lit by the changing light of mountain sunset.

I wrote in my journal, *"It is very satisfying to be here with these two good men who happen to be my sons....Snow pings on the tent. Fog obscures the night. Time to sleep."*

Wind blew. Snow fell. I rose twice and slept poorly, but night passed quickly and at 5:30 a.m. we rose. We made hot drinks and ate and dressed and packed, leaving the tent up in case we needed it on the way down. We were moving before 7 a.m. in very cold temperatures. Clear skies, but it felt and looked more like February than June on Mt. Shasta. New snow had blown off the ridge and the old snow was frozen and crampon perfect hard. We carried skis on our packs and used ski poles and crampons, and we moved quickly and well. I wore pile long underwear, Marmot bib overpants, a capiline shirt, a pile sweater, a hat, wool gloves and snowboard mittens over them, and even working hard carrying a pack I was not overheated. A blister on my left ankle expanded its domain.

By 8 a.m. we were at 10,000 feet and feeling good. The sun was out but an unusual cold wind blew out of the east. Billowing clouds moved down into Strawberry Valley and the town of Mt. Shasta from the north. We donned parkas and kept them on the rest of the day. At that point rock gendarmes plastered with wind driven snow forced us off the ridge onto a steep, snow basin to the north. Scott and Richard chose to continue using crampons and ski poles. I decided to exchange ski poles for ice ax for the steep, hard, upward slanting traverse ahead. Scott went first, me second and Richard last, perhaps thirty feet apart. Three things were evident:

My fears about Richard's fitness were groundless; he was at least as strong as me, probably stronger;

Scott, while still stronger than Richard or me, was obviously aerobically human and feeling the altitude (in later conversation we joked that before future joint endurance excursions in the mountains Scott should be exiled for three weeks to sea level and France); and being off the west facing, wind swept Casaval Ridge proper and in the northwest facing basin presented us with a totally different set of snow conditions. Irregular ridges of hard packed powder snow, laid down and sculpted by wind, covered the perfect crampon snow like psychedelic waves on a pure white sea. The condition is called sastrugi, and sastrugi can be a bitch. The crampon may bite into the perfect, secure, confidence inspiring ice of the sub layer, or it may sink into the sastrugi layer which had the consistency and stability of a block of chalk bonded to ice by a few crystals of frozen water and air.

The wind picked up. Very cold. It was a day worthy of any February on Mt. Shasta.

Our pace immediately and drastically slowed. There was little talk, as there was not much to say. I used a traditional technique called *piolet ramasse*, used for moving on moderately steep terrain which to an alpine skier would be double black diamond. Ice ax planted with both hands, step, step. Ice ax planted with both hands, step, step. Ad infinitum. Repetitious. Tedious. Efficient. Safe.

After about half an hour something happened that.....ahhhhh.... should not have happened. But it did. We moved up to the right, and my left foot was downhill. I stepped carefully with my left foot onto a ridge of sastrugi, stomped out a foothold, tested it, felt it was solid and stood on it. As soon as I picked up my right foot to move it ahead, the left foothold crumpled like chalk under pressure. The unexpected drop pulled me off balance and out of position. Eight inches lower the left crampon found solid footing and stopped. My pack, attached to my back, continued downhill with a rotation to the right, my left ankle being the axis of the system. I felt the ankle on the verge of breaking.

Despite its many standards of measurement, time is an imperfectly understood phenomenon. Human perception of time is inconstant, and in times of crisis may alter dramatically and differently for each individual. This was not the first time in my life that time has slowed down (or do perceptions speed up?) in a moment of action crisis. In measured time it took only a few seconds, but it seemed much, much longer.

My mind sorted through the limited options with the clarity of slow motion film. Perhaps thirty years before I could have stopped everything with an act of strength and balance and just continued climbing with an extra burst of adrenalin; but that is neither certain nor in any way meaningful to 1995, though it underscored the eternal refrain of the uncomfortable mountaineer: "What am I doing here?" As it was, my entire body and pack, except for the left foot which was firmly planted, were heading downhill in a twisting motion. My options were to let my left ankle break and then fall off the mountain or to just fall off the mountain and see what happened. The latter seemed my best choosing.

I pulled the left foot off the snow and fell, rolling in the process to my backside, pulling my feet into the air. When you are sliding at a high rate of speed, a crampon catching could have unfortunate consequences for everything between ankle and hip.

Time speeded up. In a flash I was rocketing down Mt. Shasta, the pick of my ax plunged into the snow by my right hip. At least a thousand feet of steep snow lay below me before the first flat. I was able to steer myself into a pile of avalanche debris 150 feet below, hoping it wasn't frozen into blocks of ice. It wasn't. I hit a couple of the debris pieces with my feet. They exploded. I slowed and then stopped. The tails of my skis on the pack had helped slow my descent. My mini misadventure was over.

Richard saw the whole thing. Scott didn't even know I was no longer behind him until Richard told him, so quickly did it happen, so silently did it go.

"Are you alright?" Scott asked.

"Yeah," I replied, though the left ankle was sore and the right thumb was sprained from a death grip on the ice ax, and I properly felt more than a little foolish. And I did not relish having to regain lost altitude. Otherwise, I was both alright and keenly aware of what some call 'luck' and I call 'grace' in my own life.

The mountain didn't notice. The wind didn't pause. The cold did not diminish. The three of us continued our separate ways up the mountain, me, of course, a bit behind. Our pace slowed considerably. The influence of altitude, the cumulative effects of fatigue, began to be felt. The wind increased and the wind blown snow mounted. Footing was difficult. Movement was slow. I was last, but no more than five to ten minutes behind the boys. I noticed their tracks in the new snow were obliterated or barely visible by the time I reached them. I noted this without analyzing clearly its meaning....that the strong east wind was loading the west slopes very fast with future avalanches. What was evident to my eyes was how slowly we were moving against the wind in the difficult snow.

Richard and Scott stopped at a couple of rocks sticking from the snow. I saw they were talking, but they were too far away to be heard over the wind. I checked my watch. It was past noon. We were about even with the summit of Shastina, which meant we were above 12,000 feet. It also meant we had climbed the first 2000 feet in just over an hour, and the next 2000 feet had taken over four hours. June 20 is the longest day of the year, and we had more than eight hours of daylight remaining. It looked to me like we were in pretty good shape.

But we weren't.

As soon as I caught up to them, Richard and Scott both started telling me about the large avalanche they had just watched break loose, slide several hundred feet and then come to a stop directly above us, perhaps a thousand feet higher. They were surprised I hadn't seen it, but I was occupied placing one foot in front of the other.

The wind was not interrupted. The snow continued to load the west slopes.

"What do you guys think?" I asked.

"No," they replied in harmony.

That was all the discussion necessary. Many times in the mountains the decision to turn away from the intended goal is fraught with regret and ambivalence. This was not one of those occasions. It was a bad place to be at that moment. It was time to leave the mountain, shut down the marketplace for the day while we still had something to barter.

We quickly exchanged crampons for skis and began a descent of more than 5000 feet. The snow for the first 2000 feet was ice and sastrugi and wind blown slab and very steep. All of it was eminent skiing as long as the entire turn was made on the same medium....ice, sastrugi, and slab. A fall could result in a nasty and long slide. A ski going from ice to chalk consistency snow in the middle of a turn, or, worse, vice-versa, could easily develop a mind of its own; and who could blame it? The skiing was wonderful if hard, but place and radius of turn were chosen carefully. Scott performed photographic duties and Richard and I were the best, most careful models we could be.

After 2000 feet of fine, attentive skiing we got back to where my fall had occurred. Just past that we had to traverse and then climb back on the ridge. As soon as we did we found the snow we had come to Shasta to ski. The lower elevation and the western exposure and the time of day had coincided to give us the snow of a skier's dreams....untracked, smooth corn in a wild and magnificent setting. The morning's exertions, mishaps, ordeals and lessons had put me in an appreciative state of mind that I have learned to find most readily in the mountains. I was not alone in my appreciation. The three of us swooped and carved and floated and in some sense flew down the beautiful slopes of Mt. Shasta. That run was one of the great pleasures of my life. The slopes grew friendlier and friendlier the lower we got. By the time we got back to Bunny Flat, after stopping for lunch and to pick up the tent, the avalanche that turned us around seemed irrelevant and of another world and time. Indeed, it was, and I was reminded of what I'd written in my journal two days before we went on the mountain: *"Avalanche is the ever present ogre on this and most other mountains. You do not 'conquer' the ogre. You can, with attention and knowledge and luck, avoid him. The ogre may block the way, but if you let him have his way without burying you, then you can return and try again when his fury has melted enough."*

CHAPTER SIXTEEN

Solo en la Sierra

SOMETIME IN THE EARLY 1970S I was talking to my friend, Doug Robinson, a gnomish-looking mountaineer of fine sensitivities and clear sensibilities in matters of mountains, when he mentioned the beguilement of a solo ski tour. We talked lotws about "processes" in those days, and he was curious about the process. I filed the thought and in my own, slow way waited nearly 10 years until I was ready to move on it. But I picked up the idea from Robinson. I wonder where he got it. I wonder what he did with it.

This is what I did with it in the spring of 1981.

DAY ONE:

My California home then was at Soda Springs on Donner Summit. It suits someone interested in skiing and climbing and being in the Sierra Nevada Mountains while keeping ready access to the depraved delights of Truckee, Reno and San Francisco. It was home, but there were and are vast areas of the Sierra unfamiliar to me.

Accordingly, I began my tour by walking a few hundred yards from my house on Old Highway 40, across the overpass above Interstate 80 where the road ran out and the skiing began, into a part of the Sierra I knew only by maps.

First day packs are always monsters, but this one felt worse than usual. It seemed the heaviest I've carried. The thought must be explored that the loads don't change; it is only the aging body telling pride to ease up.

Just as I reached the freeway a car let out a hitch-hiker. The driver asked and got directions to Sugar Bowl. The hitcher, an abused looking man in his mid-twenties, was poorly clad in thin shoes, an ill-fitting seersucker suit and carried a large cloth bag of his belongings.

I thought to myself, "Poor bugger, he's on hard times." I said, "Hello." He asked where I was going and I told him "Into the hills." He looked at me and my load as if thinking, "Poor bugger, he's on hard times," and said, "Good luck to ya." I said "Same to ya," and those were my last words for several days.

Two travelers passing on the road, each with his own destiny.

I stepped into my skis and with the terrible pack on my back headed west, following the power lines downhill as far as the bridge across the South Yuba River. From there I headed north. And up. The day was fine and the South Yuba gurgled with spring runoff, transforming the dying snow into itself with irrevocable rhythms.

Two skiers had crossed the bridge earlier in the day. An inauspicious beginning to my solo tour, but I was not too proud to use others' tracks to ease the strain of breaking trail. Give the overloaded body any advantage over the situation, which consisted of more than a foot of new snow on an uphill course powered by a 42-year old body guided by a mind of indeterminate age.

An hour later my solo chagrin affected acumen and I decided the tracks contoured higher than I needed. I deviated along a sidehill which soon proved too low and landed me in a steep, narrow gully that was not easy to escape but certainly awakened a few napping judgmental capabilities. It takes a day or two to clear out the cobwebs from the most experienced mountain instinct. After a couple hours of intense bushwhacking, I ran into the tracks again and gratefully followed them. They ended at a point where the skiers had, apparently, frolicked in the snow before turning around and going back out.

The afternoon began to tire and I had no intention of exhausting the poor devil. As soon as a suitable site with running water presented itself I set up camp. The camp dinner was delicious, washed down with lots of tea—but I'd forgotten my toothbrush.

The last words in my notebook that night: *"It is extremely beautiful and peaceful here. How do I get so far away from this feeling when I'm in civilization?"*

That question alone is worth the trip.

Another question: What is the answer worth?

DAY TWO:

A crisp, clear day dawned upon frozen snow. North Face, my camping equipment sponsor, hadn't let me down. Tent, bag, booties and over-booties for nighttime urination excursions had worked perfectly and I was rested, but the body ached and pained in unusual places.

First camp sounds—a woodpecker pecking on a dead tree. A breeze over the snow and through the trees. A tiny stream behind the tent. In the night the trucks gearing down on Interstate 80 and the train over Donner could be heard. A new-morning California zephyr put such things out of auditory range.

From my notes that evening: *"The most northern point of Fordyce Lake. Tired after a difficult day. Tough terrain with variable snow and much breakable crust. Fatigue is nothing in return for the beauty here today. I am happy. However, I am moving slower than anticipated.*

"I came out by Buzzard's Roost and dropped down to North Creek and followed it here. A nice creek. I was whipped hours before stopping, and when I arrived at Fordyce Lake there was no lake, only a stream wandering through a snow-covered meadow. I was perplexed. Had I been mis-reading the map? And then it struck me—a series of slim Sierra winters and the rising population of California had combined to reduce the lake to a fraction of its 1955 United States Geological Survey Topographic map size. After a perilous crossing of the creek, I had a late lunch and skied another mile before setting up camp.

"I haven't spoken a word since yesterday except a tight-spot grunt and a loud squawk when I fell once. Unlike Don Juan, I haven't mastered turning off the internal dialogue other than on rare, special times. My mind goes into the past and then jumps ahead to a possible future, and when it stays in

the present it enjoys itself. My mind right now is out to enjoy, not necessarily excel, though certain standards will be maintained out of pride. And today I noticed that every decision was not made by me alone. 'We' made the decisions. 'We' is here. Being alone in this state is never lonely.

"Colors and lights change continuously. White, grey, blue and then orange and gold. There is wind and an occasional airplane. I keep thinking I hear a large engine or generator, but it must only be the sound of my own head."

That night a coyote called for a long time and I woke. Stars filled the black sky and the snow sparkled.

DAY THREE:

Tracks showed a coyote had paused in his travels to sit down 150 feet from my tent. A good omen. An owl hooted throughout the night, but so far only one tree squirrel and a few small birds had been sighted.

I breakfasted on cashews and oatmeal and Ovaltine and took my time watching a Sierra spring day slowly warm the morning. I broke camp. My body was stiff and sore. My back carried the weight, but the mind was clear, the spirit happy and my heart as light as the pack was heavy as I headed northeast up 1,500 vertical feet over gradual terrain to a little meadow called Bear Valley.

It's hard carrying loads up or down, no matter what the tool of furtherance—ski, snowshoe, crampon, jumar or unaided human foot—but there is always advantage in the exact tool for the job. By the third day I knew I'd chosen my equipment well. In the past I'd used alpine skis with mountaineering bindings and double mountaineering boots—reliable, sturdy, functional but heavy gear. But a year earlier three friends—Galen Rowell, Kim Schmitz and Ned Gillette, on anybody's list of the best American mountaineers—completed a grueling 300-mile ski tour in Pakistan's Karakorum using lighter gear. I took their advice and acquired metal-edged cross-country skis (Kastle Trail 2) mounted with Rottefella three-pin bindings. I used Kastinger double cross-country boots. The system is easily one of the best for moving through snow-covered mountains with a load, and control on the downhill sections is excellent.

After a long morning of uphill effort, alleviated somewhat by easy waxing for consistent corn snow under a bright day, I reached Bear Valley. The change from hill to flat was welcome. After skiing its length I gobbled down a lunch of cheese and bread, chocolate, roasted soy beans, raisins and water flavored with sugared lemonade. Most enjoyable.

The morning's exertions had focused my restless mind on the economics of solo ski touring. I had done plenty of ski mountaineering in the company of friends, but never had I moved so slowly. With partners no one person breaks trail for more than an hour at a time, allowing long rests from that most grueling of ski mountaineering chores. The solo skier breaks trail all the way, and that is both debilitating and slow.

It was a steep and dicey descent into Perazzo Canyon. Fear became the awareness of a couple of potential avalanches that, fortunately, didn't happen. The exposure of the lone mountaineer is somewhat cushioned by a preparatory awareness of the process of mistakes. I carried enough food, fuel, shelter and clothing to survive anything up to two broken legs, medium grade pneumonia and acute hallucinations until friends got worried and sent somebody out to check on me. However, you don't sit out, ride out or get out of even small avalanches without a luck no one should count on.

After I skied off those cliff bands and was striding across the secure flats at the head of the canyon life without devitalizing fear flowed warmly back into my system, and I knew that I was lucky that time. Luck feels good.

It was a long afternoon getting to Perazzo Meadows. Snowmobile tracks appeared and I used them immediately, but I reached Perazzo Meadows on reserve energy. I camped in an appealingly dry patch on the north bank of the Little Truckee River. I gave myself an invigorating bath and dried out naked in the late day sun. Four snowmobiles roared by several hundred yards away. One waved and I returned the courtesy. I also saw one squirrel, several small birds and a hawk.

Though normally a voracious reader, I brought no books. I carried only a blank notebook to write in and a book on map reading in case I got in trouble.

That night a coyote barked but did not howl. I slept poorly, too tired to properly rest.

DAY FOUR:

I explored the meadows without changing camps. After a few hard days, the luxury of skiing without a pack is like vacationing in a favorite location after a long but successful work session. I skied about 10 miles before lunch.

I scouted the approach to the next day's route and I examined beaver dams. I saw two geese and ten ducks and blackbirds abounded. Western America had a tough snow year, and at 6,500 feet Perazzo Meadows held just enough to ski upon.

And, unfortunately, to snowmobile upon. I saw, and heard, nine of them, one as close as a hundred yards. My notes that afternoon read: *".....the snowmobilers have reason and rationale, but it certainly is shocking to be in a place like this, listening to the stream and the wind and the birds and to be suddenly interrupted by those fucking engines. I'm sure they're fun, but I wish they could be kept out of the backcountry. Let people walk there if they wish to see. The land is worth the effort."*

There is a road to Perazzo Meadows but it is closed in winter, and I was being petulant. Also, in many matters I am an incorrigible snob. It seems to me that man will always be a visitor in the bush because his nature demands he 'civilize' any place he settles. But he needs wilderness for its lessons and just to know it's there, even should he choose not to visit. Man must discipline himself to ensure the integrity of this earth. It is essential to sanity, and the snowmobile is inimical to the mental health of the outdoorsman......God, the places the mind gets to.

I took another bath and sat in a private place to dry out and be naked in the sun. There is great freedom in doing things alone, none in doing them lonely.

DAY FIVE:

On July 15, 1964 I fell while competing in the Kilometro Lanciato in Cervinia, Italy. At the moment I fell I was traveling just over 100 mph.

I broke a leg, bruised my body, permanently altered my perspective of high speed, and did something mysterious to my back that caused it to be never again quite right.

On the morning of April 6, 1981 the ghost of that fall visited. My back went out as I landed from a jump across the Little Truckee River. 'Out' means intense discomfort, difficulty moving with or without a pack, and the consequent splintering of concentration that accompanies pain. A past mistake dropped in to say "hello." Don't fall at 100 mph. Be careful jumping across streams with a pack on your back. There are many things to learn in the woods.

The Gods of gadabout mountaineers decreed that April 6 was to be the most demanding day, injury aside. The route ascended a steep ridge from the meadow to Mt. Lola at 9,143 feet and back to White Rock Lake at 7,900. I had trouble breathing. Climbing on skis and shouldering pack caused bizarre, involuntary sounds to emerge from my self-imposed silence. The meadows were safe and regularly visited by humans, even if riding those damned machines, and I admit to considering re-establishing camp with the aim of recuperation or rescue. The injury of backcountry solitude has a grander proportion in the mind and perhaps in fact than that of home and family and friends and safety. But.....

Tough day. Ice. Slush. Good corn. Powder. Breakable crust. A wide range of snow types. My time was good but by the time I crested the ridge at about 8,300 feet my back hurt badly and I was moving slower than ever.

As I contoured through trees east of the crest I was amazed to hear snowmobiles. I encountered their tracks when I regained the ridge and found them about 400 yards from the summit of Mt. Lola. I joined the snowmobilers for lunch. Larry and Jerry were Reno firemen who worked with an old ski racing/school mate of mine, Tom Nicora. They offered me wine, beer or a pop. I took a pop. We had a pleasant lunch and good conversation and they agreed to phone a friend to let the world know I was still in the game.

The firemen roared away on their plastic/metal monsters and I slogged on to the summit of Mt. Lola, rising nearly 3,000 feet above Independence

Lake and offering a spectacular panorama of the Sierra Nevada.

I walked 300 yards down the west face to Mt. Lola to find snow. My back was killing me and the snow was rotten and it was a beat-out to White Rock Lake. The frozen lake was snow covered, but caution told me to ski around the south shore to the west end where I set up camp.

DAY SIX:

From my notes that morning: *"Awake before sun up to photograph the sun hitting the mist above the lake. I slept the best of the tour last night despite back pains which woke me when I moved. Both water bottles and the cook pot were frozen solid this morning.*

"It is incredible to watch the metamorphosis of the lovely and fragile and intricate and myriad snow crystals on the snow and trees, left by last night's temperature acting on the moisture in the air. When the sun hits they slowly die, returning to the indistinguishable snow pack. But the snow crystal doesn't die; it only takes on another form in the ceaseless cycle. Nature's way.

"My back is a mess. I dread my pack today. Every so often a qualm of pure fear creeps in, fear that I might blow out entirely. How vulnerable we are to our weaknesses and to the non-malevolent tides and quirks of nature.

"A man alone is allowed little error. No wonder tribal societies developed.

"Meanwhile, I must get myself to the Peter Grubb Hut, and I'm a bit worried about it."

From my notes that evening: *"Peter Grubb Hut. I made good time despite my back and two painful falls. Descending into Paradise Valley was the best downhill skiing of the tour. Windy with scattered skies and cold when the sun goes behind a cloud. (I wonder why we never describe a cloud moving over the sun.)*

"The condition of the cabin is shocking. Garbage is strewn everywhere. People have defecated in the middle of the trail only 30 feet from the outhouse. I've never known a place in the woods treated like this. The snowmobile crew makes noise and leaves tracks, but I've yet to see them leave a mess like 'backcountry skiers' have left here.

"*Same old story. The Peter Grubb Hut is too close to the highway and to too many people who refuse to learn how to take care of themselves and the world they inhabit.*

"*Still, despite visiting slatterns, it's a good hut. A wood stove provided direct heat to a tight back. I read the log book, cleaned things up and chatted with two guys who had skied in for an hour. A photo of Galen Rowell's was pinned to the wall and it was nice to be reminded of my friend.*

"*Andy and Donna, a young Reno couple, arrived not long before dark. Donna was inexperienced and exhausted. Andy had plenty of time in the woods and at the Grubb Hut and he was ecstatic to be there. We had friends and acquaintances in common and had a nice talk, despite their disappointment at having to share the hut.*"

I slept well on a mattress. My back pains dulled the joy of pushing hard, and I couldn't concentrate on skiing. I was tired and missed home. Besides, talking with six different people in a few days had coarsened the charm of solitude and raised hell with the consistency of introspection. And that mattress sure felt good.

DAY SEVEN:

Up early to a clear but cold day. Time to go out. I was anxious for the familiar things of home, but I delayed departure to drink hot coffee and watch the growing morning make over the land.

My hut mates arose and we had a hot drink before Andy helped me on with a considerably lighter pack that still felt heavy. I headed for Interstate 80 on a trail I'd never seen, but it was downhill and not far and clearly delineated with hundreds of ski tracks and the droppings of pet dogs.

Even skiing cautiously I reached 80 before the lifts at Boreal Ridge opened. I walked under the freeway overpass to the gas station next to the Western America Ski Museum and phoned for a ride. I bought a coffee from the dispenser machine and sat outside in a chill sun to await my return home and to contemplate the mountaineer's eternal process— that the cherished lessons and experiences of the back woods are invaluable, but they must always be brought back to civilization and put to use.

I was happy. I was peaceful. And I knew that for awhile I had earned that feeling.

CHAPTER SEVENTEEN

The Great 1975 Wind River Ski Touring and Life Experience Expedition

AN IDEA CAME INTO BEING and the idea required action, but it took nearly three years to unite them. The idea entered my mind in the summer of 1972 during two weeks of climbing in the Cirque of Towers in Wyoming's Wind River Mountains—"This is amazing country; I'd like to see it in winter."

The Wind River Mountains run southeast to northwest through a hundred miles of western Wyoming, some of the most beautiful, spectacular mountains in America, including Gannett Peak, at 13, 785 feet the highest point in the state. Part of the Wind River Indian Reservation, on which rests Sacajewa's grave, extends into the eastern side of the range. The Winds contain the headwaters of the Green River, a host of peaks above 13,000 feet, lots of wind, thousands of lakes, some fine forests, abundant wildlife, low temperatures and enough snowfall to keep the range relatively inaccessible for all but three months a year.

The most practical, acceptable and aesthetic means of transportation in wintertime Winds is the ski. Snowshoes are limited and slow. Snowmobiles have both limitations and advantages, but, in my opinion, used in any other way than as tool of necessary evil, make too much noise, frighten the wildlife, befoul the air, deafen the rider and destroy the natural world. My prejudices against the internal combustion engine in the wilderness are extreme and deeply ingrained, though I have flown by airplane into the wilderness of Alaska and the Yukon to gain access to peaks I wished to climb. My prejudices are neither pure nor consistent, but they are real. The dog sleigh might be within the bounds of decency but is outside my experience and knowledge. As a life-long skier only skis were considered, and in the evolutionary course of 'idea' a ski tour in became a ski tour of the Winds.

Over the next two years I knew I'd do the tour and talked too much about it and then talk ran down and it had to be done. The seed idea had taken root.

Many people were interested and they passed in and out of the picture with astonishing regularity, but just a few weeks before starting Kenny Corrock was the only person I was sure was in. I wasn't worried. There are always good reasons specific people come together to do whatever it is they are going to do, even if those reasons never become evident to you. I felt confident the right people and the balance between them would work out if I just let it be.

Preparation reached commitment level when Ski Magazine agreed to buy a story about the tour. My friend Stephen Jarrell of Santa Cruz persuaded The North Face to donate tents and sleeping bags. Hexcel offered to donate skis and they were the lightest skis made at the time. With a magazine assignment and equipment in hand the idea had moved to action.

Each person was responsible for the remainder of his own equipment. We all used Silveretta bindings and a wide and individual assortment of boots, packs and clothing. I suggested double boots and all but two of our group used them. The two who used single boots suffered frostbite of the feet before the tour was finished.

Six of us came together in April 1975:

Kenny Corrock, 25, and I had known each other for several years, not always as good friends. We knew each other peripherally and had many mutual friends when I went to work as a coach for the U.S. Ski Team in the fall of 1970. We had our differences, as they say, in the coach/athlete relationship. It took a couple of years after the U.S. Ski Team working together as coaches at commercial race camps in Argentina and in Wyoming and some climbing in Idaho, but by 1975 we were fast friends. At the time Kenny was a professional ski racer and lived in Sun Valley. He read our maps and "The Big Sky" by A.B. Guthrie during the tour.

Jim Fox was next in. An old friend from Bear Valley, Fox had phoned me during the winter at my home in Truckee to inquire about some winter climbing. During our talk it struck me that he would be perfect for the tour. I asked him and he was interested but had to run it by his lovely wife, June, the Bear Valley school marm. Jim and June had not been apart for more than a few days since they had gotten together, and we were talking about a month. A few days later he phoned and he was in. Fox is a survivor of the marines and the kind of combat in Viet Nam the rest of us do not want to know about. A southern California beach boy, Jim was one of the original big wave surfers of the '60s, an endeavor he quit when it became too crowded. Jim read "The Grapes of Wrath" by John Steinbeck.

Duane "Sharkey" Cornell and I taught skiing at Bear Valley together for two years. We were never close friends there, but he was solid, reliable, fun and always one of my favorites on the ski school. Fox phoned a week after he had agreed to go and asked, "Why not Sharkey?" Why not? And so we were four. Sharkey, 26, is a survivor and graduate of the University of California in Berkeley in the late '60s, a musician, pilot, ski mountaineer, reader, world traveler, life student, ski instructor and river guide on the Green and Colorado (He later literally took Ed Abbey down the Colorado). He read a biography of Trotsky.

Lance Poulsen phoned me less than two weeks before we started to ask if he could go. I had known Lance since he was a small boy and had spent a lot of time coaching him during his ski racing career. He had always puzzled me because I felt he had the skills and mental qualities to be the best ski racer in the world; but he never did as well as I knew he could and I wasn't able to figure out why. He was a survivor of, among other things, a family and life devoted to ski racing, Denver University, the U.S. Ski Team, and Australia's Mainline Corporation which took up Lance's life savings and bought Squaw Valley just before going bankrupt. His Canadian wife was having immigration problems and Lance didn't know if she would be home in Squaw Valley when he returned. (She wasn't, but eventually was allowed back to the U.S. and her family.)

Lance was easily the straightest and closest to the mainstream among us. He had never toured and borrowed all his gear and was the most unlikely member of our group. We celebrated his 27th birthday during the tour. He studied for his realtor's license.

Jim Talcott phoned me in a nervous state from San Francisco just a week before we left. He clearly wanted to go but couldn't say so and talked all around the people involved and the equipment and touring and his recent trip to Sun Valley with Sharkey and what an outrageous tour it was going to be and........... "And would you like to go?" I interjected. "Yes," he said, "yes, of course. Could I?" I laughed for my reasons and he for his and he got even more nervous because now he had to go. Talcott was a 27 year old survivor of the road, the seas and the spaces and places American wanderers and seekers had taken in the previous 10 years. With only three years experience, he was the weakest skier. I had known him when I lived in Bear Valley and had skied with him a little and liked him a lot. Talcott and Sharkey were very close and traveled in South America together. He read James Joyce.

And me, the eldest, a survivor of 36 years of fortunate life on Earth. I was the only member of the group who knew all the members. I read "Steps to an Ecology of Mind" by Gregory Bateson.

On an early April night Jim and June and Sharkey and Talcott drove from Bear Valley and after dinner in Truckee we retired to my tiny cabin between Truckee and Squaw Valley to organize our piles of gear under the bemused, incredulous eyes of ski writer/photographer Peter Miller who was visiting from Vermont. It was midnight before we retired on every available bed, couch and floor space in the cabin and in my 1938 Chevy truck with the redwood camper on the back.

At 4 a.m. Fox said farewell to his beloved June, we all said goodbye to Peter, and we got in the Chevy, Sharkey and Talcott asleep in the back, and headed east in a wet, silent, spring blizzard. Despite the '38 Chevy's max of 50 mph we were at the City of Rocks in southern Idaho that night. Corrock joined us and we spent a few days rock climbing and power hiking in the snow and sagebrush before moving on to Jackson, Wyoming where Lance was flying in from California with all the skis. After a furious couple of days in Jackson getting organized, buying food, arranging for a friend to leave a food cache in the Winds, getting to know each other and more carefully reading the maps of our proposed route, we were ready.

APRIL 18, 1975

Kenny and I dropped our vehicles at Craig Shanholtzer's in Jackson and our friends Grace and Carolyn jammed all of us and our gear in Grace's VW bus and droved us to South Pass along Highway 187 on the west side of the Wind River Range. The mountains passing by looked bigger and more isolated than they did on maps. It took most of the day with a lunch stop in Pinedale to reach South Pass at the southern end of the Winds.

Clear weather, high winds, uncomfortable cold. We were sure spring would come, but one should never be too sure about anything.

South Pass is high desert country, a point on the road between Farson and Lander. Snow drifted across the road. We got out of the van at three in the afternoon, took a few photos, waxed, said farewell to Grace and Carolyn, remembered to remember the feeling of a 70 pound pack, and began moving north, grateful for the movement to keep warm.

Jackson was a long, long way away, about 130 miles as the crow flies; but humans on skis are not crows except for Don Juan who, like any rational brujo, was down south where it was warm. We figured it was around 200 miles to Jackson as the ski turns. But such statistics are irrelevant to life experience.

Fox, the high-strung Viet Nam vet whose intensity and propensity for nighttime urination interfered with his sleep, was in the best physical shape, but he was slowest the first day. He had taken on the four man tent and the additional weight literally drove him into the ground.

Lance, the lifetime skier but novice ski-mountaineer, immediately displayed a trait that manifested itself the entire trip—taking his own path in apparent oblivion to what the rest of us were doing. This characteristic made the tour a little harder than it needed to be for his mates and a lot harder than it needed to be for Lance. But that's Lance.

Our first mistake quickly showed up. We had sealed our ski bases with alpine wax and Nordic wax was reluctant to stick to it and only did so for short distances. (It was several years before we embraced the more convenient, but, it can be argued, less adaptable in undulating terrain, skin in place of wax.) We re-waxed quickly in biting cold and pushed northward on a course that would intercept the mountains the next day. After five miles of fighting cold and our first day fatigued bodies, stunned by and unused to the loads they were carrying, Sharkey and I found a protected valley filled with willows and set up camp. Talcott cruised in and had drawn first blood with a scraped and bloodied nose in a fall. A herd of wild horses grazed in a clearing on a hill above camp. Lance came down from the direction of the horses. "Where you guys been?" he asked with a huge grin. No one answered. We were all busy building a fire of dead willows, setting up tents, cranking up Svea stoves and working out the patterns of reality in a new existence that was less forgiving of inattention than others we knew.

For sleeping there was a four man and a two man tent. For eating we broke into two equal groups, one of us squeezing into the two man at meal time. Neither arrangement was ever static except that Lance never left the four man after two nights in the smaller tent.

We melted snow for water over the fire to save gas. One group cooked over the fire, the other in the big tent over the Svea. Experience had caused me to abjure freeze-dried foods in favor of the real thing. That made packs heavier but worth carrying. Necessity limited variety of fare but no two meals were the same and nothing was thrown away. In deference to my vegetarian diet, the entire group agreed to a meatless diet, no small sacrifice on their part. The first dinner set the pattern: tea or Swiss Miss hot chocolate; one of a variety of packaged soups mixed with nuts, noodles, part of an onion and an enormous variety of spices all cooked together; a piece of cheese; a hot drink after. On occasion, Corrock the popcorn wizard served popcorn with melted butter.

APRIL 19, 1975

Up before the sun, already feeling the benefits of a night divorced from what Ed Abbey termed 'culture.' A clear, cold day. The rivers of wind arrive with the sun. The first of 18 breakfasts—quick cooking cereal (Oatmeal, Wheatina, Zoom) loaded with nuts, raisins and honey, and a hot drink. Breaking camp reveals another mistake—two ski poles used as tent pegs broken removing them from the snow which had solidified overnight. Fortunately, we had four spares.

A difficult day. One hundred yards out we found running water. A hundred yards later I had to re-wax. While involved in this chore Talcott began yelling and whistling from behind. The urgency of emergency in his voice made me think of a broken ski or leg, a herd of enraged moose, a deranged cowboy with shotgun, but, no, Talcott had the four man tent and the extra weight pressed on his body and mind like Sisyphus's rock and he wasn't going to roll it back up the hill.

I took the tent and spent the morning trudging across a snow-covered, bitterly cold Wyoming desert, hoping that my own avarice in life had been less than Sisyphus'. In due time, Sharkey rescued me and his pace immediately snowed to the four man tent shuffle. Later in the day we distributed the tent parts between two people. That helped. The tent was only ten pounds but proved the proverbial straw atop our already maximum loads. One of the difficult ironies of a long ski tour is that the heaviest loads are at the beginning, when you're not in the best shape, and lightest at the end, when you are.

We encountered a herd of about 30 elk, survivors in a state where a sizeable portion of the economy is based on their destruction at the hands of hunters, most of them from other states. They fled our presence, leaving elk shit everywhere to lighten their loads, enabling them to run faster but burning up precious stores of scarce energy they cannot afford at that time of year.

Not long after spooking the elk we dropped into the canyon formed by the Sweetwater River. Relief from the wind. Running water. Warm sun. A perfect place and time for lunch, the ingredients of which never varied: rye crackers, cheese, butter, salted soy beans, prunes, nuts, raisins, chocolate and, sometimes, a packaged tea or sugared drink.

During lunch conversation we agree to follow the wind protected

Sweetwater so long as it goes in the right direction. We wanted photos of the wild animals in the area and were sure they, too, would seek wind protection. I finished eating first and began breaking trail up the canyon, Lance right behind. At some point the willows got thick and Lance took off in his own direction, winding up on the rim in the wind. When the others reached the fork in our trails neither of us was in sight and they followed Lance. I spent the next two hours in warmth and solitude, moving north along the Sweetwater. I heard crashing in some trees to my right and 50 yards away a huge cow moose thrashed in belly deep snow to get away from me. We were heading in the same direction and I tracked her until she climbed out the other side of the canyon and stopped. Were I a brave white trophy hunter with small cannon instead of ski touring photographer with adventure in his mind she would have been dead. As it was, I unpacked my 300 mm lens and took some photos while she posed broadside.

When the river turned east I climbed out the west rim into the unyielding western wind, grateful for the two hours relief from this scourge. Four of my mates were sitting on their packs a couple hundred yards away doctoring their feet. The dreaded blister had arrived and it looked like an outdoor hospital. I was grateful for the five year intimate relationship that existed between my feet and my well-worn double mountain boots.

Lance was a half mile ahead.

Fox was having trouble keeping his skis on. Kenny and Sharkey were the most cheerful. All of us were adapting in our own ways to the new conditions of reality. Rest stops were more like collapses than rests.

We lacked three topographic maps and two of them were for this first part of the trip. That afternoon we got onto the maps we had and into trees, valleys, rolling hills, varied terrain—the mountains. The wind was less debilitating in the trees. We camped in a clearing surrounded by cottonwoods whose bark showed the often beautiful carvings of many years of Basque sheepherders expressing themselves to the future through the only art form available.

A fire of dead cottonwood branches accompanied the nightly

serenade of inter-stellar songs by the wily trickster coyote who has survived man's entire violent effort to annihilate him. We saw and heard coyote nearly every day and night of the tour, his song the perfect lullaby to exhausted bodies and refreshed minds.

APRIL 20, 1975

A fine day with two bad times: a difficult section of downhill bushwhacking through impossible trees on a vertical cliff in terrible snow where Lance, who took more falls (though it could be argued he was the best skier) than everyone else combined, fell and broke the waist strap on his pack; and a minor but uncomfortable snowstorm in the afternoon. There was wonderful downhill skiing on hard snow in the morning, all of us beginning to adapt to making turns with heavy packs, learning about the minute forward/backward range of balance with a load. For the first time the touring was beautiful in gentle, low mountain terrain in cold but reasonable weather. Conditioning was coming along and each move wasn't simply a gut struggle. The physical cadence of touring—left pole-right foot/right pole-left foot—takes over in a constant, fluid pace and the rhythms of the body free and elevate the spirit, as the simplest workers of all time have always known.

From my journal: "....*we do things like 200 mile ski tours through isolated, lovely mountains because it is adventure. There is no other reason and he who seeks further deceives himself. Adventure is as basic and deep in man as his need for food, warmth, shelter, challenge and to love and be loved. Adventure starvation among the people is one of the reasons governments owned by industry owned by a handful of sly fat cats have always been able to round up so many universal soldiers to fight their wars for them—man jumps at the chance to escape the offices and shops and factories and workrooms he has been committed to against every biological, psysiological, psychological and emotional molecule in his being.*

"And adventure is not the same as thrills. Adventure cost more and lasts longer.

"Beauty is adventure; power tripping is thrill.

"Experience is adventure; stature is thrill.

"Falling in love is (the greatest) adventure; an affair is thrill.

"Commitment to the environment is adventure; profiting from the environment is thrill.

"Balance is adventure; oscillation is thrill. (The middle road, the middle road, take the middle road, said the Buddha. To adventure, I might add.)

"Cooperation is adventure; competition is thrill.

"The mind is adventure; the flesh is thrill. The spirit encompasses them both.

"How far out we are forced to go for adventure is a measure of how far off the mark is our culture and time. Yet, everything in the universe is perfect in its own way—like the patterns made by wind on untracked snow—and going through its own paces, like our own growing awareness, to keep the balance of the whole."

APRIL 21, 1975

We broke camp early by beaver ponds in the foothills due west of Mt. Nystrom. The weather was ideal. The sun burned. The country was low rolling hills with pine forests, aspen and cottonwood groves, clearings, frozen lakes and willowed valleys formed by tiny, iced over streams.

Waxing skis on a tour is an art, a science, a challenge and sometimes a bummer. In just a mile it is not out of the question to encounter windblown hardpack, powder, corn, slop, breakable crust, sugar and ice. Fox's tirades on the matter would have been funny were he not so serious and his discomfort so real. In truth, they were funny anyway, just not to him. Sharkey fell on a rock and hurt his knee but hobbled on until he worked it out. Lance took the most spectacular fall of the day when he went for a long, fast schuss without first checking out the snow. And I was reminded of the season when he fell in 17 straight races.

"It is amazing how enjoyable it is to carry a heavy pack and be enveloped in putting one foot in front of the other. The mind needs vacations from the complexity of modern life (even modern mountain life!) and a return to the simplicity and innocence to be found in an adventure such as ours. The mind is free to roam at such times. There must be a correlation between

innocence and freedom."

By the end of the day we were vaguely lost between Independent Mountain and Big Sandy Campground. We were having differences of opinion about our position and what the maps meant, so Corrock was made 'Map Man.' He was a good choice, never erring even in snow storms.

Just before finding camp near a sulphur tainted spring we stopped on a knoll. To the west was open desert covered with snow; to the north was rolling hills and forest; east was abrupt mountains above tree line; to the south was all the country we had just passed through. This perspective of vast horizons gave us a good charge of energy.

The sulphur-mint tea that night couldn't have tasted better.

APRIL 22, 1975

A bushwhacking morning from which we emerged to find culture in a snowmobile track on the road to Big Sandy which we followed. About three miles from Big Sandy Lodge we waxed with klister. Fifteen minutes later a snow storm leapt from the ether upon us and we quickly had four inches of powder clogged to our bases. Cagoules on. Snow scraped off. Spray klister remover (very handy item) applied and klister removed. Re-wax. Move on.

We pushed past the regular lunch stop time to reach the lodge. We were dragging beneath a good storm, but we found shelter at the closed up lodge front door and had lunch. We were cold, wet, tired and stormed upon. Also, a few years before Fox had fallen fifteen feet (Fox's Folly?), landed on his back and broken his coccyx, and this old injury was giving him a great deal of pain.

Naturally, we did the logical thing and broke into the lodge and into cabin #5 to take care of our immediate needs. The operators of big Sandy Lodge have enough sense to lock their place during the winter but wisdom enough to leave it so that the *determined* intruder can get in without having to break anything. As Talcott said, "We didn't break any *natural* law."

We stoked up the wood burning stove in #5, dried out, ate and drank extra rations and rested. My mates went to work on their feet which all looked bad. Each had to do some serious taping. Lance, the novice and least prepared for the trip, was in the worse shape. All his equipment, including boots, was borrowed, and his clothing mostly consisted of old, ragged U.S. Ski Team uniform issue. The soles of his on loan boots were coming off and he had ugly blisters the size of half dollars down into the flesh. He looked like a refugee from ski racing, an image with humorous aspects, but we were all concerned about his feet. However, like the others, he taped his feet and epoxied and taped his boots and persevered.

In #5 we found three Mountain Gazettes with articles of mine and one by Doug Robinson about touring. We laughed, talked and argued over the articles, particularly one about skins versus waxing for touring, and we had a wonderful time expounding on and defending our positions. The cabin was so warm that we had to open the door before sleep would come.

APRIL 23, 1975

Up before the sun. We cleaned the cabin, re-closed it, left a note of explanation and enough money to cover Big Sandy's contribution to the expedition in the lodge, re-closed the lodge and skied across the new snow on Mud Lake in a crystal clear, primordial mountain morning. The short day before allowed us extra energy and we made outstanding progress to the pass above Dad's Lake where we had our first look at Mt. Geikie and saw a coyote. Our commitment to the mountains was really in effect and our work was enormously fulfilling and easier.

"How fortunate the birthright of life, to be in this place—exquisite mountains—at this time—NOW—doing what we are doing—skiing—with these good people (Jerry Garcia says there are no evil people, only victims)—friends. Feeling fortunate about being alive is the birthright of every man. And take the lessons home when the tour is over for in wilderness is the preservation of the world, but man can't live forever in wilderness. He must create a balance between the warmth of civilization and the hardship of the wild. He will not survive long exclusively in either."

That afternoon another storm moved in and we were quickly lost among innumerable identical canyons, ridges, trees, snowflakes and clouds. We followed the compass until that time of day and fatigue when little things—getting lost, the leader breaking trail with feet too close together, a branch catching on a pack—are taken personally. Then we found a flat spot, set up camp and crawled into our nylon shelters for dinner, conversation, reading, keeping notes and being lulled to sleep by wind and snow upon the tent.

APRIL 24, 1975

A bitter cold night had us up at dawn. Synthetic sleeping bags, unlike down, dry out from body heat, from the inside, and in many ways are superior (and less expensive and easier on the geese of the world) to the less bulky down bag. On several nights the temperature put us right at the limit of our bags' effectiveness, and even a little over. Cold or not, it was wonderful to be up and to watch the first sun strike Mt. Geikie. Within seconds of the sun hitting the peaks the first plums of snow from the morning winds could be seen. Every blessing has its price.

We began the day with a half mile of outrageous downhill skiing in fine powder. Sharkey got so carried away he dropped his pack and climbed back up for seconds. Later in the day he paid in the coin of fatigue for his enthusiastic energy expenditure. Fox and Talcott, the weakest skiers, struggled in the trees where it was steep.

Then came a long climb through sparse trees where we rested on an enormous, mostly treeless plateau west of Mt. Geikie and an unnamed knob we christened "Commander Cody Peak" after a band we favored. At 10,000 feet it was warm and bright and burned exposed skin. Lance, the non-bearded, really suffered. Talcott lagged. Fox and Sharkey practiced telemark turns.

The rest of the day was downhill and easy, steady touring across frozen lakes and gentle country with remarkable peaks looking down upon our movements. Once Lance charged blindly into the lead and guided us into some unnecessary bushwhacking. We collectively reminded him that the whole is more than the sum of its parts.

During lunch Kenny and I got into talking about Lance's

extraordinary skiing skills, and we spoke of some of his finest ski racing moments. Lance shrugged it off and remarked, "Yeah, but so what?" I flashed on the suicidal dentist in the film "Mash" who had told his priest that poker was "only a game," and I had a sudden insight into why Lance's abilities had never taken him to the level I believed was rightfully his.

Kenny discovered a useful water gathering device on frozen lakes. We knew we couldn't chop through several feet of ice to water and never tried. But Kenny found that above the thick ice is about a foot of water, an inch of ice and then the most recent snow on which we walked. This discovery simplified life.

I, too, made a discovery. I had been equally concerned about Lance's propensity for charging ahead and Talcott's always being so far behind. That day I figured out that Jim didn't stay back because he couldn't keep up. He liked being by himself to check out the scenery, get into his own head, set his own pace and enjoy the tour. Except for a few dangerous sections when I worried about everybody, I never worried about Jim's skiing after that.

We had worked to the point on that fine day that we could see the sun refracting to a sea of colors off the white snow. The views of Geikie, Hooker, Bonneville, Reads and Pyramid were alone worth the week of labor.

"The first skis were tools, enabling people to move through country which would strand them otherwise. After hours of gut-straining labor a spurt of downhill skiing is tremendously exhilarating, a fitting reward for endeavor. The next step of the mind was the one Sharkey had taken: "That was so much fun I'd like to do it again, without my pack." Thus, the first true sidetrack in skiing. The sidetrack off the sidetrack came from the desire for the rush without the labor, a pattern of mind we all know—instant enlightenment for a dollar a hit or $10,000 a course, canned laughter on TV, tickets on the 50 yard line, and the ski lift. Modern skiing is a refinement of the first sidetrack and is quite degenerate. Every skier knows this intellectually, different knowledge than experience, but sooner or later everyone has to get back on the main track."

APRIL 25, 1975

A long, uncomfortable day in marginal to miserable weather with little sun and an afternoon blizzard. One of Lance's short cuts got us lost for a couple of hours. All of us feeling the effects of pushing hard for a week without rest. Talcott, Sharkey and Kenny singing the lethargy blues after getting stoned the night before. After a waxing stop I took off without my pack which inspired lots of laughter from the group, mine included. Ha ha. I took my first fall of the tour, burying my face in the snow between my tips, a 60 pound pack atop my head. We began to take little things *really* personally. Fox claims that every time a person loses his temper his body burns up all his vitamin C. I ate 1250 mg of C as soon as we set up camp on George Lake in a howling snowstorm.

APRIL 26, 1975

Our first rest day. Snowing. Cold. Windy. Tents ice caked and damp. The day is spent sleeping, reading, writing, talking and savoring relaxation. Our bodies thanked us for the rest.

APRIL 27, 1975

Fox, the insomniac and nighttime prowler and urinator (two to four times a night) had us up by 4 a.m. Clear skies and a morning moon hanging like a white pendant in an emerald void. As cold as any of us could ever remember experiencing (We later learned it was minus 30 degrees F). Breaking camp and rolling up tent was challenging and miserable and I was very concerned about my hands for the first two hours. We moved fast but it was terrible until the sun came up, and it only stayed an hour and a half before the weather turned stormy.

What happened to spring?

Our route took us over 11,200 foot Lester Pass. Our lunch at 9,000 feet was cut short by the numbness that entered our hands as soon as gloves were removed. Sharkey, Talcott, Kenny and I ate ginseng root to help us over the pass. It was all uphill and sweat froze when we stopped and chill seeped to the bone. Snow flurries and wind increased with altitude. By 10,000 feet breathing was difficult, spurts shorter, rests more frequent and longer.

A mile below the pass I made sure I took over the lead. There was some very real avalanche possibility and I wanted first look. We had already put in twelve hard miles that day and I didn't want the couple of suggestions about camping before the pass to become reality. If one gets over, all have to get over. I found a good solution to the avalanche problem up a nearly imperceptible ridge to the right of the bowl below Lester Pass, followed by a spooky forty foot traverse through the only flaw in the protective cornice at the top. My mates didn't have my close up perspective on the matter, and I was later explicitly informed that hey were unhappy and questioning my judgment until they got there.

We skied down the other side in poor visibility to an unnamed lake above Little Seneca Lake just below Indian Pass. It had been a fifteen mile day in miserable, cold weather over our highest pass. Energy was low. We dropped packs and while the others set up camp Kenny and I went to look for the cache of food we hoped our friends had left. We saw nothing and quickly realized that it is one thing to draw a couple of X marks on the same spot of two identical topographic maps back in warm Jackson a couple of light years away, and quite another to correlate the X with bunches of trees in a mountain blizzard with darkness coming on and exhaustion already filling the body and brain with images of empty hands and certain difficulties about the remainder of the tour. After an hour or more of looking and wandering a mile and a half from camp, there it was—a tree decorated with streamers of red survey tape and loaded with food and white gas. No Christmas tree was ever more beautiful. Just then I broke the first binding cable of the tour, the only time I wasn't carrying my pack with extra cables. Fortunately, Kenny had one in his rear pocket.

April 28, 1975

Sharkey and Kenny picked up some ugly frostbite blisters on their toes from the previous day. Sharkey was hurting pretty bad. We had a leisurely morning organizing and distributing our new loads before getting a late start to one of the best mountain days any of us had known, and between us we had known many. Good snow, clear weather, really cold. The views of Mt. Warren, Bob's Tower, Skyline Peak, Mt. Woodrow Wilson and the Sphinx were reminiscent of Chamonix without the people. It was high mountain touring between 10,500 and 11,000 feet through lovely, inhospitable for the body but nourishing for the spirit, country.

"Commitment is irreversible, real, vibrant, and our commitment to the mountains is evident in every stride, each pump of the human heart and breath of the clean air in freezing wind, unending reminders of the relationship between man, the mortal, and his environment, also mortal.

"Our commitment is a fine adventure worthy of Snowshoe Thompson, but our margin of error is far wider than that of the good Sierra mailman of the 19th century. We are six instead of one, all wearing Vuarnets and ski equipment of space age sophistication and carrying shelter and warmth that old Snowshoe would envy or, at least, marvel at. More, we have the knowledge that if worse comes to worse thirty miles to the west is a major highway. Even commitment is relative.

"Still, one must pay attention to every move."

The late start and rejuvenated packs kept our progress down to eight miles, the least daily distance of the tour. The day was spent above 10,000 feet in winter weather reminiscent of January, in no way connected with the Aprils of my dreams and youth and fantasies and other unrelated unrealities. Just before stopping we went over Shannon Pass under the spectacular Stroud Peak which looked like a miniature Fitzroy. We thought of naming it "Mick Jagger Peak" until learning that Stroud already had the honor. The north side of Shannon Pass is steep and the avalanche possibility obvious, but we managed somehow and then climbed back up Cube Rock Pass to Dale Lake, the headwaters of the Green River, where we camped in the first flurries of a storm.

APRIL 29, 1975

Lance's 27th birthday. A terrible, high mountain (Dale Lake is 10,685 feet), alpine, snowing, blowing, cold, dangerous day. Our path down Green River Canyon involved inescapable risk, and we put it off a day. Sharkey made an outrageous bisquick birthday cake with nuts, raisins and chocolate bars. After lunch the entire expedition congregated in the four man tent for a birthday celebration and general good feelings full of war stories, dreams, fantasies and fun. We talked mostly about surfing, sun, the ocean, the season of summer and southern California's beaches of bikinis.

Sharkey's frostbite had turned black and his pain interfered with sleep. He constructed some amazing, bulbous 'overtoes' from sleeping pad ensulite and duct tape. These got him through the tour but frostbite is frostbite and black toes are ugly and we were all concerned and wondering how far Sharkey would push the useful quality of stoicism. Fox was sick with diarrhea but in good spirits. Talcott, always in good spirits, was having breathing difficulties in the night. These concerns joined the avalanche possibilities of the Green River Canyon to flow like frozen oil through my mind.

APRIL 30, 1975

Up early to beat a sun that never showed anyway. The first mile down was one of my spookiest mountain experiences. The canyon bottom is less than a hundred yards wide. Fifteen hundred foot walls laced with obvious avalanche chutes loaded with two feet of fresh snow shot up on both sides. I went first, Kenny last. Except for Lance who said he didn't see anything so dangerous no matter what the rest of us said and came right behind me, we spaced ourselves several hundred yards apart. 10,000 years later we dropped into the safe trees and the exhilaration of the aftermath of adrenaline high, except, I suppose, for Lance who didn't see anything so dangerous.

The rest of the roller coaster ride down the canyon over enormous boulders covered with perfect powder was the purest of hard-earned fun. Talcott and Fox had their problems with the intricate, precise skiing. Lance took several falls caused by imprudence and the sole of his borrowed boot which detached itself whenever he sat back. The first six miles passed quickly as we lost 2500 feet. The imperfect weather was warm and comfortable. For the rest of the day we crossed flat, gentle terrain, and by the time we camped on the north end of Green River Lakes

Dale Lake was 17 miles of skiing behind. We had left the Wind River Mountains.

MAY 1, 1975

May Day. The worker's holiday. We celebrated with hard, enjoyable work, 14 miles along the Green River and into the east side of the Gros Ventre Mountains which are older than the Winds and, therefore, mellower and easier to get along with. Superb weather. We saw coyotes, a herd of over a hundred elk, moose, the first wolf any of us had ever seen, geese, ducks, cranes, hawks, a domestic dog, two horses, and a man who fed hay to the herd of elk to keep them alive through the fierce Wyoming winter. The economy of the state depends on their living—and dying.

We noted a curious phenomenon—throughout the Winds abundant animal life is visible up to 8500 feet, then almost none until 10,000 where animal life appears again.

Leaving the Wind River Mountains made us a little like horses heading for the barn.

We had lives in different worlds to return to. Lance and Fox had wives waiting and wondering with no word. Sharkey had a job as a river guide. Talcott had a girl friend in San Francisco and needed to find a job. Kenny had a fireplace to build in his North Fork house before the summer ski race camps began. And I had lots of writing and climbing I wished to do before going to work as a coach at those same camps. Yet, individually as a group we were so happy that we could have gone on and on.....

"...into Jackson and along the Tetons and over to the Absaroka Range and into the Crazy Mountains and on to the Lewis Range and into the Canadian Rockies and through Canada and over to Alaska and across the Alaska Range and over the Bering Straights to Siberia and.....and it could be and maybe should be done.....a reversal of the path of the beautiful people called by white man Indian and who call themselves according to their tribe.....but such is not our fate. Ours is to use our small tour to put our spirits in the sacred trust of relationship and harmony with the trees, rocks, animals, birds and streams and mountains of this exquisite land, to

translate that trust into the language of human civilization and the mind of those who live in oblivion on the brink of destroying the wilderness that sustains everything on this lovely planet that is home."

We camped in warm weather by a spring at 8,000 feet a mile above the Moore Ranch where we saw snowmobile tracks and horses. An abandoned snowmobile sat under some trees two hundred yards away. Our friend coyote serenaded us to sleep.

MAY 2, 1975

Re-entry to American culture was shocking. Two miles after breaking camp, right above Kinky Creek Airport, the silence of a beautiful day was shattered by the blare of four snowmobiles. They stopped, two fathers and their twelve year old sons from Rock Springs, amazed to find anyone on skis so far from a highway. "The only way I want to come in here is on *this*," one of them commented, giving a couple raucous revs with the throttle as illustration. Those guys were friendly folks and told us the best way down the aptly named Kinky Creek to the Darwin Ranch, but I can't relate to the snowmobile scene. Until they were out of sight, sound and smell we couldn't get into the skiing and the mountains, and we thought of their effect on the sensitivities of the local wildlife.

We had fine skiing down to the Darwin Ranch, a magnificent two-story log ranch house with impeccable cabins, a dude-ranch for hunters, fishermen and snowmobilers. The caretaker, Tom Allen, about 30, was a vegetarian and had been at the ranch for two years, most of that time alone. He was pleased to see us and invited us in for the longest, most memorable repast of the tour—soup, homemade bread, cheese, chocolate, coffee and three and a half hours of animated conversation about our collective adventures, follies, travels and times. I remarked that he had a magnificent library. Tom replied, "Yes, but I'm getting a little tired of reading good books."

Thanks to Tom Allen, the Darwin Ranch was the most relaxed time we had known and we could easily have spent the night. Kenny snapped out of it first and got us on the trail. During the entire tour when some of us would start dragging one of us would keep the group pushing. That day it was Kenny.

While saying farewell to our new friend I discovered that my wind shirt had blown away in the wind and was not to be seen. Tom immediately took the Levi shirt off his back and insisted I take it as his contribution to the tour. I accepted.

A mile up the Gros Ventre River we came across a band of mountain goats, an endangered species. None of us had seen these creatures before, and we delighted in spending a half hour watching them while they posed with no obvious fear. A hundred yards further on two moose spared no efforts to put as much possible distance as possible between us. The trail had been partly packed by snowmobiles and the four miles we made before camping would have been grueling without the track in the rotten snow.

MAY 3, 1975

The worst snow conditions of the trip on a day harder, longer, colder and more dangerous than we had anticipated. We made good time to the headwaters of the Gros Ventre at 10,000 feet where the wind came up and our wax clogged. That combined with cold and my impatience caused me to push through without re-waxing to earn my first and only blister of the tour. We ate a frozen lunch in a small clump of trees a few hundred feet below a 10,400 foot pass above Swift Creek, the route we had chosen to Granite Hot Springs.

This was another Poulsen short-cut but, unlike all the others, one we all had agreed to. It was a hard, dangerous and bad choice. From the pass we dropped more than 3000 feet into Granite Creek Canyon on snow that changed from breakable crust to unskiable heavy powder to the rottenest corn on terrain that only a lack of alternatives allowed conscience to accept.

We were more fatigued by the descent than the ascent. Fox, big wave surfer, combat marine in Viet Nam, climber, survivor, said, "That was the hardest thing I've ever done."

We rested at a bridge a mile from the hot springs and immediately encountered the guide/rancher/hot springs keeper and his wife in a two-track, tank-like snow machine. They lived in a house by the bridge. He charged us a dollar apiece to use the pool, informed us a 'young couple' was camping there, and implored us to 'dress decently' while in the pool because of the young lady.

The idea of the six of us—tired, grubby, smelly, bearded, uncombed (uncouth?) and sixteen days in the mountains—dropping in on the lovebirds who had assumed privacy in paradise was funny enough to give us the energy to make the last mile to Granite Hot Springs. Fox's feet hurt badly and he was complaining and verbalizing fantasies about spending an extra day at the pool. The rest of us were as tired as we'd been on the tour. We straggled into the campground one by one, much to the dismay of our fellow campers. I went to the couple, introduced myself and did my best to convince them of our friendliness, attributes of civilization and relative lack of depravity. His name was Steve Lundy, a Jackson ski coach who knew of Corrock, Poulsen and me through the small world of ski racing.

The hot springs kept the camping area dry and grassy. As soon as we were immersed in the hot water the day's trials were amply rewarded. We spent a delicious hour in unaccustomed luxury and comfort before drying out in the cool air. Then I dressed in clean underwear, knickers socks and shirt that I brought just for this occasion. I called it my Jackson crotch. It felt fabulous, better than corn starch or talcum powder.

We stayed up late eating and talking and we slept on bare earth beneath the stars, a bed and bedroom with no peers.

MAY 4, 1975

The hardest day of the tour. Up early because we knew a difficult, strenuous time awaited us in the 20 air miles to Jackson. We had a morning chocolate and chat with Lundy and his lady. They had skied in from the south but intended to follow our westerly path to Jackson. They planned to do it in a day and it seemed to us they lacked an appreciation of reality, but we wished them luck and tackled the first problem—a 2400 foot climb out of the canyon. We didn't see the couple again but were assured that no one on cross-country skis would be following our path. (Three months later I was photographing a professional ski race in Bariloche, Argentina. One of the racers hooked a tip on the gate coming off the second jump, turned upside down and took a spectacular fall. I was close and was helping him get his equipment back in order when he looked at me and said, "Oh, hi, Dick. I heard you were here. How are you doing?" I looked at him, as surprised to hear him speaking English as to realize he knew me. "My name is Steve Lundy and I met you at Granite Hot Springs last spring." Just then Corrock was side-slipping the course. "Hey, Kenny," I said, "Come here. You won't believe this one.")

Our route was possible only because the cold kept everything in place. It was physically hard, technically demanding, and dangerous as hell and, for anyone I know, impossible on cross-country skis. One section was a smooth, icy, very steep wall that would drop the first mistake well over a thousand feet to a rocky stop that encouraged me to be as attentive as I've ever been on a pair of skis.

Lance, following his own mysterious reasoning, took a route between two wide and easy to see fracture lines. The rest of us were too concerned with our own immediate situations to do more than silently wish him luck and be grateful none of us were below him.

Once the altitude was gained the gut-straining work was over and we became involved in the longest right-hand traverse any of us had ever traversed—13 miles of contouring. My left leg felt a yard longer than the right. We told stories of the mythical 'Side Hill Wampus' who lives in southern mountains and can only move in one direction around the sides of those mountains. It was a particular form of working on patience.

And patience is invaluable. A man who had to ski tour for three weeks in order to develop three seconds of patience to use in the right situation would have done himself and the universe a good turn, joining the brotherhood of the visionary Rimbaud who prophesied: "In the dawn, armed with a burning patience, we shall enter the splendid cities."

After eight miles of side hill we made our last camp in a blizzard.

MAY 5, 1975

The last day. Ten inches of fresh snow, more arriving every minute, too cold for idle chit-chat. We continued the traverse on the new snow which made it easier to hang onto the side hill, as did the knowledge that we'd be in Jackson for dinner.

After five miles we stood on the pass above Cache Creek Canyon which runs eight miles and drops 2400 feet into Jackson. The first two miles were as good as powder skiing gets, an enjoyment we had earned. In the enthusiasm of the moment I shamelessly neglected my photographer duties. The snow became heavy as we bushwhacked to the Jackson mine road where we stopped for the tour's last lunch. We had estimated our food well enough that we skied into town with an excess of one soup, some noodles and a little cereal.

The last six miles took only a couple of hours. We saw one moose. It was foggy and damp and finally felt like a wet spring. Snow ran out just on the edge of town and we walked a mile through Jackson carrying our skis. Lance walked a hundred feet ahead, impatient of our pace and conversation about the adventure we had just shared and of our reluctance to let go of the tour. The first people we encountered was a construction crew of beer-bellies in hard hats laying asphalt on Mother Earth. We rented motel rooms, bought beer and snacks, turned on the TV and learned that the Viet Nam war was over and the country returned to the Vietnamese. We watched Arlo Guthrie, Don McCann, Rita Coolidge and Kris Kristoferson on the Smother Brothers Show. We ate huge salads (our bodies craved fresh vegetables the past ten days) and drank expensive wine in the Wort Hotel. We stayed up late drinking beer in the Cowboy Bar, listening to a rock band called "The Wings of Freedom," turning them on with nothing more than our vibe and presence and they told us so. We slept late the next morning before scattering in our own, different directions. We had returned to the American culture, but we were more civilized and better people than we were before the tour.

CHAPTER EIGHTEEN

Around Tahoe

APRIL 17, 1978

AT LAST, AFTER SEVERAL MONTHS OF PLANNING and three years of waiting for enough snow, we are beginning a proposed 200 mile ski tour circumnavigation of the Lake Tahoe basin. An idea in motion. For me, a lifelong skier and Tahoe resident, a sentimental journey through a vital and beautiful part of my heritage. An attempt to establish a Tahoe Haute Route, a safe and close-to-civilization ski mountaineering route easily available to city-bound weekend mountaineers. A time in the back country performing the repetitious drudgery of humping heavy packs through snow-covered country on a pair of skis powered by nothing more than sweat. Time to recharge the batteries.

Following the normal packing, farewell, procrastination delays, our friend, Susan, loaded us into her old bread truck and drove a couple miles outside Truckee to Cold Stream Canyon. We piled out, took photos, said our good-byes and began walking south along the dirt-mud-water-snow road leading up the canyon. It was more than a mile before we found enough snow to ski upon.

We were a diverse group—

Craig Calonica, 24, has lived his entire life at Tahoe. Craig is an Alpine ski racer, climber, carpenter and lover of good times. With his long hair and frizzy beard he looks like Tahoe's main Rastaman. He spends a couple weeks each year in Cervinia, Italy and Portillo, Chile, seeing how fast he can ski. Two months after the tour Craig fell face-first between his skis at 118 mph in Italy, and, while not seriously injured, he was in the Turin hospital for awhile.

Otis Kantz, 36, was raised in an Ohio orphanage and appreciates the good things in life. Otis was part proprietor of Truckee's *Squeeze In* where the best omelets I know are found, and that morning omelets were on Otis at the Squeeze. Otis is one of those people who will have the mundane and not so mundane chores done before the people around him realize or at least admit the job *needs* doing. Ski mountaineering was new to Otis and his fatigue the first days was as real as his amazement at the experience.

Tom Lippert, 38, is sometimes called "The Walrus" for his big round smiling face and droopy mustache. Tom is one of the better skiers at the Squaw Valley Ski School and is the consummate professional photographer—dependable, in focus, energetic and right where he says he is. He's an old friend of many facets and miles (including the time we talked our way in carefully chosen French into France and out of Switzerland with a van load of Warren Miller's very expensive camera gear we could not account for.) A few years ago Tom was well into his 30's and unmarried and no prospects in sight. A friend of mine asked him, "Tom, why haven't you ever been married?" He replied, "Well, I just never met anyone I thought I could grow with." Good answer. Thoughtful mind. However, a year and a half before our tour Tom married Laurel and they've both been growing ever since, and the tour was the longest they've been apart.

Bill McKinley, 25, was a stranger to us all, but a friend of Otis' said he was a good man and wanted to go, and somehow that was enough of a recommendation. Bill is cheerful, intelligent, strong and incredibly knowledgeable about maps, mountains, trees and the back country in general. A forestry graduate of Northern Arizona University, Bill had worked for the U.S. Forest Service and was in the process of getting out of bureaucratic government life into the more classical hand-to-mouth existence of the non-governmental person of the mountains who is not there to protect, rape, govern, capitalize upon, escape to or commune with the mountains, but only to live in harmony within them.

Steve McKinney, 24, is, was, and will be for quite sometime one of the better-known people in the ski world. I've known Steve since he was in the cradle and his family since not too long after I got out of mine. Within six months after our tour he had set two more world records for speed on skis. He is the only person to have traveled over 200 kph on skis. Steve is, mentally and physically, one of the strongest humans I know. He is not by any means outside the common experiences, but McKinney has resources you can count on which all people have but most do not know how to tap. He's one who sets the standard and the pace, and he's a hell of a trail breaker when the snow is deep, the pack heavy and the body tired. McKinney used that tour to begin conditioning for the speed runs.

And me, Dick Dorworth, 39, the elder. It's impossible to describe yourself in less than a lifetime of work, and hard enough at that, but I will say I find it intensely rewarding to immerse myself in the simple task of getting from Point A to Point B on a pair of skis. It's excellent therapy for the aches and pains encountered in the civilized world. I mean, if I was a musician I'd be a *blues* man. As it is, instead of picking notes and howling hurtin' words, I spend lots of time picking my way up and down and around the mountains of the world and listening to the wind howl in the trees and through the passes and over the lakes of those mountains.

On this first short day we made only a few miles before camping by the south fork of Cold Creek about 2 miles NNE of Anderson Peak. It was nice to be out. Lippert's brand-new boots had blistered his feet. Old friends are better than new when carrying a heavy load. The rest of us were tired in the good way.

Sierra Designs had generously given us six sleeping bags and two dome tents, a three and a four-man. Steve christened the smaller one by spilling hot water all over the inside while trying to cook a brew. Tom, not to be outdone, kicked over a pot of soupy rice inside the larger tent. We finally ate and collapsed into restless comas, emanating snores and farts and belches and the sounds of the uncomfortable movements of the first night in the woods sleeper.

APRIL 18, 1978

A perfect Sierra day. Up early after a poor sleep. Tents are preferable to nothing, but it takes a day or so to get used to a new sleeping situation. Otis complained of stiffness. Tom's feet had lots of tape. The rest seemed okay, but a difficult day was upon us. Our route was one way—up— from 6500 feet to 8700 feet just east of Tinker Knob; and there's no way to get in shape for humping heavy packs in deep snow except by doing it. Fortunately, we had luck with wax and our equipment (Hexcel Alpine skis and various models of the Silveretta binding) worked perfectly.

Backbreaking work. The labor of touring with pack through the back country is liberating, exhilarating, fascinating and positively healthy. It clears the mind, elevates spirit, fatigues body. But people are different and Tom, the slowest, cracked us up during one rest stop after a particularly tough stretch when he commented he was "periodically overcome with fits of acute depression." Tom needed lots of encouragement at that point.

Otis, too, was extremely tired when we reached the ridge by Tinker Knob. The rest seemed all right, and I was pleased with how well the group interacted. We then lost nearly a thousand feet to some outrageous late afternoon spring skiing on south facing slopes of corn snow before setting up camp in a huge clearing at the base of some cliffs. There was running water. A marmot sat in the mouth of his snow hole sunning himself, and he was one amazed marmot when we six skied by and set up camp in his neighborhood.

APRIL 19, 1978

A strange, hard day. Windy and cold. We made excellent progress and Lippert and Otis had more life. Craig and Otis wore old lace-up leather ski boots which were coming apart and always wet. One concern gives way to another.

All of us work and ski at Squaw Valley and are connected to the area on several levels. Four days earlier the tram at Squaw had wrecked, killing four persons and injuring many more; and we were shaken, saddened and subdued by the accident. My six year-old son had been in the tram car an hour before it went down. We hadn't talked much about the wreck, but it was in all our minds; and as we climbed the ridge leading to Granite Chief we could see the entire upper mountain at Squaw. It was incredibly eerie. The immobile tram car dangled in the air like a smashed toy. We had all ridden it many times, and four people had died there. The mountain was freshly groomed, the skiing looked fantastic, and every lift we could see was stopped. Abandoned. We knew the wind had shut the lifts, but it was surreal to see the mountain smooth and clear and empty. We considered skiing down to the Shirley Lake lift, firing it up and taking a few runs, but better judgment prevailed.

Steve, the philosopher, remarked on the irony of starting this tour right after the tram wreck. We go back to the basic leg power when the mechanical fails. My mind dwelled on that thought and its ramifications. It extended back to my skiing roots. Back to my first experience on skis at the south shore of Tahoe when I and my childhood buddy Doug Gaynor climbed up and slid down a small hill, over and over. Rope tows were the first lifts we used in the late '40's and early '50's, and my grammar school friend, Kenny Burdick, lost his arm to a rope tow. The mechanical failed then too, causing me to examine the possibility that perhaps it is not progress which fails but mechanical means to human ends.

We crossed under the face of Granite Chief and over the col on the back side of Emigrant, a place we'd skied many times; but this was the first time up instead of down. Then we dropped into Whiskey Creek. After the long uphill grind it was wonderful to ski down and maneuver through trees. Also, it was a relief to be again in the back country, away from ski resorts and the reminders of all we had left behind. Overtones of escapism.

There is a cabin at Whiskey Creek and we decided to track it down just to see and know its location. A couple of dead skiers who accidentally wandered off the back side of Squaw would be alive had they known about Whiskey Creek cabin. It was cleverly concealed in trees and mostly buried in snow, but we dug it out and decided to spend the night. Though several hours of daylight remained, it was a good decision. The two-story cabin has a wood-burning stove, a huge saw, a table, emergency supplies and shelter from the storm which arrived that night, much to our amazement.

We spent nearly two days at Whiskey Creek. I kept notes and read a marvelous book by Farley Mowat, "A Whale for the Killing." McKinney read Abbey's "Desert Solitaire." Tom took photos. Bill kept notes. Otis, the worker, kept things in order. We ate and drank unrelentingly. Steve played his harp and cracked us up with imitations of Jimi Hendrix playing "The Star Spangled Banner." It was Hitler's birthday in the heavy cabin at Whiskey Creek.

APRIL 21, 1978

From my notebook: *"Near the top of Little Powderhorn Creek in the gathering dark, we are just a few hundred yards below the ridge leading into the Rubicon, but we were forced to stop in view of a threatening storm and Tom's slowness. Our precarious camp is on a tiny knoll under trees in snow so soft we used ski poles as tent pegs. Storm seems to be dissipating. Lippert real grateful we didn't continue. Snow must be melted for water. The team is tired and no one wants to cook.*

"Everyone is stronger. Tom is slowest, but his wit and good will and very presence make up for any delays. After all, he's never done this before; and we all got to learn.

"Bill and I got us lost on Powderhorn Creek, but we came out right where we wanted. We've ·checked the maps and still can't figure out where it went wrong. Nothing is lost. The light meter on my new camera doesn't work, so Tom loaned me his light meter. Pissed at the camera. Pleased with Tom.

"Since I started writing here, Otis, who was comatose in his bag, has rallied and is having a great time with my spice kit preparing dinner. The stove works poorly."

APRIL 22, 1978

Up early but all reluctant to enter a bitter cold, clear morning. We made excellent time over the pass and for several miles mostly downhill on a long traverse through dense forest. Wonderful touring. We were getting fit and seeing the mountain mileage unfold. We took a snack rest about 11:30. Otis and Tom were a bit behind. It was hot and we sat on our packs in T-shirts or bare-chested sunbathing and watching our mates. A strange thing occurred. About 30 feet away, Tom shifted his weight in a weird way, his leg buckled and he fell like Troy. He couldn't get up without Otis' help and I knew we had a problem. Tom has had the knife taken to his knee twice and he was hurting in his bad knee.

We rested awhile, but Tom was rightfully fearful of pushing further damage onto a painful knee. We checked the maps, found a convenient escape route via McKinney Creek and cajoled Tom until we were at the head of the route a couple of miles behind Sourdough Hill. Bill and I hurried the eight miles out to the roadhead. On the way we ran into Malcolm and Todd, two Squaw Valley Ski Patrolmen, who were out touring and had a car at the road. Within four hours of leaving the back country, Bill and I were at my house enjoying Dos Equis. Two different worlds.

We called my old good friend, Jerry Smeltzer, who, among an infinitude of things is involved in search and rescue circles. The *last* thing we wanted was to call out the rescue freaks, bless their Red Cross souls; all we wanted was a Ski-doo to give Tom a ride out. Jerry tracked it down.

APRIL 23, 1978

By mid-morning Jerry, Bill and I were back at the trailhead with the gas-eating, ear-splitting, raucous, harmony-destroying dreaded machine affectionately known (with a copy right) as the Ski-doo. It was raining. None of us have ever driven such a contraption. It seemed simple and since Jerry borrowed the thing he decided to go in. We told him to follow our tracks, gave him map and compass, wished him luck and waved adieu as Jerry and the metal monster roared into the back country in a blare of cacophonous noise and exhaust.

Bill and I breakfasted and then spent the day drinking beer, reading, talking and sitting in the truck to avoid the ever-falling rain. A few other Ski-dooers were also up McKinney Creek and late in the day Jerry and two Ski-dooers emerged from the wood. Jerry's day was awful.

He learned a lot. So did we. He overturned his machine three times, got it stuck in a creek and a tree well and would have had a tortuously lovely walk out if the two experienced Ski-dooers hadn't found him. We learned several things—(1) Just because aesthetically, morally, practically, philosophically and environmentally we hold that Ski-doos in the back country used for cheap thrills is indefensible, doesn't mean that a skilled, experienced and intelligent operator isn't necessary to guide one through the woods. (2) *Nobody* goes into strange country alone on a Ski-doo. Travel in company. (3) Getting Tom out wasn't going to be the piece of cake we had thought. (4) We didn't (don't) know as much as we thought (think) we did (do).

We retired to the nearest pub to invent Alternate Rescue Plan B.

Meanwhile, our mates enjoyed a restful day reading, talking, swimming and sunning between rain squalls. They wondered what the hell had happened. We were not back as agreed, and there is always the possibility that something had gone wrong to prevent me and Bill from getting out. Those sorts of thoughts are easy in the mountains when mates are overdue.

Accordingly, they made plans for Steve and Craig to follow our tracks out in the morning, leaving Otis with Tom.

APRIL 24, 1978

Alternate Plan B went into effect. We rounded up a second Ski-doo and two people to operate them. Dennis Dunn is the local telemark turn champion and is *hot* on the Ski-doo. Tim Tilton is a professional ski racer who got the other machine and volunteered to drive it. While we were unloading the machines at the trail head McKinney and Calonica showed up. We saw Tim and Dennis off, gave Steve and Craig beers and sat down to wait. Smeltzer showed up. It was raining. Jerry was going back to work and Steve and Craig, both restless for civilized diversity, went with him. Soon, charming Laurel Lippert arrived to await her husband's return. Bill got restless and skied halfway in to meet the rescue party. Laurel and I drank beer, talked and watched it rain. I preferred to be where I was than stuck in a tent.

It was after 4:00 in the afternoon when the machines, their drivers and Otis and Tim and Bill, all drenched to the skin, arrived. Tom was happy to be out and even happier to see his wife. We returned the machines and retired to our favorite Tahoe City dining establishment.

The next two days were spent watching it rain. One of the machines had inexplicably incurred $250 worth of damage. Calonica managed to get arrested and thrown in the slammer within 24 hours. Life in the woods, while chock full of certain difficulties, is simple and clear and enormously healthy compared to the usual life we live and leave from and always return to.

April 27, 1978—Compared to our original beginning, we got an early start. Tim Tilton, the 20 year-old ski racer, replaced Lippert. We left McKinney Creek and made excellent time in clear weather and good snow to the exit point. Instead of staying on the ridge to the east we dropped into the Rubicon Canyon, a dreadfully frustrating mistake.

We enjoyed several hundred meters of downhill skiing through open terrain before running into a *wall* of manzanita. An omen. After that we skied a few times, sort of, but the next five hours were spent carrying skis through impossible woods, across impassable rocky areas, and into chest-deep brush which grabbed at packs, skis, poles, legs, belt loops, *anything* it could snag to frustrate progress. Tiring. Perverse. Slow. Shitty. It became a *personal* matter. A month later we reached the lovely Rubicon River. Sunny and warm and clear and we found a perfect camp—a large flat smooth rock ridge to sleep upon with out using tents. We were tired.

Otis immediately stripped and had a sun bath. Craig embarked on an unsuccessful fishing expedition. He lost his drop line and took an enormous kidding for previous immodesty about his fishing skills. Tim sat and stared with a bemused smile into the west. Bill took photos and relaxed. Steve stretched out and napped. I explored the area and then sat down with my notes. The terrain ahead is mostly granite slabs covered with rapidly melting snow. Avalanche potential was clear.

That night we built a great fire and ate like kings before bedding down under stars that shone bright and clear in the black depths of space. I slept like the rock I slept upon.

April 28, 1978

Sleeping bags covered with thick frost. We drape them over small trees to dry while we eat. A fine morning. We arranged ourselves without talking about the continuing bushwhack before us. I started first and hadn't gone a hundred meters before finding Craig's dropline. It was returned with much humor. The Rastaman is able to blush.

We carried skis and crawled over boulders and streams and the Rubicon River and thrashed through brush and rotten patches of snow until, at last, we could don skis and resume ski touring. Everybody worked well together and Tim was going through the breaking in aches and pains.

It wasn't Calonica's day. At Rubicon Reservoir he announced that we were at Rockbound Lake and he had fished it often. We stopped for lunch on the dam and told unmerciful Craig fish stories. It clouded up and cooled down and before we had gone a mile it started raining-hailing-snowing-raining with such ferocity that we nearly set up camp. It cleared and we made fine progress to a camp a few miles north of Mosquito Pass. Open water hole. Flat terrain. Dead trees for firewood. Outrageous scenery. A huge fire was built on the snow. As the night progressed, it became a five-foot diameter receding pit belching flames into the night. After dinner we stood around the fire drinking home-made kahlua until the exertions of the day, the kahlua and the hour forced retreat to tent and bag. Steve and Craig, sturdy youngsters the both, stayed up a quart of kahlua longer telling raucous stories, giggling, and laughing and the next morning we found them sleeping on the snow, bags and boots and clothes covered with beautiful thick frost.

April 29, 1978

Up early to a cold, clear morning. Start delayed while the two speed demons organized hangovers. Then we hit it hard. I went first in a sprint to Mosquito Pass because of avalanche concern. I wanted across the west facing slope before it softened. In the beginning I couldn't have worked that hard. Still, I was exhausted from the drain of physical and nervous energy. I thought the snow would hold and it did, but sometimes in the mountains you never know for sure. The same applies out of the mountains.

We lunched on the pass, looking down on Lake Aloha and the lovely, aptly named Desolation Valley, covered in white. After a good rest we had fine downhill skiing on perfect corn snow into the valley. While crossing Aloha Lake we saw two climbers descending from the summit of Pyramid Peak to the west, the first people encountered. Familiar ground to me from many other times. I put myself on cruise control and took a mental sentimental journey. I remembered climbing Pyramid Peak 20 years earlier with two friends, and I thought about those friends now. I recalled hiking in Desolation with certain people and spending training weekends there in ski racing days. I thoroughly indulged my sentimental fantasies and by the time I came to my senses we were in the woods above Echo Lake, a milestone on our journey. A larger milestone than we realized.

The skiing to upper Echo Lake was composed of long traverses in soft snow followed by a kick turn. As we skied across the lakes other skiers appeared. Proximity to civilization. From the south end of Echo Lake the east side of the Tahoe basin was visible, and not enough snow remained then to complete our tour without an inordinate time in the bush. Rubicon Valley had given us all of that endeavor we needed. Those days of rain and rescue had postponed our plans. We agreed to finish the tour another time, got to the nearest phone and called Clyde Calonica, Craig's father, and sat down beside the road to await a return to the gyrating mainstream of the civilized world of man and a few hits of Clyde's home-made wine, *very* affectionately known as "white lightning," "white death," and "Clyde's revenge." The tour is not finished.

CHAPTER NINETEEN

And a Mile Climb Back Up

"...the modern mind...has yielded to the inferior magic of facts, numbers, statistics, and to that sort of empiricism which, in its passion for concreteness, paradoxically reduces experience to a purely abstract notion of measurable data, having cast aside the 'immeasurable wealth' of authentic experiences of the spirit and imagination."
Eric Heller

In the Warm Springs Lodge at the base of Sun Valley's Bald Mountain is a bronze plaque commemorating the large number of vertical feet skied by a nice old man in one day. The number is less noteworthy than the fact that he spent his entire day riding Sun Valley's high speed lifts up and then skiing down Baldy as fast as he could go, all for the sake of the experience of a number. It epitomizes modern alpine skiing.

There is no way to cast in bronze the immeasurable wealth of authentic experience.

"...the mountains speak in wholly different accents to those who have paid in the service of toil for the right of entry to their inner shrines."
Sir Arnold Lunn

When I was a boy and had just started to ski I read somewhere what was called 'an Indian definition of skiing:' *"Wheeeeeee, and a mile climb back up."*

As a boy developing my own modern mind of the early 1950s, I interpreted this as praise and thanks for the modern ski lift and an end to the toilsome (and, largely wasted) hours of the climb back up, contemporary triumph over stone-age adversity. Though we always did some back country skiing, some cross country skiing and plenty of climbing to get up jump hills, slalom hills without ski lifts and to the starts of some downhills, my skiing friends and I grew up primarily as alpine ski racers who rode lifts in pursuit of good race results. That is, numbers, "a purely abstract notion of measurable data."

Number one, of course, was always best, abstract or not, and, without denigrating or missing the point of Heller's assertion, we had lots of authentic experiences of the spirit and imagination (and body) in its pursuit. Alpine ski racing, especially downhill, provided a lot of wheeeeeee without the mile climb back up and I loved it. At the time, the effort and focus of ski racing brought me higher and deeper into the mountain experience than could any other vehicle I knew.

After competition was done I continued to alpine ski. Even now, nearly 60 years after it started, I ski and ride the lifts on Bald Mountain most winter days. Like a junkie, I still love it. However, among a (small) circle of my old alpine skiing friends I have noticed that we are spending more days each year skiing the back country, savoring the climb back up as much as the wheeeeeee down, away from lifts, far from crowds, seeking the mountain's inner shrines. Many life long skiers mark the success of their skiing season by the number of days skied at which resorts, not by the quality of their experience, and it occurs to me that passion is best experienced fluid and hot, not concretized by the number. While the back country snob waving the banner of "earn your turns" in the face of alpine skiers is as big a turn off as an over crowded ski hill, it must be admitted that his pretentious passion has some heat and can't be cast in bronze unless, of course, he keeps track of vertical feet skied in a day.

My expanding appreciation and practice of back country skiing of the past few years feels like a return to roots, though I rode lifts whenever possible as a boy. Climbing back up does not get easier with each year, so the coin of toil required needs budgeting, but the inner shrines of mountains in winter are no longer accessible through alpine ski resorts. I think they once were until the merchandising of mountains, too many people, and the corporate world that defines today's alpine skiing clogged the entrances.

A few summer past I visited an old friend, Pepi Stiegler, in his Montana home. Pepi has spent his life alpine skiing, directing the ski school at Jackson Hole for more than 30 years. Before that he won three Olympic medals in alpine skiing, including gold in slalom, but we did not talk much about racing or alpine skiing except for his daughter's budding slalom potential. We talked about literature, about the path in life that led an Austrian Olympic gold medal skier with a high school education to pursue a degree in English literature late in life at Montana State University in Bozeman. We talked about his growing appreciation of the 'beats,' particularly Kerouac, and how reading them gave him a better understanding of me. We talked about his admiration for America's southern writers, the horrors of slavery and its shameful legacy, and about the difficulties of reading Faulkner when English is a second language. I assured him that Faulkner is difficult if worth the effort for the most erudite native speaker of English. But mostly Pepi wanted to talk about the back country tours he has been doing in the Tetons the past few years, showing me 8 x 10 photos of some of his favorite spots, inviting me to join him this winter for some tours. He leaves the ski area and heads to the back country at every opportunity, and there is passion in his voice and eyes when he talks about it. He clearly is not jaded about the authentic experience of skiing.

I commented that it was interesting that lifetime alpine skiers like he and I are turning to the back country for their skiing highs. What did he think about that? "Ahhh, Dick," he said, "It's like it was in the beginning. It's pure. Skiing in the back country is like going home."

We evolve in circles like snowflakes returning to the sea. The back country in winter feels like home to an old skier.

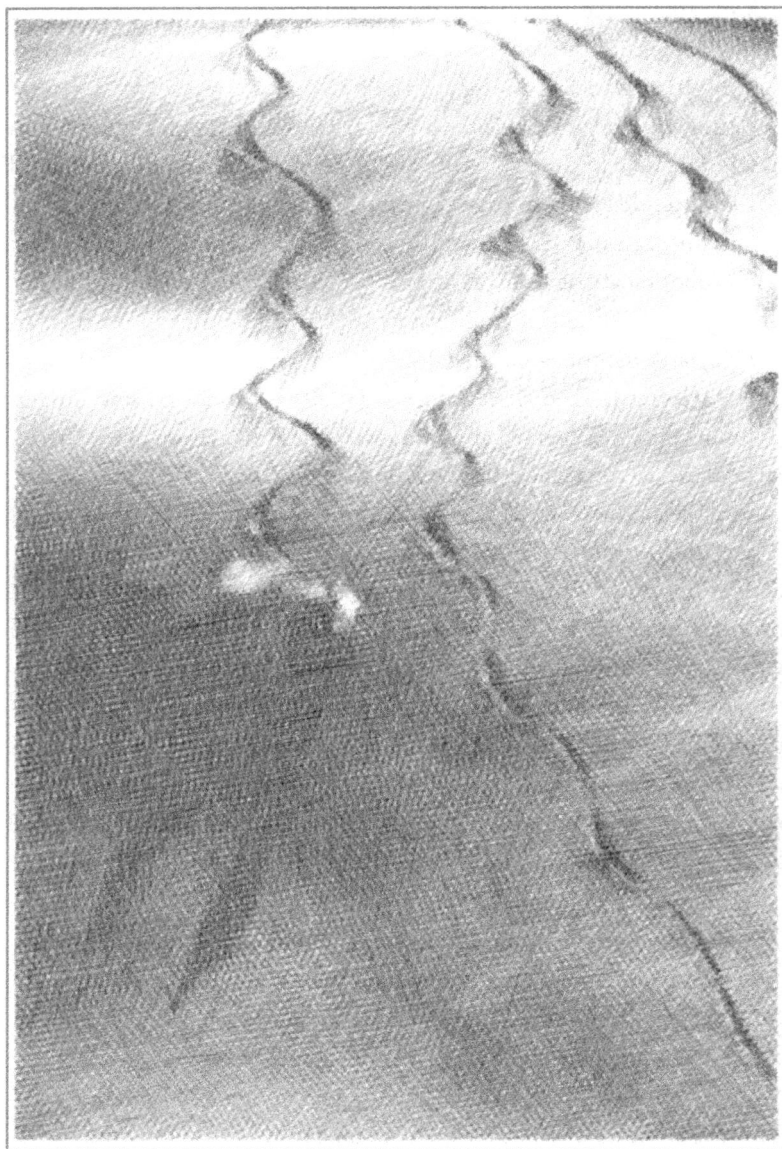

PART FOUR

Fiction

CHAPTER TWENTY

The Perfect Turn

YEARS OF SUN HAD PURIFIED SKIN into a permanent crust tan with strong creases of long life in a face around peculiar blue/green/gray Pacific Ocean eyes. Bill Clarkson's hair was white, befitting an old man, but his hair had lost color at an early age. He looked the same for so many years that friends and colleagues in the ski school tended to think of Clarkson as without age, but of course he wasn't. He was an enthusiastic old man with a reverence on his mind he seldom chose to talk about.

Skiing provided much of his livelihood. His mind and spirit had been largely molded by it, and he was on a private quest for the perfect turn on a pair of skis. He had been conscious of it for 20 years, but age had revealed to him that his path was the same from boyhood; the perfect turn. It existed in that place where snow and ski meet to sculpt man, the connector. Clarkson had come close many times, but he never quite made it around the perfect turn. The prospect excited him.

His manner, reputation and appearance, with fathomless peaceful eyes encouraged others to attribute lofty aims and levels to Bill Clarkson. Few imagined his inner expedition. He was no longer allowed the athleticism of the good young skiers on the mountain, but he was respected for the style that comes only from a lifetime's work. Serious students of skiing sought his advice, demonstration and that form of energy called encouragement, but few persisted. He spoke only of essentials. The truly determined would figure it out, and Clarkson knew he could not shorten their process of discovery. The dilettante, too, always figured it out.

His students often wound up talking about two of his interests, science-fiction and submarines. Sometimes lessons continued beyond skiing to several glasses of red wine in The Avalanche, a dining/drinking spa across from the lodge at the base of the mountain. Clarkson loved conversation, but he rarely spoke of his privately perfect turn. He liked to talk about the ideas of Heinlein, Herbert, Dick, Bradbury, Clarke and Wells, and he made impassioned verbal solo runs on the importance of the submarine to man's evolution, though he had never seen a real submarine. True students don't mind eccentricity, and the coquettes were content to be in the presence of Clarkson's reputation and personality.

From November to April his days were regular and similar. He rose early and breakfasted with Eileen, his religiously minded wife of more than 30 years and his closest friend. Their marriage had ridden the storms and endured the slack times of that institution to reach the safe harbor of familiarity, self-acceptance and habit. Their two grown children had married and moved to the city. Their favorite ongoing intimate jokes were built around the theme that while Bill hadn't quite worked out the perfect turn, he was doing as well as Eileen's God was with His world. The joke had innumerable variations.

After eating and morning talk, Clarkson kissed his wife and walked the mile from their cabin to the mountain. He enjoyed the walk. The last few years he needed it to loosen up for the day's skiing. He knew he had a fine instinctive feel for skis, snow and terrain, polished with solid technique and many years. Still, he felt his age. Certain runs—Elevator, No Deposit Chute and Larry's Bowl (named for a man killed there in an avalanche)—Clarkson wouldn't ski anymore. He could ski them if he had to, but he neither enjoyed fear nor saw merit in imposing it on himself without interest or necessity.

At the lodge he drank coffee with others in the ski school, talked about the weather—always a prime topic—the world news, the latest ski, local gossip and how the snow was likely to be that day. He relished this part of the morning, especially if Hal Sanders was pleasant. Bill and Hal were friends and skiing companions of nearly 40 years. Sanders felt like a comfortable old coat to Clarkson, warmth against the chill of unfamiliarity Clarkson felt around some of the young skiers. Most of the younger instructors were too abrasive, abrupt and insensitive, both on and off skis, in Clarkson's educated opinion, but he remembered being stupid from fighting identity battles that were no longer his concern. He was comfortable with people and things known, and his living enemies had abdicated or aged with as much élan as his own in the face of the falling inevitable. Morning coffee with Sanders was like a favorite and old piece of music to the mind and spirit of Bill Clarkson.

Then he went to the crowded ski instructor's room. People changing into uniforms. Many voices at once. Heavy ski boots stomping on a concrete floor. A ritual preparation for the day's skiing encompassing several meanings: sport, business, craft, meditation, and goal. It was a bit of each to Clarkson and the path toward a balanced mystery he thought of as the perfect turn. He believed in the grace and worth of the self-indulgence of guiding a pair of skis upon a field of snow with precision and intelligence. He bet a part of his life that the turn existed. It presented itself to his mind, over and over and over, as if it had happened before and would of necessity again. The perfect turn was wonderful to contemplate. Deja vu.

Ski lifts started an hour before classes gathered in clusters before ski school signs of ability—A*B*C*D*E*F—stuck in the snow before the lodge. More than many instructors Clarkson used that hour for his own skiing. Often he skied alone, sometimes with colleagues who had no idea of his deepest mind. It wasn't their fault they didn't know.

Nor was it his.

It was just that way.

Eileen knew. Sanders had an abstract comprehension. Sometimes at instructor's gatherings when talk turned upon the theory or purpose or some such armchair concept of their profession, Sanders pontificated in the manner of the righteous that Bill Clarkson embodied the substance of skiing and knew something no one else did. Sanders was unable to determine what that something was.

During the savored morning chair lift ride, a portion of his mind took in the matutinal mountain—light on the ridges and the white/blue snow and the green frosty trees and the clunk-whirrrr of the cable passing over the lift support towers and the motors of the sno-cats working ski runs into a smooch, soft blanket and the easy breeze rustling trees and gently swirling across the snow and the stark cold air that hit the face like a slap encountered nowhere else but in the high mountains. At such times Clarkson felt extraordinarily lucky.

At the top came the best part, first run of the day. He felt titillation as if he had never stood upon a pair of skis, and surging doubt quickened anticipation as he debarked the lift. He knew he could ski, but it was a special sensation to incinerate faint anxiety in the purifying flame of action. The act of skiing transmitted a familiar pressure to the skilled soles of his feet and up his old bones to his brain. Skiing was in that moment the entire reason for his existence. He guided his skis down the mountain along the smoothest line of least resistance, for that time master of his destiny. Excessive exertion was a waste, a sloppy turn a mental and moral lapse in Bill Clarkson's soul. Skiing is composed of pressure and angles in constant flux. Like leaves, rivers, snowflakes and people, no two turns are the same and once made can never be retracted or redone. Each turn in life is a complete statement, and Clarkson was sure the integrity of a turn persisted. It was important to make correct turns and to never give up the work of refinement, the process reaching toward the perfect turn. Two runs of several hundred turns each could be fitted in before classes.

A popular and good teacher, the consummate "old pro," Clarkson lived off his knowledge that there's more to skiing than recreation. When business was brisk he often worked the entire day until lifts stopped, skiers left the mountain and the afternoon light began its fade. If Clarkson missed lunch, evening surely found him in The Avalanche, eating, drinking red wine, talking. He preferred to be with Sanders, another friend or an old client, but a festive mood infectiously followed him, and many a late night grew out of a sandwich and a glass of wine with Clarkson after skiing. He had a celebratory quality, but he opened only to those he chose according to the private standards of a private man. Kitty Reese was one, a 20-year old girl whose passion was photography, whose love was skiing, whose friend was Bill Clarkson. They were a sight. A pretty girl with long, light blonde hair and deep brown eyes and a quick, easy smile, and an old white-maned man with a weathered face and unfathomable, strange eyes. Easy talkers had the two as lovers, but it was not so. If he were younger or alone perhaps it could have been, but that is no more sure than the vagaries of all relationships and statements beginning with "if." Their friendship grew from Kitty's eagerness to photograph his skiing. She was a nuisance at first, but he was kind and by consenting to ski for the camera he learned appreciation for the photographer. She took up reading science-fiction. He critiqued her work with the unbiased eye of the non-photographer.

Kitty once told Bill she would "give anything" to ski like him. He looked at her and said nothing, his Pacific Ocean eyes flooding her with embarrassment, and Kitty never said anything like that again. She settled for being pleased when he granted her skiing or photography a word of approval. Conversation between them revolved around such topics as the possibility of intelligent life in other parts of the universe, what lived in the depths of the sea, astral projection, the ethics and significance of transplanting parts of the human body, the concept of good and evil, and of the necessity to strive for the perfection which includes both the seemingly unattainable and the presently possible. Like good friends do, they spoke of the contradictions and difficulties of life.

When the skiing/photographing day ended, Kitty usually retired to the darkroom in the basement of the lodge. As a photographer Kitty was a throwback to an earlier time. She saw and searched for an essential clarity and beauty in using monochrome film to make silver halide black and white photos that, to her eye, were not available in digital photography. That search set her apart from other photographers and was part of her connection with Bill Clarkson. After she was finished with negatives, proof sheets, prints and enlargements, she studied and evaluated accomplishment and failure for that day. Then she often joined Clarkson, and usually Sanders, in The Avalanche. They joined a larger mass of skiers discussing the latest ski or ski boot or exploit of the hero of the hour, as necessary to any endeavor as bread to the Sacrament. In the altar of The Avalanche they drank red wine and enjoyed each other's company and conversation.

One clear day near season's end Clarkson volunteered to ski for Kitty and her camera. It was the first time Kitty hadn't suggested the filming, and she was happy for the unforeseen chance. He was relaxed and talkative and joked that she would never see him ski so well as he would that day, green/grey eyes reflecting his private laughter at her pretty surprise.

While they rode the lift he talked about his favorite ski runs and he pointed out for her once again the beauty he perceived—the texture of snow, the vibrancy of living trees, the contour of a ridge, the honorable struggle of skiers battling their own fears and limitations, blue sky streaked with wispy cirrus clouds presaging a storm two days hence. Shadows. Peaks. Valleys. Sharp clear air caressing lungs. Bill Clarkson told Kitty Reese that she was very pretty, as pretty as the mountain with a new mantle of snow on a cold sunny day with color spectrum snowflake diamonds dancing in the air. And he laughed at her blush and at his own sentence.

Bill Clarkson was in a very good mood, the best Kitty had known of him. She watched his skiing through the camera viewfinder, and the elusive thought slithered through that the skier and the skiing had danced together so long that the two had become the same one. The idea passed. Clarkson chose the spots to ski and Kitty noted the light was excellent. She shot several rolls of film. At one point she stopped photographing to simply watch him maneuver through an old burn of scattered dead pine trees standing nakedly branchless. Free of the camera eye, she saw him with her own. Her admiration and attention was tinged with an electric feeling of ephemerality, a sense that Bill Clarkson's skiing existed on its own, while the man himself had stepped out for lunch or a date with his love. A chill passed through her body and mind like a cloud from nowhere crossing before the sun on a warm day. The moment passed. Clarkson skied up to her and stopped. Warmth returned.

"That's beautiful," she said. "Bill, that's lovely skiing."

"Yes," he said, smiling wide with his whole wrinkled and weathered face. "I've got it today. But I told you. I've really got it today."

They parted when the late afternoon mountain sun bathed the passes and peaks in golden contrast to the dark blue valley shadows of imminent night. He kissed her on the forehead like he sometimes did and looked into her eyes and then he skied away.

Kitty went to her darkroom, excitement and nagging anxiety floating like corks on the quiet, strong currents in the rivers of her innermost mind. For a couple of hours she was completely involved in the celluloid/chemical/time/light world of the film development process. By the time the negatives were ready to inspect, Kitty was filled with charged anticipation. Using a magnifying glass, she began peering first at the individual frames of the strips of film she had taken that day of Bill Clarkson.

Nothing in her young life could have prepared her for what she saw. Frame after frame showed the mountains, snow, trees, the great open sky and the exact scene she had photographed in the perfect reverse focus of the negative—except that Bill Clarkson and his skiing were not there. No skier was visible in any of the film.

Kitty looked with mounting perplexity through half the negatives before the tears burst from her brown eyes and flowed down the face that Clarkson said was as pretty as the mountain with a new mantle of snow on a cold sunny day with color spectrum snowflake diamonds dancing in the air. She dropped the magnifying glass. It made a dull thud landing on the work bench. She ran, leaving the darkroom door open behind her. A growling, short breathed sob escaped into the night air as she emerged from the lodge and sprinted across crunchy frozen snow. With blurred, sorrowed vision she saw through the tall, plate-glass windows of The Avalanche a scene from a world that would never be the same: a brightly lit, smoke-tainted room; the long table in the alcove covered with beer and wine glasses and ash trays and empty pizza trays and surrounded by ski instructors; the animated movements of conversing people, as if seen upon the silent screen of an old movie house.

And in the corner of the alcove furthest from the window,

unnoticed by the others, sat Hal Sanders on a bench holding in his arms the slumped form of Bill Clarkson. Sanders looked straight ahead, his eyes wide and red, and tears streamed from them and down his old face like spring run-off from the mountains.

———————————